Balancing Acts

D0220459

In this book, counsellors, trainers and supervisors discuss the tensions, conflicts and complexities involved in many of the aspects of being a trainer, being a trainee and the elements of counselling training itself. Through innovative research and lively first-hand accounts, *Balancing Acts* explores both individual trainer development and course design and management in counselling and other training contexts in the helping professions.

The first section of the book examines the balancing acts involved in being a trainer: managing the content and context of the training programme, being responsive to the needs of groups and individuals and being accountable for the ethical protection of clients with whom trainees might work.

Contributors go on to consider the various settings in which training takes place and the differences between training professionals and volunteers. They discuss negotiated and reflective learning, assessment, the needs of adult students and issues arising from the functions of groups.

Finally, three experienced counsellors relate their experiences of the training process: the difficulties and fears they encountered, and the personal growth and satisfaction that helped them to survive as trainees.

Using both research and the reflections of experienced counsellors to explore issues that affect their professional practice, *Balancing Acts* is a valuable resource for all those involved in adult learning.

Hazel Johns is Senior Lecturer in the Department for Continuing Education, University of Bristol, and a Fellow of the British Association for Counselling.

Balancing Acts

Studies in counselling training

Edited by Hazel Johns

London and New York

First published 1998
by Routledge
11 New Fetter Lane, London EC4P 4EE

Simultaneously published in the USA and Canada
by Routledge
29 West 35th Street, New York, NY 10001

© 1998 selection and editorial matter, Hazel Johns; individual chapters,
the contributors

Typeset in Times by
Ponting–Green Publishing Services, Chesham, Buckinghamshire
Printed in Great Britain by
Creative Print and Design (Wales) Ebbw Vale

British Library Cataloguing in Publication Data
A catalogue record for this book is available from the British Library

Library of Congress Cataloguing in Publication Data
A catalogue record for this book has been requested

ISBN 0–415–16545–8 (hbk)
ISBN 0–415–16546–6 (pbk)

To the memory of my mother, Beryl Patricia Johns,
and for all our mothers, in life and in counselling training

Contents

Contributors

Trish Edwards is a lecturer in further education, a counsellor, counselling trainer and supervisor.

Christabel Fey is a freelance counsellor and supervisor working in private practice, the NHS and a variety of organisations. She is writing under a pseudonym.

Emma Fletcher is a freelance telephone counsellor, counselling skills trainer and supervisor. She is a former social worker with mental health service users in the voluntary sector.

Hazel Johns (Editor) is Senior Lecturer in the Counselling Education and Training Unit, Department for Continuing Education at the University of Bristol. She is a Fellow of the British Association for Counselling.

Celia Levy is Head of the Counselling Unit at the City Lit. Adult Education Institute, London. She has a background in speech and hearing therapy and is also a counselling trainer and supervisor.

Alison Maybank is a staff counsellor/group facilitator with an NHS Health Trust and a freelance counsellor, supervisor and trainer.

Arthur Musgrave has been a counsellor and advice worker with young people and manager of a well-established advice, guidance and counselling centre in Bristol. He is currently a freelance counsellor, supervisor and trainer.

Larry Parker is a probation officer of many years' experience, specialising in the psychology of addiction. He has training as a counsellor and now works in a newly created drug therapeutic community set within a prison for young offenders in Dorset.

Jane Speedy is a lecturer in the Counselling Education and Training Unit, Department for Continuing Education at the University of Bristol. She has particular interests in the field of counselling at work, adult education principles in counselling education and research methods in counselling training and supervision.

Anne Stokes is an independent counsellor, trainer and supervisor working in private practice, with business organisations and with a drug and alcohol rehabilitation charitable trust. She is an ex-deputy head of a comprehensive school.

Alyss Thomas is a freelance counsellor, supervisor, trainer and writer in the south-west of England. She is on the editorial board of *Self and Society*, a journal of humanistic psychology.

Introduction

Chapter 1

On the tightrope

Hazel Johns

Introduction

This book represents some of the work of a Counselling Education and Training Unit, based in a well-established Department for Continuing Education, in the University of Bristol. The contributors (already experienced counsellors) have all been mature students or tutors, or both, on the Master's degree course in Counselling Supervision and Training, the only one of its kind in Britain. All the chapters have evolved from the counselling trainers' experience, research and reflection on their practice.

Those three introductory sentences could stand as a metaphor for counselling training. They reflect a number of complex inter-relationships, potential conflicts, competing demands and possible – or impossible – paradoxes. Similarly, the writing of this book has spanned a time filled with exhilarating beginnings and sad endings, both personal and organisational. The department in which our Counselling Unit exists is to close within the year; my mother has died, as have the mothers of three of my close tutoring colleagues; and numerous individual students on many of our courses have faced the costs of unemployment, relationship break-up or losses of various kinds. Yet, we have begun new courses, engaged with fresh student groups, struggled to capture and express creatively old and new ideas. There have been many innovations in trainees' work settings; at least three students and two tutors have also produced babies, while others have made life-enhancing decisions and risked change of all kinds. In the face of such emotionally intense, personal and professional challenges, it is difficult to sustain energy, commitment, personal integrity, ethical soundness and appropriate focus – yet that is what counselling trainers and trainees have to do.

Counselling training is a complex process. Participants have to tussle with ideas, philosophy and constructs. There is a demand for constant effort to hone perceptions, extend practical skills and give and receive feedback. Most critically, at its heart is the management of personal change, transitions and growth of all kinds. Students and tutors puzzle over conundrums of theory and practice; few concepts are absolute and paradoxes confront at every turn; gains and losses abound. This is true of any kind of adult education with mature students. It is intensified in counselling training by the subject matter and necessary emphasis on the person and personal awareness of both tutors and trainees. A vivid picture comes to my mind of the brave – or foolhardy – man on a tightrope precariously inching his way across Niagara Falls: a balancing act in the extreme and one with which I – and other trainers of my acquaintance – often feel great affinity. At the same time, much of the activity on training courses is mundane. Tasks have to be completed; administration and 'housekeeping' attended to; and the minutiae of social interaction flows through and round the group. Trainers and trainees have to develop the ability of a 'Janus' figure: the capacity to face in (at least) two directions at once and respond appropriately.

This chapter will outline some of the key balancing acts which both frame and are at the heart of our work. The subsequent chapters explore some of the challenging aspects and complex issues of counselling training which have engaged, fascinated or puzzled the contributors. The writers have their own fascination with the adrenalin and vertigo induced by tightrope walking over dangerous and uncertain depths or over the mudflats of daily demands.

Chinese boxes

In addition to the immediate tasks of counselling training – the intentional preparation of appropriate individuals to become competent, aware and ethically sound counsellors – any trainer or training unit must also manage the 'Russian doll' or 'Chinese box' effect. Each individual trainee and trainer exists within the specific course, within learning and teaching methodologies, within the training context, within the funding system, within the developments of the wider counselling world, within the political and social culture of the time, and within transpersonal belief systems. All of these elements may demand at particular moments accurate perceptions allied to swift intellectual and emotional footwork, combined with a wide range of skills. Such competencies are necessary in order to make rapid and sensitive responses, based on clear understanding of often-competing concepts or demands, both mundane and highly complex.

The training issues, paradoxes and experiences described in this book exist in two main contexts. One reflects the setting of many counselling courses in the academic world: a Counselling Education and Training Unit, within a Department for Continuing Education, in a large, traditional, civic university, at a time of funding changes and harsh prioritising of resources. The second aspect involves the evolution of a particular course culture (the M.Sc. in Counselling Supervision and Training), in a counselling training setting with specific values and priorities. This operates in the wider world of counselling developments, in a rapidly changing period of professionalisation, during considerable social and political change at the end of the millennium. There are many balancing acts necessary both within and between those inter-connected facets.

Counselling training in universities

Counselling training takes place, of course, in many contexts and much of what follows has parallels elsewhere: conflicts of interest and tensions can and do occur in any setting. There are, though, some particular issues pertaining to the academic world.

Counselling courses have existed in universities in Britain since the early 1960s. The first courses were based on American models, taught, in general, by psychologists and aimed to train counsellors for educational settings. Since then, courses have proliferated, counselling has evolved into a discipline in its own right and methods of counselling training have become more sophisticated and specialist. There has been increasing debate among counselling educators about the 'fit' of values, techniques and resources, so that Berry and Woolfe (1997) can legitimately question whether 'counselling ... and the activity of teaching and learning in universities can ever be congruent with one another'. Many universities are developing innovative, creative curriculum design, teaching methods and assessment. Traditionally, however, universities value intellect, external knowledge, cognitive assessment, objectivity in research and analysis; counsellors place a higher value on feelings, knowledge from within, synthesis, interpersonal skills and self-awareness. In reality – and in an ideal world – students and teachers of any discipline should need and respect both modalities. Counsellors certainly need effective heads and hearts, while scientists, artists and social scientists are more ethically and humanly effective when they ally sensitivity to cognition. Such values and skills should not be seen as in opposition to each other or in a hierarchy of status, but should complement and inform each other. Where counselling courses exist in a conventional academic context, however, tensions, competition and mutual antipathy seem to be all-too-familiar companions. A further disparity might lie in the way in which the organisation's purpose is defined. Traditional universities may see their main aim as 'teaching difficult subjects to the ablest young people' (I quote a vice-chancellor!); counselling training offers a variant of vocational education to mature students, mostly on a part-time basis, linked intimately with practical experience.

Since 1986, when the embryonic Counselling Education and Training Unit at Bristol University began, our own experience has reflected many of these tensions and strains. Being in a university has been both an advantage and a struggle, as we have gradually developed a programme containing a progression of courses at all levels. The courses range from introductory to Masters': they include short courses for the general public, Open Studies courses carrying credits, a Certificate in Counselling Skills, three postgraduate Diplomas in Counselling, and the M.Sc. in Counselling Supervision and Training. We also offer consultancy and continuing professional development courses in counselling and supervision for experienced practitioners. The Unit has had first one, then two full-time academic staff, who engage and supervise a very large number of part-time tutors. A continuing education department, with its roots in part-time adult education, might seem an appropriate home for counselling training, yet many of our ways of working, especially in the early days, triggered critical reactions in our academic colleagues. Some found surprising the active nature of our teaching and learning methodologies; our staff-intensive teaching and tutoring ratios; and our need for extra small group rooms as well as flexible, large teaching spaces. Others, at times, seemed to regard as unreasonable or inappropriate our insistence on practical skills and personal development (less susceptible to formal, quantifiable assessment methods), as well as on academic theory. Our emphasis on mutually respectful, student-centred, adult-to-adult negotiated working relationships appeared to be something of a puzzle to some staff, since it potentially challenged our own role (and theirs) as experts. It was wounding to hear of negative comments from a few colleagues undermining or undervaluing our work, based not on knowledge but on prejudice, usually expressed indirectly, and often assuming on our part a lack of rigour and intellectual substance.

In reality, funding alterations and political ideologies were forcing all members of the department to face rapid change. Many of the new demands seemed to be an attack on the academic staff's established values and practices, leading to a general feeling of threat and vulnerability. Counselling was a 'new' area of study, representing the new wave of self-financing courses. Some colleagues welcomed our fresh approach and enjoyed exchanging ideas, while some of the negative responses were a reflection of people's anxieties or stemmed from their ignorance of the counselling field, rather than from specific hostility. Counselling staff reactions to the negativity ranged from hurt and anger to righteous paranoia, from irritation at colleagues' hypocrisy (since they were often only too willing to use our counselling skills in their own interests!) to indifference and reciprocal antagonism. It was difficult, at times, to resist a bunker mentality; certainly, in the early years, it felt like a struggle for survival, both emotionally and in practical resource terms. It certainly involved a constant balancing of effort: optimising energy for course development, tutor and student support and high-quality learning, while building relationships in the department and the university, devising strategies to change attitudes and ensuring high standards of student performance. Students had to demonstrate appropriate academic and practical competence and adequate personal development. As tutors, we had to be seen to be intellectually able, rigorous in assessment and efficient in managing the demands of the academic system. It was difficult, at times, not to become overly defensive or unhelpfully attacking; even harder not to encourage hostile negativity in both students and tutors to the institution on which we were dependent for resources – limited and hard-won though those were. At the same time, counselling staff were somehow expected to be good at relationships, skilled in negotiation and (almost) saintly in tolerance, whatever the provocation. This was, as counselling has been described, 'no easy task' – and we often failed miserably on all counts.

Over time, creative tensions, as well as frustrations, were released by the necessary striving to articulate in debate our teaching and learning philosophies, the comparison of values, the dilemmas and collisions over priorities. Counselling courses in universities can and do stimulate academic work of high intellectual quality, in addition to producing professionally and ethically competent practitioners, who have well-developed self-awareness. The trick is to manage it all without huge personal cost on the part of the trainers and students, without distorting, denying or abusing key counselling precepts and without colluding with students in 'splitting' about the organisation. The gains of working in an academic setting can be substantial: access to adequate libraries, cutting-edge research, expectations of intellectual rigour and an established system of academic boards, quality assurance and course development procedures. Counsellors do need theories to inform and challenge their practice; as long as personal and skills development receive equal attention, the university can be a fruitful

setting for stimulating high-quality counselling training. The contributions in this book, mostly evolved from personal research at Master's
level, are testament to this potential.

The counselling unit has felt, at times, a lonely, if immensely productive, place; now, after twelve years much has changed in colleagues'
attitudes towards and respect for our programme. As university attitudes
to teaching, learning and students' needs begin to adapt, it feels as if we
are pushing at an open door; indeed, there is much more acceptance that
we have led the way in terms of course design, learning and assessment
methodologies, and student support. By modelling ways of working, by
being proudly 'different' and by engaging in dialogue, we have stimu-
lated considerable developments in departmental practices and provision. We have also learned from some colleagues' expertise in related or
even quite different academic fields. Some 'balancing acts' are worth the
effort – indeed, as we are preparing this book, we are living with the
irony that the Counselling Education and Training Unit is to survive while
the Department for Continuing Education is to be closed. There is, though,
no satisfaction in that, but rather a deep sadness in the loss of a valuable
resource (albeit with both strengths and limitations) for thirsty adults
seeking opportunities to learn.

Counselling training and the counselling world

Just as we have striven to integrate and satisfy the academic demands of
the university setting, so we have attempted to sustain a respectful relationship with the emerging professional world of counselling. Over the
last thirty or so years, counselling in Britain has developed rapidly (Bond
and Shea 1997). The British Association for Counselling (BAC) has also
grown from a delicate fledgling to a powerful late-adolescent bird – whether
watchful, wise owl or hunting hawk is currently under debate. Much
work has been undertaken by the members and officers of BAC in developing codes of ethics and practice and schemes to accredit both courses
and individual practitioners (counsellors, supervisors and trainers). To
demonstrate our support for and valuing of these efforts, all our students
are encouraged to become members of BAC; all students are introduced
to the relevant codes, and courses work within them. Our generic postgraduate Diploma in Counselling was one of the first university-based
diplomas to apply successfully for BAC course recognition; and the university and the department are organisational members. In developing a
progression of courses at all levels, we have also worked at differentiat-
ing training for counselling and counsellors from that for counselling

skills, while affirming both volunteer and paid activity in the many settings where students operate.

This effort to be full and co-operative members of the counselling world has not been without its tensions. At times, practitioners in other contexts communicate a sense of suspicion about the credentials of university-based training, as if the necessary emphasis in our setting on academic standards might somehow preclude adequate attention to skills, professional practice or personal development. Similarly, there is pressure from BAC to have at least two trainers co-leading any substantial course, for discrete and consistent course membership, and for some course elements, such as personal growth, to be non-assessed. To meet these expectations, trainers in university settings have to fight constant battles about staff–student ratios and against modularisation and formal, traditional assessments. Some counselling trainers in universities have felt strongly that such demands are unreasonable or even irrelevant. They have even formed their own organisation to discuss training issues, a development seen by some as unhelpfully divisive. Yet, at a time of rapid development, BAC still has no trainers' group or division and the need has been strong for support and peer discussion. At Bristol, we have tried to stay in tune with BAC and accepted the need to challenge university assumptions where they clash with counselling values and concepts. Willing partnership does not, though, always mean complete agreement or a peaceful mind!

There have been many benefits from our decision to place the Counselling Education and Training Unit within rather than outside the concerns of the wider counselling world, yet issues of acceptance and respect for difference create at times a potential element of conflict. Although these are in theory conventionally sacred concepts at the heart of counselling, the struggle to define and protect the emerging profession has led to some ambivalence around 'must' and 'should' in evaluating training. Both BAC and the United Kingdom Council for Psychotherapy (UKCP) stress, for example, that all validated training courses must have a consistent core theoretical model, adherence to boundaries as essential, confidentiality as pre-eminent and so on (Feltham 1996). The British Psychological Society (BPS) has similar demands in its guidelines for course development. Such mandatory demands might be sometimes inappropriate, irrelevant or simply a matter of opinion. The core values of the Counselling Education and Training Unit are person-centred; these values and attitudes pervade the integrative theoretical model that underpins our courses, influence the teaching and learning methods that we espouse and affect the way we behave as tutors. Representatives of the wider counselling field (for example, in the BAC course accreditation process) have at times disputed some of the specific outcomes of those approaches, even though the particular training practices are fully congruent with our beliefs and within our competencies. Instances of such tension include the appropriateness of course tutors facilitating personal development groups in diploma courses or students engaging in contractual counselling (to extend their experience) with members of other courses. Some of those who disapprove of these practices tend to present their arguments as having absolute validity; in reality, the differences of view stem from differing theoretical perspectives with contrasting understandings of ways of working with issues of power, authority and assessment. To debate such differences in a climate where all views have equal status and where power is shared can be stimulating; to feel that, at worst, a rearguard fight is necessary with a dismissive, autocratic potential enemy is frustrating and wasteful of energy. Similarly, where little regard is communicated for existing organisational quality assurance procedures, and a tone of suspicion, mistrust and negative policing pervades discussion, it is difficult to sustain positive relationships. Counselling trainers in universities sometimes feel trapped in two shotgun marriages – and neither is consistently productive. The struggle to maximise trust and resist mistrust is constant – and an irony, given the central values of the counselling field.

In contrast with those occasional difficulties, the relationship between our work and the wider counselling world has, in general, been fruitful. It has been extremely educative to put our courses through BAC course accreditation procedures and to navigate our own explorations as tutors and students through the range of individual accreditation challenges. There is much discussion at present about the relationship between training and professional accreditation and new developments will undoubtedly be agreed in the next few years. It is particularly important to explore whether accredited courses should also be responsible for awarding individual accreditation.

Meanwhile, much of the work of counsellors and those who use counselling skills continues to operate outside the still relatively narrow parameters of formal accreditation. All these participants work with clients of all kinds and may or may not have experienced training, in settings either professional or voluntary. Client groups emerge or are re-defined, contexts change and society throws up new or newly visible challenges. In our unit, we continue to develop supportive and stimulating training, with all the attendant opportunities to discuss current developments, ethical issues and personal training needs. Many people have academic ability and an interest in counselling and are drawn to our training programme because it is in a university setting. Perhaps our most difficult task is to support those who lack the psychological sensitivity or personal flexibility to reach the level of emotional intelligence (Goleman 1996) which we and the professional counselling field think is essential.

Counselling training and adult education

Perhaps the most fertile balancing act reflected in the chapters which follow is that between the content and process of counselling training and the learning and teaching methodologies of adult education. We have consciously harnessed these two forces in all aspects of our training programme. The M.Sc. in Counselling Supervision and Training, in particular, was designed specifically so that experienced counselling practitioners, supervisors and trainers could reflect on the potential in the partnership. The course allows critical exploration of key concepts from adult education, such as the needs of mature students, the variety of learning theories and learning styles, the significance of times and theories of transition, the value of what Heron (1989) called 'intermittent chaos' and the creative power of learning to become a 'reflective practitioner' (Kolb 1984). These are interwoven with the now generally accepted methods of active, experiential counselling training (Inskipp 1996; Johns 1996) and explored through the range of purposeful relationships posited by Clarkson and Gilbert (1991). Underpinning those intellectual, cognitive or theoretical frameworks are the three core elements of our approach to counselling training: a student-centred ethos in which Rogers' (1983) 'prizing, acceptance and trust' are central; the willingness to be alongside students' unique learning journeys; and the valuing of 'readiness to learn' as the starting point of all.

This combination of elements allows students to review critically their own experiences, assumptions and understanding, evaluate the meaning and purposes of counselling education and make connections of all kinds between theory and practice. The course operates as a community based on negotiated learning. Within the clear parameters and standards already agreed with the university, detailed content, structures and assessment processes are designed with each course cohort. A dual focus operates throughout the life of each course: attention is paid to the content and concepts of whatever aspect of counselling, supervision or training is being explored, alongside reflections on the implications for counselling education and the facilitation of learning. In addition, and inevitably, given the earlier outline of the university setting, the organisational and cultural implications of training contexts are examined (Mezirow 1991) and their potential identified as stimuli for learning. The course members are engaged in counselling training in many settings; the shared critical reflection on experiences is a rich collective resource.

All the course participants are mature people, experienced counsellors, already engaged in training and supervision, committing themselves for more than two years to demanding part-time study as 'reflective practitioners' in continuing professional development. They experience all the rewards, costs and conflicts that they are also critically defining, analysing and reviewing. Such a course offers a very different experience from, for instance, traditional approaches to studying mathematics or a modern language and necessitates a particularly high degree of self-awareness and stability. Students come from widely varied theoretical, organisational and client backgrounds; this and the emphasis on negotiated learning necessitate much attention to group processes, both in theory and in practice. The interplay between task, individual and group needs is as strongly played out in this course as in any with which I have been concerned. Tutor roles are similarly complex and demanding. It is truly difficult to maintain accountability and yet share responsibility; to model expertise, yet carry the label of 'expert' unobtrusively. It is taxing to facilitate sensitively a group of students who may have at least as much experience in certain key areas, yet who will demand at times that the tutors represent their fantasies of power and control. This chapter is not the forum for an exhaustive analysis of the experience of the course; it is, though, no accident that the strong emphasis on individual research in the course produces many sophisticated explorations of complex training issues. The chapters in this book are adaptations of some of these and reflect the puzzles, passions and paradoxes with which students become fascinated. We have not attempted to cover all issues, but rather grappled with some elements of counselling training and its adult education underpinnings, which may have relevance for trainers and trainees in a variety of contexts.

Puzzles, passions and paradoxes

The balancing acts we explore in these pages are both general and specific. Some reflect major preoccupations of the emerging profession of counselling, such as issues of power, questions of standards and assessment, access and inclusivity versus professionalisation and its consequences. Other contributors explore technicalities of counselling education, such as co-tutoring, face-to-face contrasted with telephone training, and ways in which trainees might more effectively learn and share responsibility. Yet others reflect on actual experiences, both developmental and crisis, as tutors or students, and on the joys, pains and challenges involved.

There is much missing: for example, we have said little about training for multi-cultural counselling, potential abuse of trainees or clients, ethical dilemmas (except in passing), the implications of the new Register or evaluation of training. Our aim was to capture and reflect on issues which were preoccupying us and which also represent some of the balancing acts of the multi-level and rainbow experience that is counselling training. Above all, these chapters have flowered from the personal experience of practitioners, who have reflected over time, then been willing to risk the attempt to articulate their evolving understanding and awareness. They represent true adult education in counselling training and its contribution to personal and professional development. I am grateful for all I have gained from these and the many other students and tutors with whom it has been my privilege to share the journey of learning about counselling, supervision and training.

References

Berry, M. and Woolfe, R. (1997) 'Teaching Counselling in Universities: Match or Mismatch?', *British Journal of Guidance and Counselling*, 25 (4) Nov.

Bond, T. and Shea, C. (1997) 'Professional Issues in Counselling', in S. Palmer and G. McMahon (eds) *Handbook of Counselling* (2nd edn), London, BAC/Routledge.

Clarkson, P. and Gilbert, M. (1991) 'The Training of Counsellor Trainers and Supervisors', in W. Dryden and B. Thorne (eds) *Training and Supervision for Counselling in Action*, London, Sage.

Feltham, C. (1996) 'Beyond Denial, Myth and Superstition in the Counselling Profession', in R. Bayne, I. Horton and J. Bimrose (eds) *New Directions in Counselling*, London, Routledge.

Goleman, D. (1996) *Emotional Intelligence*, London, Bloomsbury.

Heron, J. (1989) *The Facilitator's Handbook*, London, Kogan Page.

Inskipp, F. (1996) *Skills Training for Counselling*, London, Cassell.

Johns, H. (1996) *Personal Development in Counsellor Training*, London, Cassell.

Kolb, D. (1984) *Experiential Learning*, Englewood Cliffs, Prentice Hall.

Mezirow, J. (1991) 'A Critical Theory of Adult Learning and Education', in M. Tight (ed.) *Education for Adults*, London, Croom Helm/Open University.

Rogers, C. (1983) *Freedom to Learn for the 80s*, New York, Merrill.

Part I

Being a counselling trainer
Keeping the plates spinning?

There are many balancing acts involved in being a counselling *trainer*: managing the content, tasks and relationships of the training process; carrying responsibility for trainees, the organisation and oneself; holding individual and group needs, while being vigilant against any kind of oppression; and, of course, being accountable for the training programme, the proper care of students and the ethical protection of clients with whom trainees might work.

The BAC Code of Ethics and Practice for Trainers in Counselling and Counselling Skills (1996) outlines many crucial elements and is essential reading for any would-be counselling trainer. At its heart are issues of power, authority and control, ethical competence, the need for vigilant self-awareness, and the demand for continual personal and professional development. The three contributors to this section explore through personal research and reflection on experience some of the key 'spinning plates' of being a trainer: the stresses and personal costs which can dominate in what is undoubtedly a challenging role; issues of power, a central focus of awareness for all trainers; and the particular joys and demands of co-training, generally accepted as ethically and professionally helpful in the counselling training field.

Chapter 2

The stresses of being a counselling trainer

Alyss Thomas

Being a counselling trainer can be bad for you. This chapter is based almost entirely on personal experience of working as a counselling trainer in several different organisations, or conversations with many colleagues.

For my first five years as a counselling trainer, I felt continually confused, inadequate, ineffective and depleted. In fact, at one point after two particularly difficult years, I vowed I would never run another counselling course ever again, that the personal cost of being the 'ever competent ever-nurturing trainer' (Proctor 1991) was far too high and the rewards far too low. What I did instead was attend a two-year Master's degree programme in trainer-training and become more consciously aware of the nature of the difficulties with which I was struggling. I chose to continue – I am still running certificate and diploma courses – largely because the input and new colleagues I was driven to seek refreshed me and enabled me to rediscover why I had chosen to do this work in the first place. Being a counselling trainer has, perhaps, a limited life expectancy, and it may be important to find a way to move on, change or re-invent the role from time to time or burn-out will result. Of course, I often find the work uplifting, exciting, inspiring and deeply humanising as well as difficult and demanding; they go together, like yin and yang. I hope that by identifying and acknowledging some of the peculiar and unique stresses of this work, counselling trainers who read this will feel a little less isolated, a little more affirmed that difficult, stressful experiences are part of the job, and are not necessarily attributable to personal failings. Counselling training *is* difficult, demanding, complex and exhausting. Knowing this can enable us to prepare ourselves more effectively and give us permission to reach out for the help, support, insight and empathy that are essential to being an effective counsellor and trainer.

The tasks of a counselling trainer are multi-layered, and a large number of potential stressors can emerge. A counselling trainer wears many different hats, including those of designer, teacher, administrator, interviewer, assessor, counsellor, tutor, group facilitator and housekeeper. We have to do all of these well, and move fast and fluidly between them. There are many complex aspects, all of which require a flexible use of advanced interpersonal skills, such as maintaining delicate ethical responsibilities, being a guardian of the gateway into the counselling profession, holding confidential material, making difficult decisions about whether to fail students for poor quality work, negotiating a pastoral role with students who have problems or painful histories, and deciding how to handle sensitive issues that come up on every course. Dryden and Feltham (1994) list the pressures to which we are subjected as administrative, financial, time, interpersonal, creative, professional, and those arising from the relationship between work and home. This is a minimal inventory, which leaves out much of the intense personal investment and sensitivity involved in being effective.

Being a counselling trainer requires us to work in a space *between*: between being a counsellor and a trainer; between being a trainer and a supervisor; between the training that we ourselves received and the training that we are offering; between the organisation that hosts and administrates the course and the participants. We operate between the expectations of our students and our employers, and what we personally feel we want or are able to offer; between ourselves and our various colleagues; between the professional requirements of counselling training and the emotional and practical difficulties that individual students often have in putting these into practice in their own lives and work settings. We survive between the evolving goalposts of BAC course recognition, NVQs, trainer, supervisor and counsellor accreditation and our desire to go home to our own lives at the end of the day; between what we feel is important and what we have to be seen to be doing. Occupying this in-between space can be uncomfortable, partly because other people may not recognise that this is what we are having to do. A student or a colleague who requests your attention during a coffee break after a demanding session may not have pondered on the emotional and mental agility you must possess in order to make a smooth transition from one emotional and mental state to another, in order to give her the attention she requires.

Counsellor trainers can often feel we are doing our best and that it is never good enough. There is always something that needs our attention. If we are driven by a need to do things perfectly or please others, we can easily become exhausted and disillusioned, and struggle to tread water by expending more and more effort. The amount of time, care and attention to detail that we give is rarely recognised or appreciated. If all goes well we are taken for granted, and if things go badly there are complaints to deal with. A sense of humour and a shared enjoyment of irony with colleagues are essential. The relationships that also happen in in-between spaces are often what makes it worth while: with colleagues over lunch or between sessions, on the way to work, the conversation with a student in a break. Working too much alone in this field is a recipe for a lonely and stressful time. Douglas (1991) says that 'The cardinal destroyers of groupworkers ... are neglect, under-appreciation and isolation from others similarly engaged.'

When I mentioned to colleagues that I was writing this contribution, they laughed heartily, as much as to say 'You won't be needing any help from us, it's right there in front of you.' Indeed, our conversation was already highlighting several key issues. I was in the process of debriefing with them a stressful session I had run on a university diploma course. It was near the beginning of the course, and, as the tutor responsible for professional development and supervised fieldwork practice, I had just presented a session clarifying the expectations and requirements of the course and had offered a range of supportive suggestions and strategies. The session had been difficult and complicated for both the trainees and myself. The students, led by an individual who seemed particularly anxious about academic work, became anxious and panicky as a group. The student felt that he was unable to manage the course requirements, both because they were too difficult and because he felt that there should have been more detailed information about them available before the course started. Following him, many others expressed anxiety, doubt, anger, vulnerability and concern, saying that perhaps this wasn't the right course for them, perhaps it was the wrong model, or badly organised, or had the wrong tutors, or they felt inadequate in the face of its rigorous assessment requirements. The room, which, only half an hour previously, had contained a group of students working in a co-operative and friendly manner, became full of people joining in with anxious criticisms and complaints and it appeared that all trust in the course had been lost.

Faced with this kind of material, any counselling trainer has to think, feel and respond quickly and skilfully. I understand, of course, that new adult learners almost always find getting to grips with assignments a challenge, and that this aspect of the course presents an early opportunity to 'storm' in the presence of tutors who, they hope, can tolerate and manage their anxieties. On this occasion, I listened, facilitated, empathised, explained and suggested sources of support and ways of dealing with the problems. I could understand that a student at the beginning of this course could easily feel discouraged by its complex documentation, the different topic sections all led by different tutors, and all the different bodies and organisations involved in its administration and verification. I too would find this confusing and frustrating. I could see how new course members might perceive it as both demanding and disorganised and that my offers of help would appear inadequate. I knew that they were already experiencing difficulties with the authority of the course, which stood between them and the counselling qualification that many of them wanted. I knew some of them were unfamiliar with the person-centred approach to learning, with its emphasis on self-responsibility and learning from one's own experience. I also recognised this eruption of anxiety as a familiar event from many different diploma courses I had participated in. I was aware that the content we were discussing (the assessment issues) had become the vehicle for the process in which this group of students was beginning to face the realities of belonging to this course and to the group. The prospect of belonging, with its considerable responsibilities, made some of them feel as if it would be better to leave now, and prove the course to be inadequate, than to face potential failure. The difficulties about the assignments and course requirements were a rational coathook on which to hang up possibly unresolved feelings about belonging and not belonging to this group which combined professional elements, such as assessment and assignments, with emotive interpersonal forces, such as old feelings about school, or transferences with the staff.

This was all in the back of my mind – not necessarily fully in conscious awareness – as I worked with the group. I felt the full force of the anxiety and anger which I was asked to contain and manage. Over years of hard-won experience, I have learned not to take this too personally. I know that the feelings I experience inside myself in this situation contain some important – even essential – information about the group, which I need to process and give back to them in a more usable form. In this case, a large number of the students had had bad experiences at school and had little confidence in formal education, and were mistrustful of the fact that the group was facilitated rather than formally 'taught'.

I cannot be a conduit for a group's expression of difficult feelings without fully experiencing both the group's feelings and my personal reaction to those feelings (which in this case was a mixture of fear, inadequacy, guilt and confusion). This is personally uncomfortable and draining as, in a group, these feelings can become strong and highly charged. I have learned not to act from my own self-protective response – by staying away from any feelings of personal attack – but to steer a way through it that is in the group's best interests. With this group, this understanding was available to me – from supervision and therapy sessions, discussions with colleagues, reading everything I could find, and all the training I had gone through myself. Yet in the intensity of the moment, it wasn't much help. I was on my own with a barrage of unpleasant feelings, and the task of sorting out and then dealing with what was content and what was process. Few people find this easy. It is also stressful to facilitate sessions like these on your own, and the BAC's recommendations are for co-tutoring on substantial courses. When we are working on our own, we can only keep our eyes on one or two balls at a time, and it is likely that we will lose our vision of the field as a whole. Lecturers or teachers whose style is to stand in front of the group, deliver a lecture or presentation, allow a few minutes for questions at the end, and then leave, will experience groups very differently. Counselling training has become more sophisticated than this, and has tended towards experiential and interactive learning. A facilitative learning environment, where the learner is valued, respected and listened to, which has evolved from the person-centred tradition, requires much more of us than traditional teaching methods, where there is more protective distance between learner and teacher. One of the problems with working alone is that it is extremely difficult to deal with content and process at the same time. In a session that is content-based, it is easy to be sidetracked on to issues about process, and vice versa. An essential skill is being able to hold both of these, to identify which is which, at times keep them separate, and earmark appropriate times to follow up important issues. This is particularly difficult when our own strong feelings, fears or other responses have been triggered by the group interactions.

In retrospect, I think the best way to have handled the session I have described would have been to have identified the process that was taking place, acknowledged it, named and accepted the difficult feelings, and then firmly continued with my task, which was to make sure all the students had a clear idea of the assignments and where they could get support and help. This would have been more containing, and probably more useful. But there were a lot of pressures on me not to do this at the time, and instead to take the complaints about the course at face value, and to feel guilty.

Another major area of stress is negotiating the boundary between facilitating and offering counselling or therapy. Counselling courses are run mainly by experienced counsellors, who are used to modelling and offering the core conditions (Rogers 1951) in a professional and educational setting. This creates a warm, empathic environment in which people are encouraged to open up, share feelings, and take risks with self-disclosure. It also helps the facilitators to feel positive about their work, as they are doing what they enjoy doing and are good at. Good counsellors, however, are not necessarily effective trainers in all respects. A trained and experienced counsellor, highly skilled in one-to-one therapeutic relationships, may find it difficult to locate clear boundaries around the role of tutor/facilitator with students, who are neither clients nor colleagues. There are good arguments that counsellor trainers should model what they are conveying, so that the core model of the course is well integrated into the manner in which the course is delivered, as recommended in the BAC guidelines for counselling courses. However, a therapeutic 'law' seems to come into effect, which says that when therapeutic conditions are offered, the recipients will re-experience feelings from the past, for example anger or grief, which could not be safely experienced or expressed at the time, but which are waiting for the right conditions in order to surface. Therapeutic material thus becomes freely available, but the training/learning group is not a therapy group; the trainers may only have a contract to work specifically with such material during the personal development slots on the course. Trainers can experience this contract as stressful, since they are accustomed to working with this kind of material in their role as counsellors, and feel comfortable working in their field of expertise. Confusion can also arise in the students about the role of the facilitators, who may appear to behave in a tantalising and neglectful way, by seeming to elicit and encourage personal expressions of deep feelings but leave the students 'high and dry' and expect them to sort it out for themselves. On the other hand, I have known of courses where the trainers have given in to this pressure and have, in effect, turned entire courses into therapy groups with themselves as chief therapist, and the formal professional training requirements have been laid to one side.

It is not clear to the members of a group, until the group becomes more experienced, what is a useful and appropriate level of self-disclosure, and how therapeutic material will be handled. This strongly emotional experience of learning does not make for an easy ride for anyone involved in it. Once it is known that feelings can be expressed, they will be, and the tutors will have to take the full impact of some of them. In the personal example I have recounted, I was strongly aware that some of the anger and fear people were expressing had first arisen during their childhood experiences of 'education', which had left some of them feeling like failures, that assessments were some form of trap, that they were going to be judged by autocratic, externalised standards, and that they would be powerless to gain or contribute anything positive. At the same time they wanted me, the 'teacher', to tell them exactly how to sort out their difficulties. I had an intuitive grasp of this – but was unable to go directly to the source of the pain as I would be able to as a counsellor with a client. In my attempts to reframe some of this by listening and facilitating, I was stepping into therapeutic territory, but I could not go in all the way. But even simply acknowledging it made me more available as a target for transference feelings of all kinds. People could appreciate me for listening, or resent me for not giving them enough attention and for neglecting their real needs.

Some of what is stressful about being a counselling trainer is the result of the intense demands it makes on our inner resources. This is often hard to understand for people who work in different fields. We have to work from our own personality just as much as when we are being counsellors. Usually – unless a trainer has a particularly extrovert, robust and confident personality and feels especially at ease in groups – we are working on the edges of our 'comfort zone'. Often people who have trained as counsellors, and who later go to teach on counselling courses, have good one-to-one skills but have to learn the skills of facilitating a group. Most people have little specialist training in this, but are expected to understand and work with group dynamics, administration, programme design and so on, as if teaching, facilitation, interviewing, assessing skills or being able to operate video equipment are supposed to come naturally, like mothering skills, without any effort or tuition. There is a general lack of resources and training programmes for trainers, which implies a lack of recognition of the needs of counselling tutors, who may work in isolation on some courses. Outside the main cities, trainers may not be able to find the kind of specialist supervision or further training that would really help them to develop, offered by people with combined experience in group work, counselling and counselling training. The more competent and experienced trainers become, the more they are on their own, with few people with whom to share their special understandings. A shared body of professional practice and thinking is only slowly emerging: for example, BAC guidelines for counselling courses are often not followed in rural areas because of pressure on resources and the reliance on relatively untrained staff. Books like this one, which acknowledge counselling training as a discipline in its own right, are still unusual compared with the quantity of material available on almost every aspect of counselling. It is essential that counselling trainers get together with other counselling trainers and exchange experiences and ideas. Many counselling trainers are not aware of how their work compares with general current practice.

This loneliness can be amplified if trainers work in a setting, for example a college of further education or a university, where the special requirements of a professionally run counselling course – which are expensive and inconvenient – are not recognised, or are fulfilled grudgingly. Often there is a lack of library resources, supervision sessions are not paid for, accommodation is uncomfortable or noisy, there are not enough rooms available, and secretarial staff can experience counselling students as unreasonable, emotional and assertive. The other side of loneliness is more personal, in that even our partners and closest friends may not understand why we are tired and stressed, why we do not want to relate to our own family who are waiting when we come in the door, why we need to talk about our work so much, why we are so emotional about it, or why we think it is so important. The special, intense experiences that can occur on a counselling course are hard to talk about with people who have not experienced anything like it, or who do not have any personal experience of counselling or groupwork. And, as in counselling practice, the requirement of confidentiality puts us under further pressure.

There are, of course, other facets of stress. I believe some of the stresses I and many colleagues experience in this work are embedded in our personality structure, or in the underlying reasons why we chose to take up work that involves such intensive and demanding interpersonal contact. Often we became counsellors partly because of a desire to help ourselves and help others. If we develop to become counselling trainers and/or supervisors, it is often because we are good and effective counsellors; we know that we have the skills to facilitate others and to help them develop, and we want to push ourselves forward in our own development and careers. For some of us, counselling courses offer a bigger, more extroverted canvas than one-to-one practice, with more variety and opportunity and the chance to work with a wider range of colleagues, and perhaps with students who do not have the same presenting problems as our clients. This quest leads us up to some solid-looking inner obstacles: perhaps that is why we choose it, so that we can learn to surmount them. As suggested earlier, many counselling trainers could be described as being afflicted with stressful emotional 'scripts', such as Get it Right, Try Harder, Please Everyone, Work Hard for No Appreciation, Always Give Your Best, and Never Ask for Support. If someone has any personal issues around competence – having too much at the expense of other qualities, or having too little – then being a counselling trainer will certainly bring them out into the open. It is the kind of job where, however hard we try, and even if we do not try, we will inevitably make mistakes or have to make difficult choices where the path of action that we take can be criticised. Students and colleagues will sometimes either be angry with us or idealise us, and our personality and its limitations will become painfully transparent to the entire learning community in which we work. Learning to let the plumbing show on the outside – that is, to be congruent, self-critical and reflective but not self-denigrating – and finding ways to grow through mistakes and difficult feelings are no easier for counselling trainers than they are for anyone else.

We are not exactly immune to inter- and intra-personal difficulties of our own. Many of us inhabit the 'wounded healer' archetype from time to time and suffer the fragile aspects of our personalities that led us into the world of counselling in the first place. When we are feeling vulnerable, mistakes such as accepting on to a course a student who is not yet ready or suitable, or omissions such as forgetting to pass on information, can set off complex chains of events. Often we do this work because we enjoy the combination of contact with people and the learning about and conveying interesting psychological ideas. Having to spend time doing increasingly complex and boring administrative paperwork doesn't necessarily suit us, and it is easy to feel overwhelmed by marking, preparation, meetings and administration, all of which are unpaid unless you are in a salaried full-time post. Many counselling trainers do not enjoy the more administrative aspects of the job, and find it unpleasant to be trapped in the role of Feelingless Administrator. They handle the complex administrative responsibilities because they have to, but this part of the work can be tiring and unfulfilling.

Co-tutoring, as mentioned earlier, is generally regarded as offering some answers to these difficulties. In reality, it is a source both of great reward and of great stress. I have heard colleagues on other courses complain bitterly that their colleagues pull in different directions to them, refuse to spend time in collaborative meetings, compete with them for the affections of their students and so forth. I have found my relationships with co-tutors to be as complex as my primary family relationships, and they have required just as much time and attention if the working partnership is to be enjoyable and productive. It is impossible to cut corners on this. You have to spend a great deal of time together, planning, debriefing, discussing the students and their current needs, and discussing any feelings or reactions you have which are affecting your work. If you don't really like or respect your colleagues, or you have major philosophical differences, or differences in facilitation styles which divide you, it is extremely difficult to enjoy the work and be creative and effective as part of a team. The co-tutoring relationship, where you are responsible for holding a course between you, is as intense as a marriage or partnership. You have to communicate with each other clearly. As soon as any difficulties arise in your relationship, they can be reflected in the course and the students will pick this up.

Proctor (1991) refers to counselling trainers as inhabiting a range of archetypal roles or personalities, and states that a full deck of these is required to manage a course successfully. Archetypes she refers to include Earth Mother, Jester, Whore and Sheep Dog. For her, these roles provide 'rich opportunities' for trainers to develop skills and aspects of their personalities. There is also another side to the tendency of groups to hold their members and facilitators in certain fixed positions. The archetypes I have come across include Nurturing Mother, Neglectful Mother, Ill and Preoccupied Mother, Over-attentive Parent, Absent Father, Aloof Academic, Empathic Incompetent. These seem to be culturally embedded roles or attitudes which are ready and waiting in the group for one of the trainers to occupy from time to time, through a process of projection or projective identification by the group. It can be painful to be typecast in this way. For example, a trainer may end up as Neglectful Mother: she stayed up late writing course materials, but she was tired and had a lot to do before leaving home and forgot to buy housekeeping supplies for the course on the way to work. A trainer is competent, takes a lot of responsibility and spends a lot of time preparing and planning; but this seems to be taken for granted and his unavailability and uncaring qualities seem to be experienced by the students much more vividly than his warmth and care. On the other hand, a colleague who does not spend so much time perfecting her competence and who often comes unprepared, who goes with the flow and cannot remember when the assignments are due, occupies the role of Empathic Incompetent. This role is more appreciated by the students as they enjoy the empathy and contact and this trainer's greater personal availability, and they can sympathise with the stress she is under which prevents her getting all the details right. This can cause both trainers a lot of pain and conflict unless they can identify what is going on and find a way to share these roles between them, rather than becoming typecast into polarised positions. It can be constructive to share and exploit these opportunities, with joint awareness and agreement.

Often students prefer one trainer to another. It can be equally stressful whether you are favoured or disliked, as both can put a strain on your working relationship. If one of you gets landed with all the positive feedback and one of you with all the complaints, it is important to process this together. How much is it that the group needs to keep a 'good' and a 'bad' object, both separate; or how much is it to do with the fact that one of you is giving more, or is more skilled, or more experienced, or one of you has a less accessible style of personality, or is having a difficult time in her own life, or is unwell, or doesn't contribute as much warmth and positive feedback? All these issues become transparent to the course members; sometimes they can even become grounds for complaints. Then you have the unenviable task of establishing what is a genuine cause for complaint and what belongs where, and how this will be handled in full view of the group.

As an end-piece I would like to offer a short reflective exercise which readers might find useful as a starting point when evaluating the personal process of their work. Training can be more exciting and rewarding if we use it consciously as a means to our own ongoing development and growth, so that we can learn at least as much as, if not more than, our students from the sessions we run. My students have taught me most of what I know; it is a matter of consciously accessing what the learning is about. We need to be able to reflect on our experience as a practitioner in order to change the experiences we have been through into insight, maturity and wisdom – or into the precise do's and don'ts of hindsight. A helpful pattern is to keep a course journal or log, and use the following headings, or creative ones of your own devising. The important thing is to take the time to reflect fully on a session every so often, and to explore the edges where you felt unusual or uncomfortable feelings. If you can, do this with a colleague or in supervision as well as on your own. These questions do not cover content and presentation, how adequately you prepared, or the quality of your materials, but you may want to look at this as well.

- How did the session go?
- What did I feel good about?
- What could I have handled differently?
- What happened that I didn't expect?
- What did I particularly notice during the session?
- How was I feeling in myself, emotionally and physically?
- What am I feeling now, while in reflection on the session?
- What images or metaphors or words would best describe this session?
- Was there anything significant happening during the session (inner or outer) that you couldn't pay attention to during the session? Can you give it attention now?
- Imagine yourself in one or two of the student's chairs. Imagine yourself as the entire group.
- What was happening between me and my co-tutor?

- If there was a lesson for me in this session, or series of sessions, what would it be?
- What role was I playing/what archetypes was I inhabiting? What was my facilitator style?
- Where did I go beyond my comfort zone?
- What is my growing edge here? What do I need to help me move on?

Most of the stresses I have discussed in this chapter are already all too familiar to experienced counselling trainers. In fact, many of the very best trainers I have known have found the work too stressful to continue for more than a few years on a full-time basis. Perhaps acknowledging the reality of what training work is like and finding ways to support and prepare ourselves are far more constructive than merely trying to survive and cope; we can initiate further discussions, and develop further creative solutions. Most of all, it is not your fault if you feel worn out and inadequate from time to time – we all do – but it is our responsibility to learn to take better care of ourselves and our inner resources in this challenging environment.

References

Douglas, T. (1991) *A Handbook of Common Groupwork Problems*. London: Routledge.

Dryden, W. and Feltham, C. (1994) *Developing Counsellor Training*. London: Sage.

Proctor, B. (1991) 'On Being a Trainer', in W. Dryden, and B. Thorne (eds) *Training and Supervision for Counselling in Action*. London: Sage.

Rogers, C. (1951) *Client-Centred Therapy*. London: Constable.

Chapter 3

Issues of power for women counselling trainers

Jane Speedy

Introduction

As a counselling trainer I am much exercised and fascinated by the issues and concerns of this chapter. Acknowledgement, denial and ownership of power and flexibility of trainer style are of pressing personal and professional interest to me. I am also a woman, doing what has traditionally been seen as 'women's work'. The overt aim of the original study on which this chapter is based (Speedy 1993) was to explore the experience and perceptions of 'power' in a group of women, including myself, working as humanistic/person-centred counselling and counselling skills trainers in the UK in the 1990s. A further aim, which emerged in the process, was to find my own place, age and stage within that network of women and to reach a greater understanding of myself as a woman and a trainer.

This chapter, then, is a brief exploration of the experiences, issues and concepts of power among thirteen women trainers in humanistic/person-centred counselling and counselling skills. It explores their meaning and language of 'power' and its use and abuse in counselling training, and looks at their definitions and contexts for 'networking' as a system of support, maintenance and transfer of power.

I interviewed thirteen women, including myself, who, I perceived, were interlinked through interpersonal/professional relationships as counselling and counselling skills trainers. Further connections emerged during the course of the study. This close-knit selection represented a significant research process since it offered an overt challenge to traditional concepts of collusion, bias, distance, detachment and 'legitimate' and 'illegitimate' inclusions. All the interviewees knew something, or a great deal, of the interviewer and, it transpired, of most of the others in the group. This shared membership of the same group gave the interviewer an overt and deliberate ownership of the role of participant/

observer. Indeed, one of the interviewees concluded her interview by thanking me for conducting 'our' research. The investigation was conducted in a style that was congruent with our shared humanistic values, involving a commitment to warm, equal, open and genuine relationships. It also matched my own search for valid experiential methods implicit in the belief that: 'intimate knowledge/personal knowledge is likely to teach us more than impersonal distant knowledge' (Mair 1989). This holds particularly if that intimacy is rigorously acknowledged as part of the research paradigm.

The members of my intimate research 'sample' were aged between 37 and 72, ten out of the thirteen being in their forties, and had all been involved in counselling training for between five and twenty-five years. They came from a variety of cultural and family backgrounds and sexual orientations, which were referred to during the course of the research, but were not central to the study. The relationship between race or class (to name but two key areas) and power in counselling training is fascinating, but not the main focus of this chapter.

Conclusions cannot be drawn about all counselling trainers, or even all women counselling trainers, from my findings. This exploration can only be seen as tentatively opening a window on a particular network, and in learning something about their experience, asking questions about the experience of others from different schools of counselling training, or of a different gender. This chapter is all about gender, and all about power, but time and space precluded any gender comparisons. I hope that it is of some interest to both men and women and that what this particular group of women have to say, not least in their perceptions of men in the counselling training field, resonates with men and women alike, and perhaps stimulates similar explorations across a wider spectrum in the future.

Gender and power in counselling

An analysis of the politics and gender/power relations of counselling in Britain is beyond the remit of this chapter, but it does provide a significant backdrop to its more specific theme. Counselling has expanded rapidly in Britain from its small barefoot beginnings. The BAC is now the largest counselling organisation outside the United States (Bond and Shea 1997), and, alongside expansion, have come professionalization, a publications boom, a high media profile (for better or worse) and an increase in academic visibility and status. The BAC has maintained a commitment to counselling being an inclusive, rather than exclusive profession. None the less, a subtle change has been happening in the 'currency' of counselling qualifications and there has been a growth of second-tier training in counselling at Master's and research degree level. These courses tend to be numerically, at least, more male dominated (Speedy 1996). The specific concerns that this chapter addresses emerged directly from my experience of gender/power relationships on the M.Sc. course in Counselling Supervision and Training at the University of Bristol. The course community comprised equal numbers of men and women, a high percentage of male students for a counselling course. This balance, however, did not lead to gender equality and there seemed to be a consensus among both men and women that women were more 'powerful'. The course tutors and the majority of external workshop facilitators contributing to the course (five out of seven) were also women. Counselling training, it seemed, was a world turned upside down, in which women had skill, experience, status and power, and men felt disadvantaged.

This sense of women's powerfulness, in the world of counselling training at least, amid a backdrop of rapid structural change and transition into a 'new' profession, provided me with an impetus. I wanted to describe and understand the nature of these women and their 'powerfulness', not only as an oral history, but more importantly, in order to notice how and in what way we (as women trainers) construct, experience, own and use the power that we have. To be so informed, at a time of transition and 'coming of age' for counselling in Britain, may prove extremely useful.

In this chapter I shall offer verbatim comments from the trainers to capture some of the core issues. In using my power as a researcher to record something of the nature of this network, I was, to a certain extent, establishing my own place within it. I had the editorial powers to make choices, cuts and changes. In their absence, I have frequently cut people off in mid-sentence, and left much of what they said unheard. I have tried, as far as possible in this chapter, to enable the women interviewed to speak for themselves, and to give readers a chance to hear the richness and diversity of their voices. The limitations of time and space, however, have resulted in a distillation of thirteen voices in concert, sometimes in harmony, but with insufficient 'solo space'. This sounds remarkably like counselling training *per se*.

Different kinds of power

In their definitions of power the women that I spoke to became clearer (or I became clearer as I listened to them) about distinguishing between power as a *possession*, something tangible, that could be gained or lost, and another different meaning of power as a *process*, as an energy field to be tapped, or as 'agency'.

Power as a possession, power the noun, has tangible roots in the traditional political meaning of power as something that can be seized (as in a coup), maintained (as in the status quo), redistributed (as in socialist theory), or even shared (as in a 'stakeholder' society). Stephen Lukes (1974), the political theorist, developed a three-dimensional model of political power as something either overt, covert or latent. It seems that women in counselling training might also construct a three-dimensional model of *ascribed*, *owned* and *disguised* power, any or all of which might 'belong' either to their role as trainer in a group, to their reputation as a trainer within counselling as a 'system', or to themselves as a person and/or as a woman.

Ascribed power

Having power ascribed to them as trainers in a group was generally recognised as an everyday occupational hazard:

> 'The trainer is seen as and is expected to be powerful.' ... 'at the BAC conference the person running the workshop has assumed power.'

This ascribed power and status was seen as very tempting, seductive even:

> 'I could feel that happening to me – people in the group gave me knowledge/power/expertise, a transaction that is hard to resist in a trainer.' ... 'people sometimes give me power over them – how seductive that can be.'

Somehow, it was in the acknowledgement and ownership of this power, a recognition of what Egan (1994) would describe as the social influence of the 'attractive expert', that they were able to feel comfortable with the power and able to use it well:

> 'The role does ascribe power, and personal power needs to be used to make choices about the powerfulness.' ... 'I have to acknowledge an imbalance to start with, and work towards a more balanced distribution of power.'

Owned power

On the whole, social influence owned and initiated by themselves, rather than that ascribed to them by others, was regarded as of greater significance, or was, perhaps, a mantle worn more comfortably. Decision-making power about the parameters of training, for instance, was seen as a legitimate use of trainer power:

> 'I have the power to structure. How you structure training is important. If it is open it is power sharing by consent.' … 'I use power at the beginning to say this is what I think is a quality course – so that people can see very clearly what is there – people may not agree with it, but they know the contract if they agree to come.'

For the most part, it seemed hard to separate their trainer power, or more precisely, trainer ability to empower others, from their personal power, and also from their professional skill and expertise as a humanistic trainer:

> 'If you are going to be able to empower other people you need to be able to use first stage skills well.' … 'How empowering can you be if you don't first acknowledge your own power?' … 'real trainer power means to be able to be genuine, to be able to assess and respond to any situation you are in.'

These views are perhaps not unexpected from a group of trainers with core person-centred values. The core conditions first identified by Carl Rogers have received almost universal recognition in recent times as being necessary (if not necessarily sufficient) requirements in the establishment of counselling relationships. None the less, person-centredness continues to be misunderstood, or at least misrepresented, in the literature of counselling, as a rather 'Pollyanna' approach that encourages practitioners to give away their power (Howard 1996). This is clearly not the view of the practitioners being interviewed above, who did not deny the enormous impact that they might have, but rather acknowledged that this influence increased when power and authority were shared. As Rogers (1978) stressed, this: 'struck such an outrageous blow to the therapist's power. It was in its *politics* that it was most threatening' (italics in original).

Would a group of men with the same core values have anything different to offer? These women were very clear that they experienced gender-specific powers as trainers, both ascribed and owned. It seems likely that in a generally male-dominated society, women might have greater ease acquiring the twin skills of counselling, support and challenge. Women are likely to have a greater ease and familiarity with challenge (a 'male' virtue) than men with support (a 'female' value). In order to enter the world of counselling, men may have had to become feminised (Johns 1988) or to have claimed the high-status ground in order to keep their identities intact. In terms of gender-specific perceptions of their work as counselling trainers, the interviewees tended to assume that women were more 'powerful' than men:

> 'Women, on the whole, are much more balanced in terms of male/ female values than men.' ... 'I do feel fairly balanced. Women do this better. Women are very much further on than men. Women have taken a lead.'

Some interviewees, by no means all, had fairly negative views about maleness or male power:

> 'I do have massive stereotypes about male power being abusive and female power being much more nurturing.' ... 'Male power is about physical strength. FART. Something male about that word. It's like FUCK – powerful, short, aggressive.'

Not all perceptions of women as nurturers, whether ascribed or owned, were regarded as particularly helpful, or empowering in the trainer role:

> 'I and "women" exercise power subtly, and controllingly by being helpful. This creates over-dependency and does too much. I don't trust the growth potential of the person I'm so busy helping.' ... 'My hardest learning is that my helpful intentions have been experienced later as oppressive.'

If Carl Rogers, and more recent feminist writers, have put 'personal power' on the map of therapeutic discourse, it was principally Guggenbuhl-Craig (1971), a Jungian, who dissected 'the problem of the power shadow' in therapeutic relationships, and used the sorcerer and apprentice archetypes to explore fantasies of therapists and teachers as 'oppressively helpful' authority figures. The women I interviewed were acutely aware of a particular kind of 'bossy' power ascribed to them, particularly by male course participants, and conscious that this had an impact:

'The last woman they met with this much influence and authority was probably their infant school teacher.' ... 'Male groups see me as hag or little cutie. I don't fall easily into little cutie.' ... 'When I work with men (especially youth workers) I feel a real teacher/bossy woman/Mrs Thatcher. I fall into all of those in relation to their counterdependence.'

Disguised power

The third dimension, the 'disguised' level, was very clearly regarded as a potential misuse of power and perhaps linked most overtly with this 'problem of the power shadow'. Descriptions were littered with words such as 'abusive', 'sneaky' and 'oppressive':

'I could be sneaky and get things my way. My brief is to clarify, hold the mirror up, but I don't want to fart around forever, there are some that give up. I have power too for insinuating and sneaking things in.' ... 'Things can be unexpected. This work opens up so much – it is a potential area of abuse. It is possible to force or push the students.'

Another way in which trainers could disguise power was by 'turning on' a particular trainer style, without making the parameters and purposes transparent to the students:

'I find it all too easy to turn on the all-singing, all-dancing charisma trainer tap ... and am equally capable of an overweeningly self-denying student-centred style that covertly leaks "trainer-power" from under the carpet.'

Some interviewees recognised that they were often 'given' or expected to take this kind of 'covert' power by trainees, who have gone along with it in the moment, and perhaps only realised their discomfort later:

'It's a need for some people to fit in with my values because they feel safer.'

while others seemed to feel almost 'sneaked up on' within themselves:

'The word power connects with fear, fear that I might have it and I might misuse it.'

Power as process

The web of constructs and responses to 'trainer power' is being woven, in response to immediate training relationships. There is, of course, a rich and parallel seam connected to counselling training as a system (of which more later). For the moment, however, I would like to stay in the training room and explore the other meaning of power offered by these women trainers. This understanding of power seemed to be a different kind of word, not so much a noun, almost a verb, with close links to the notion of 'empowerment', and very different from a power that could be 'given' or 'possessed':

> 'like something in the room that is more than the individuals, almost like electricity. It seeps out of the walls (that's my fantasy about electricity anyway) and it's there to be harnessed, and also there to be damaging.'

This power seemed less tangible, its nature and source being described in terms of imagery and metaphor:

> 'It's like some kind of fountain.' ... 'It comes from within, non-external like plumbing.' ... 'It comes from here (solar plexus) up into your head.'

The ways of tapping, or harnessing 'circulating' power seemed to vary. For some, it had a direct relationship to feeling grounded within themselves (perhaps not surprising for a 'power source' like electricity!):

> 'It has to do with feeling well balanced and centred.' ... 'I know I can fill a room with energy – I have to feel okay.'

For others, the 'channelling' of this power had a transpersonal, external quality:

> 'It does not belong to me. I am like a conduit, through which something flows.' ... 'There is a thread of spirituality in this, and that is also about trainer responsibility.'

It seems that the first meaning of power, as a possession, is used by these trainers to describe the differences in *roles* in the training relationship, in an arena where it is of paramount importance to notice the 'crucial element of the difference in the balance of power between helper and helped' (Dainow and Bailey 1988). The second meaning, power as source, as a 'something in between', is used to describe potency and potential in the interaction. It is a 'doing word' which outlines the process that might take place. Power is not invested in a particular role, or individual, but rather, is simply available.

This concept of power as part of relational, circulating energy is akin to Foucault's (1980) model of 'social power', that is not located anywhere, but available to any 'agency' to define, and also to Carl Rogers' portrayal of 'personal power', which is of significance, not so much in its possession, as in its universal human potential: 'it is not so much that this approach gives power to the person, it never takes it away' (Rogers 1978).

Feminist theorists have suggested that women have a particular ease and facility with this 'process' model of power. Starhawk (1990) differentiates between power over (authority), power with (social influence and responsibility) and power-from-within (the awakening of potential); the last of these three she imbues with particularly 'female' qualities. There was no evidence from these women that this particular source of power was seen as intrinsically female, but they clearly believed that the ability to use it improved with experience:

'When I do it well, I manage it well. The role of conductor (in the lightning sense). I can use it. Harness it. I have become more aware of it more of the time – and more of the time over time as a trainer.'

Experience

Experience, in counselling training, as in life, was a core construct for the majority of interviewees and also something that would be shared from one to the other:

'I don't assume age equals wisdom, but I'd like to think I can benefit from, and use the experiences I have had in all of my life.' ... 'I have no great sense of shame about what I can't do. That will come with good use of experience, with age and with working in the field.'

The group of women interviewed each had between thirty-seven and seventy-two years' experience of life and between five and twenty-five years' experience as counselling trainers. They none the less seemed to be agreed upon the significance of experience or 'a matriarchy of passed-on experience'. As a group, they exhibited an unusual (for twentieth-century Western society) respect for age, experience, and learning from each other:

> 'As I get older and more experienced, I am more conscious of, and more want to take power seriously. The power I have wanted to exercise is less about direct power than about influence.' ... 'Being a trainer is part of my journey – not just in the here and now – being a good trainer has much to do with experience.' ... 'It is early days for me as a counselling trainer, but I will learn from my own experience, and being alongside more experienced people.'

The creative tension between 'experience' and empowerment was acknowledged in the process of the work and of 'passing it on':

> 'I wonder if the passing of wisdom is in conflict with the being empowering.' ... 'There's a tension between an empowering role and the passing on of wisdom. Sometimes I think, I'm talking too much in this training and then I think, oh well, bugger it, I've got a lot to pass on.'

There was, none the less, an immensely strong sense of experience being passed on and shared within the network, or community of trainers, which produced a rich variety of images!

> 'Elephants have a matriarchy, but other elephants change roles. Daughters care for mothers and aunts.' ... 'It's like women in the family. Trainers are sisters. Some are older, some younger, some contemporary.' ... 'Fairground rides. A sort of moving thing. In and out of dark places, light places. As the fairground moves around people loom up and fade away again, but they stay there.'

Networks

The notion of 'networking' within this 'family' was important to everybody in the group. They all had a recyclable sense of their local and national networks and 'a sense of place' within them. There was a real sense of 'passing on' of wisdom. Relationships evolved and changed, indeed, were evolving and changing during the course of my research, and then new dimensions were created:

'"X" and "y" were my gurus, then I became a peer, then I pushed off on my own.' ... 'There are still people like my parents.' ... '"X" was my supervisor, then co-trainer. She's still more experienced but the relationship has changed.'

This was particularly complex for some of the more experienced trainers who had known each other in different ways, over a long period of time:

'I don't know where to put them. That's very complicated. They would be very significant people I've learned from and they've learned from me. An incestuous, in some ways, set-up and it's gone through lots of stages.'

This sense of incest, and perhaps nepotism, was complex in that people recognised the work opportunities that had been created:

'I've always got work through the network. I rely on it for work. There are key people in my network who open up whole new networks. You were one.' ... 'It's very much through a network that bits of work have come my way.'

They also recognised, to some extent, that this was in conflict with a sense of equality of opportunity:

'Network credibility gives you a lot of power even if you balls it. I hear "x" has worked with "y". I think "x" is okay, so "y" must be as well. How do we get that right with equal opportunities?'

An interconnectedness that for some was a 'fertile root system' was for others a 'tangleweed phenomenon':

'When "x" became "y"'s trainer and then "z"'s counsellor I felt completely crowded out. I felt as if it was hard to hold the boundaries.'

One striking feature of this informal networking, as opposed to roles and connections within counselling organisations and systems, was that it was in this context that the most strongly felt gender differences materialised. A very strong sense of trainer-networking being among women in a women's world, emerged:

'My network is 100% women. I can't think of any men at all. I work with some men, but that's not networking.' ... 'My network is mostly women. I'm very fond of "x" and "y", but they don't bother. Women bother more. "X" doesn't share in the same way. Passing on what he is doing. Something about not passing on, men want to hold on to more.' ... 'I network, not to get work, but to get validated and have contact. That's different from men. I have a fantasy that men don't need this validation, are much less concerned.'

It was clear that there were men 'in the picture' of counselling training, but that networking was among women. It also connected with a sense of the networks being about love and friendship as well as work:

'There are several ways of connecting. It's usually more than one thread, not just as a trainer, there's usually a personal thread.' ... 'There are not many women with whom I have a purely instrumental relationship. It's the quality of friendship and caring that comes.'

It would be interesting to find out how (if at all) men's perceptions of informal networking were different. Certainly the literature of women in business and women in alternative subcultures suggests that women are much less likely than men to use networking as a means of marketing or gaining promotion, and much more likely to depend on outside networks for support (O'Leary and Ickorics 1992). Starhawk (1990), in describing the coven, the central network of witchcraft, describes the meaning of networking as 'intimacy and support' and the language of networking as 'gossip'. This resonates with the power invested in my own role, as researcher: as I wandered around the country, recording the stories, I also passed on the gossip, and gave and received support. In the age of telecommunications, my reputation also went before me, in that X or Y had often told Z something of the culture and process of my investigations.

Power and systems

This informal, intangible 'oral' network, has connections with the 'process' model of power. It can be tapped into, or not, in a very informal way, and perhaps has its roots in the 'barefoot' origins of counselling. It exists alongside, but very independently from the more formal counselling networks. As such, it has its links with the networking of alternative subcultures, such as witchcraft, mentioned above, and the nebulous connectedness of some political subcultures, such as the women's and ecology movements. All these movements have a rich array of underground, personal connections, and more overt and tangible arenas, such as Friends of the Earth, Green Party conferences, or, in the case of counselling training, the organisation formerly known as SCATS (Standing Conference for the Advancement of Training and Supervision).

Only five of the women being interviewed were in full-time employment with a particular institution, the rest having an immense variety of freelance and part-time working contracts. The sense of 'place' in networks, tangible and otherwise, had a very restorative quality that was felt particularly keenly by people no longer working in a team and by more isolated freelance trainers:

> 'I co-lead very seldom now, it's convenient for control, finances and organisation, but also desperately lonely. The SCATS network has been important to me.' ... 'While I taught at the college I was part of the family, talked the same language, shared the same beliefs. Working on my own I feel very isolated, I need the network, the gossip, the support.'

This sense of isolation was also experienced by people working full or part time in non-counselling organisations, who needed the 'normative' contact of a wider network within their own field:

> 'I am quite isolated. It's important to have it reinforced from outside that I'm doing reasonable work.'

Words such as 'incest', 'nepotism' and 'gossip' are, no doubt, ringing warning bells in the ears of the reader, yet there seems little doubt that the network proved immensely supportive. It was rightly unstructured, but the lack of formality brought a parallel lack of 'organised' accountability:

> 'We just have to trust each other.' ... 'It's important to be able to have a gossip, have a moan, have a brag, even, but also to be respectful, that is a paramount value.' ... 'Even a supportive network of women can be a supervision issue at times.'

Influence and professional standards

This brings us full circle to the 'coming of age' for counselling training with BAC codes of ethics and practice for trainers and the BAC accreditation of courses well established and schemes for trainer accreditation newly set up. Many of the interviewees for this study had been in at, or near, the beginning of a very young and quickly developing field of counselling and counselling skills training in Britain. The opportunities to be influential instigators have been rich and plentiful:

> 'There's BAC; SCATS; supervision. Consultancy courses coming up to BAC recognition. That's very powerful, the standards we set up there have made such a difference to so many courses and the future setting up of courses.'

The significance of the BAC in upholding standards of safety and developing codes of ethics that supported trainers and trainees alike was universally acknowledged. This was particularly so in the crucial role of upholding a complaints procedure that defended students from the kind of emotional or sexual exploitation by trainers, documented by Janice Russell (1993) and others:

> 'It's about accountability, accountability and accountability again.' ... 'Trainer power can be seductive, misused, and there need to be safeguards, like the BAC codes.' ... 'These are very real issues, and I feel very strongly about them. Trainers who seduce their students in a literal way, and I do know of some who do. I'm very clear I haven't done that.'

The trainers that I talked to worked in a range of contexts, which also brought different dimensions to trainer power as 'power over':

> 'On short courses I have been a very effective performer. Having charismatic impact that has struck/moved/impressed. At the same time I have had influence rather than power over. I think there are very different issues around power on long courses, rather than the short, fancy stuff.'

A particular dimension, that needed the overview of a 'watchdog' organisation such as the BAC, was what one woman described as the 'big deal power dynamics that qualifications bring in'. (I have discussed in Chapter 6 the complexity and enormity of the assessment task on one particular training course.) The role of trainers as assessors and gate-keepers of standards on professional training courses was seen as an inevitable 'imbalance' that needed careful monitoring:

'There is a real imbalance of power, shown in BAC complaints about course tutors. The course culture and structure is enabling and then there comes a moment that says "are you good enough?".'

The BAC, then, was both important in providing avenues for these women to influence the development of counselling and recognised as a necessarily powerful keeper of safeguards and standards. Virtually all the interviewees had taken the responsibility, at some time or another, to be involved in the workings of the BAC as their professional organisation, and some had clearly felt quite powerful and influential within it. None the less, the majority found the formality and the scale of the BAC quite alienating and disempowering:

'The BAC conference is about getting to the top of the heap. I hate it. It disempowers. I'm not a good time-server – more of a maverick.' ... 'I put a lot of effort into BAC politicking this year. I felt burned and turned off really. The wheelers and dealers are taking over from the diggers and weavers. It takes guts to stay there and does you no good as a human being.'

It is interesting that although the intimate women's networks were consistently seen as empowering (albeit at times somewhat complex and interconnected), they do not seem to have provided women with transferable skills to engage with more formal systems and organisations. Several of the women interviewed had themselves been instrumental in the moves towards professionalisation that have accompanied and been implicit in the growth and formality of the BAC. They also recognised this as something of a loss of a different tradition, that of being the 'doers' and 'passers on' in a less organised way:

'As I listen to you, and myself, I feel really sad that we might be at the end of an era.'

Many of them saw this as the end of a 'women's' era, and there was general consensus that in the current political climate of counselling, the notion of women being powerful would shift:

'As soon as an occupation becomes more status orientated there is an influx of men.' ... 'However many women you've got on the bottom rung, the higher up you go, the more men you find. That's reflected in the M.Sc. It's interesting that it's a man that's the first professor.' ... 'Probably as counselling becomes more professionalised we will see men coming forward and taking the plum jobs and the dominant ideology will change. In ten years' time, if you were doing this study the picture would look very different.'

We are not yet ten years on, but it is interesting to note that in the four years since I conducted the study, the number of professorships has grown from one to six, and only one is a woman!

Writing as power

In their role as counselling trainers, it seems clear that these women experienced and acknowledged their personal and professional power in the 'process' of training. In 'systems terms', they had their own complex, predominantly female, networks of support and had also been influential and instrumental, however uncomfortably or uneasily, in the more formalised networks and organisations of counselling training.

Another area of 'influence', about which there were very divergent thoughts and feelings, was the experience of having been 'published'. There has been an astonishing 'publications boom' in the counselling field in Britain over the last ten years. When I first interviewed them, eight out of the thirteen women had had some of their work published. As I write this chapter only one of them has yet to go into print, and some of the others have become quite prolific authors and editors:

> 'What I've written I haven't taken sole recognition for, although I've done the bulk of the writing. There are quite powerful reasons why I haven't written much. I'm on the surface lazy, but underneath terrified. This is something to work on – a really big issue!'

These are not my words, but are feelings that I can wholeheartedly identify with. It is not merely 'happenstance' that I have taken four years to get around to publishing my original findings in this chapter.

For the most part, the women interviewed recognised the power of publication, and seemed quite proud of their influence and achievements in this field:

> 'I have influence as a trainer among trainers, because I wrote a book.' ... 'And if it sells because it has my name on it, well so be it. I have some useful things to say.' ... 'They asked me to write a book. I

realised, if I could write this book it would be wonderful. It would be the most enviable thing.'

A model of power

And here we are, coming to the end of *my* chapter in this book. I have a sense of a chorus, and at times, a cacophony of women's voices, sometimes clearly raised together as women, in their sense of themselves in their work, and in their support and valuing of each other, very clear that they are operating, or being operated with, as women. At other times, they are unique, diverse, and perhaps simply human, engaged in the complex process of counselling training, as best they can. The business of being a counselling trainer is both complex and exposing, a place in which, as Connor (1994) points out, 'there is nowhere to hide'. The women who took part in this study were emotionally, spiritually and intellectually generous, almost to a fault. I ended up the richer in my understanding of myself and the network and structures that I, too, felt part of. If a core construct for these trainers, in their own understanding of their personal and professional power and influence, was a sense of self-knowledge and self-acceptance, then they, too, perhaps found the process helpful. Certainly the feedback suggests that some found this opportunity quite empowering:

> 'I didn't realise how powerful I was.' ... 'I might be surprisingly influential.'

Only time will tell whether this power and influence is of limited duration for women, whether their influence will remain or increase through their writing and their teaching or whether it will diminish and change in the systems and organisations of counselling, which will, no doubt, continue to be 'up to [their] neck in the world of money, power and politics' (Thorne 1992).

The process of this research has enabled me to construct a meta-theoretical model of power that takes account of authority and domination, as well as flexibility and transformation. This model suggests two concepts of power, power as *possession* and power as *process*, together with a three-dimensional framework of power as *acknowledged, ascribed* or *disguised*. I have found this model useful in working with men and women in exploring their potencies and responsibilities as counselling trainers. I hope the model proves of interest to other counselling trainers, and their trainees.

In time, perhaps we will learn what governed the values of this particular group, who made such strong links between powerfulness and connectedness, experience, influence and energy. Was it to do with being women, with being 'in at the beginning', with being counselling trainers, or all of these things? I suspect that we will never know and must be satisfied with capturing, 'freeze frame' in this moment, the reflections, concerns and experiences of a specific group of women on the power dimensions of their work. Given the enormous richness of the resources outlined above, I am left feeling amazed that a group with this amount of creativity, stamina and determination (three core trainer skills) has any doubts about its ability to remain influential, or feel included and central to the future development of counselling training.

'Now I can feel the size I am. All this bloody growth and where's the harvest? My power in my professional life has been my harvest.'

References

Bond, T. and Shea, C. (1997) 'Professional issues in counselling', in S. Palmer and G. McMahon (eds) *Handbook of Counselling* (2nd edn). London, Routledge.

Connor, M. (1994) *Training the Counsellor*. London, Routledge.

Dainow, S. and Bailey, C. (1988) *Developing Skills with People. Training for Person to Person Contact*. Chichester, Wiley.

Egan, G. (1994) *The Skilled Helper* (5th edn). Pacific Grove, CA, Brooks Cole.

Foucault, M. (1980) *Power/Knowledge*. New York, Pantheon.

Guggenbuhl-Craig, A. (1971) *Power in the Helping Professions*. Dallas, Spring.

Howard, A. (1996) *Challenges to Counselling and Psychotherapy*. London, Macmillan.

Johns, H. (1988) *Gender and Counselling Training*. Unpublished M.A. thesis, Open University.

Lukes, S. (1974) *Power: A Radical View*. London, Macmillan.

Mair, M. (1989) *Between Psychology and Psychotherapy: A Poetics of Experience*. London, Routledge.

O'Leary, V. and Ickorics, J. (1992) 'Cracking the glass ceiling', in U. Sekaran and F. Leing (eds) *Woman Power*. London, Sage.

Rogers, C. (1978) *On Personal Power*. London, Constable.

Russell, J. (1993) *Out of Bounds: Sexual Exploitation in Counselling and Psychotherapy*. London, Sage.

Speedy, J. (1993). 'Heroines, Healers, Harlots and Hags. An exploration of experiences, issues and concepts of power amongst women trainers in counselling and counselling skills.' Unpublished M.Sc. thesis, University of Bristol.

Speedy, J. (1996) *Gender Ratios in Counselling Training*. Student handout, Counselling Education and Training Unit, University of Bristol.

Starhawk (1990) *Dreaming the Dark: Magic, Sex and Politics*. London, Mandala.

Thorne, B. (1992) 'Psychotherapy and counselling: the quest for differences', *Counselling*, 3(4).

Chapter 4

The co-training relationship

Trish Edwards

Co-training – the process

I love co-training!

I started my career as a teacher; later I became involved in counselling and counselling training which have been fruitful activities for me both as recipient and provider. Co-training, advocated by BAC in all substantial counselling courses, has added another dimension to my learning. Each time I work with a new co-trainer I learn something new about myself; like any learning, this is not always easy to accept. As others have found, it can be painful but is always growthful (Levine 1980).

Douglas (1991) states that the high visibility of leaders in any form of group makes it almost certain that their behaviour patterns will be the single most important source of their 'real' intentions for group members, whatever the leaders' expressed intentions may be. If this is true, and I believe it is, then there is learning for trainees in the actual experience of the co-training relationship as well as in other components of training courses. How can a constructive relationship develop in the whole learning community if there is unacknowledged or unresolved difficulty between the trainers? What do co-trainers need to do to foster a congruent working relationship?

Paradox in training

Some of the dynamic tension in the training process comes from the paradoxes that Benson (1987) identifies in groupwork: each group member is his brother's keeper yet each takes responsibility for self; group members are interdependent yet autonomous; the group worker is neutral yet committed and is part of the group yet separate; groupwork is a rational activity and it is spontaneous. He likens working with groups to negotiating white water rapids, where the group worker has to roll with the waves, be prepared to switch direction suddenly, be swept along by the current for a time, then head for the bank, swerve, sway, lean and pray! My experience of counselling training is similar and I need to work in tandem with another co-trainer while negotiating these 'rapids'.

Benson sees the establishing of Assagioli's (1980) concept of 'right relations' as a powerful way of handling the different tensions and paradoxes within groups, allowing movement and growth. 'Right relations' involves engendering an atmosphere of friendship, co-operation, teamwork, sharing, empathy, goodwill, altruism, a sense of responsibility, service and understanding. This kind of relationship recognises, affirms and grows out of the essential contradictions and complementarity inherent in the paradoxes within the group. The work, values, and concerns of group members emerge out of the tensions generated by seeming opposites and the practice of 'right relations' offers a context in which the necessity of each, and the essential difference of each, can be permitted and explored without one having to dismiss or compete with the other. If the process of the training group is (ideally) to work towards this kind of relationship, then this must necessarily be modelled between the co-trainers as well as experienced between trainers and group members. If it is not evident and felt within this prominent 'group within the group' then how can 'right relations' be experienced in the whole learning community?

Negotiating 'white water rapids' while working in tandem with someone else does not just happen. Establishing a sound working relationship between co-trainers requires awareness and commitment. From my own experience as a new trainer I had been aware of the difficulties and tension I had felt as I struggled to be 'me' when working with a very experienced and supportive co-trainer. Differences in experience meant that the co-training relationship did not feel equal; I worked hard to offer something that was different yet of equal value – a key concept in co-training.

Co-training and groups

There are relatively few references to co-training in counselling training literature (Dryden and Feltham 1994). Material on group therapy offers more insight while other groupwork studies provide relevant ideas. Some of the advantages of working in tandem in group therapy have been identified by Yalom (1985) while writers from different groupwork settings (Rabin 1987, Henderson and Foster 1991, Hobbs 1992) explore the effect of co-working relationships, all of which have relevance for counselling training.

Practical advantages include the quality of planning: an increased range of techniques, strategies and experience of handling groups; greatly improved review and feedback; and more effective monitoring and evaluation (Henderson and Foster 1991). Co-training may also increase the usefulness of supervision sessions since it gives the trainer a companion on each training journey where one can support and complement the other. Two people can watch and 'feel' more than one; for example, when I sit at one side of the group during a check-in, my co-trainer sits on the other side; between us we can see much of the non-verbal interplay of the whole group in a way that one person could not. Two can generate more hunches and more strategies, and can focus separately on content and process; if one trainer is intensely involved with a group member, the other trainer may be far more aware of the remaining members' response to the interchange. Hobbs (1992) sees this as particularly useful when sensitive issues are being addressed within the group.

The range of transferential and interpersonal reactions will be broader and will become more evident as group members will differ among themselves in their reactions to each of the trainers and to the co-trainers' relationship (Rabin 1987). Most co-trainers either deliberately or unwittingly split roles; for example, one will be challenger and the other supporter. If there is a male/female partnership the image of the group as the primary family may be more strongly evoked. When there are differences between the co-trainers in race, sex, class, age, disability or some other factor, this may permit group members to work on prejudices that they have about one of the pair being able to deal with the topic or lead a group for them (Henderson and Foster 1991). For a new trainer, co-training may reduce anxiety, while feedback about each other's behaviour will help to differentiate between what is real and what is transference distortion in group members' perceptions.

Two trainers can counter group pressure more effectively than one, and the presence of another trainer may be a necessary stabiliser for the inexperienced trainer. Yalom (1985) sees two trainers as more likely to be able to deal with attack on one or both, and help the group to make constructive use of it. When trainers are 'under the gun', he writes, they may be too threatened either to clarify the attack or to encourage further attack without appearing defensive or condescending.

Openness between co-trainers may enhance the development of constructive interpersonal processes such as self-disclosure and feedback between group members (Dies, Mallett and Johnson 1979). If co-trainers express disagreement within a group, they can model for group members an ability to disagree openly, make mistakes, experience discomfort and resolve differences without permanently harming themselves. This may strengthen the honesty and potency of the group. The genuineness and congruence of trainers has often, in my experience, been a catalyst for group members' development.

Benson (1987) saw this as the key advantage of co-training: the willingness of the trainers to exploit and explore their differences in perception of the group experience for the benefit of the group. Differences in perception and response, even lack of agreement, if handled creatively, can be an exciting and enhancing experience for group members, providing more information, contrast, and alternatives, offering opportunities for giving opinions, sharing, taking stands, assessment, consideration and decision making. In certain situations, lack of agreement between the trainers may be inevitable. If the relationship is to work the trainers must be able to acknowledge publicly the other's understanding of the situation, and value it as a contribution in its own right to the total experience. When this occurs, there need be no conflict or necessity to force one viewpoint on the other.

Personal and professional growth is often generated by the co-trainers working through their relationship with one another. For myself, working with a number of co-trainers has made me examine my own levels of congruence and incongruence, of competition and co-operation, of personal safety and confidence, when and how I disempower myself, and when I feel safe enough to let go and trust the process.

Not all co-training relationships offer such a fertile experience and, as Yalom (1985) found, difficulties in co-training tend to stem from problems in the relationship. Ideally, each trainer should feel comfortable and open with the other, and learn to exploit the other's strengths; for example, one may be more able to nurture and support, the other to confront and work with anger. If co-trainers are competitive and each pursues his/her own way of working, and interrupts rather than supports a line of enquiry or response that the other started, then the group will be distracted and unsettled. A clear differential in status can lead to tension and lack of clarity about the leadership roles unless the relationship between the trainers is made explicit and each is comfortable. The more experienced trainer should encourage the co-trainer to participate in every way possible.

The combination of closeness and dissimilarity between trainers will enrich the experience of the group but other group processes may undermine the group's development. Tensions often occur in groups led by co-trainers; group members may undermine the trainers' relationship or intrude between them, much as they have done in their primary family. Factions may also emerge as group members align themselves around each co-trainer. Such alignment may occur because of personal characteristics, depending on who is seen as more intelligent or more attractive. One trainer may emerge as brilliant and stimulating while the other is seen as dull, incompetent or disorganised. This may be a form of splitting where all bad feelings are projected on to one trainer, and all the good on to the other; it may also reflect a great disparity in competency and popularity. If this feedback is known to both trainers what, ask Dryden and Feltham (1994), do the trainers do, how will they react – emotionally, cognitively, interpersonally and professionally? Similarly Henderson and Foster (1991) talk about the course members making one co-trainer out to be the 'baddie' and the other the 'goodie' in difficult times. The co-training relationship has to be strong enough to address such happenings.

Collusion between the trainers, if persistent, may also divide group and trainers; the training pair may appear to the group as powerful and hard to beat (Glassman and Kates 1990). To avoid such dangers there also needs to be time, and willingness by both, to talk before and after the session; if supervision is available then both must attend (Yalom 1985).

Levine, looking at co-training in the field of social work, points to other dangers: over-dependence on the other trainer, evasion of experiencing the full weight of responsibility for the group and its members, inhibition of professional initiative, risk and growth, and the complexity of having to work out an intense pair relationship while trying to develop one's own professional identification within the group (Levine 1980).

Establishing a co-training relationship

Inequalities in the co-training relationship are likely to be present when new and more experienced trainers begin to work together in any field. Benson (1987) sees co-training as a very sophisticated way of working and one that is not necessarily suited to the beginner, whereas Douglas argues that the only wholly satisfactory method of acquiring skill with groups is a form of apprenticeship to a skilled and experienced group worker/teacher (Douglas 1991).

If co-training is required, an apprenticeship offers a role model and some security but a number of important issues emerge. When and how do you leave your apprenticeship? If you perceive yourself (or the group perceive you) to be the apprentice, how do you come of age? What does this do for the other trainer? How, and how quickly do you become equal but different? If the group develops further and faster than the relationship between the trainers, what effect does this have on the group? Should groups be held back for the sake of the learning of the co-trainers?

My own experience as a new trainer was to work with a more experienced trainer and I felt I learned a great deal in this 'apprenticeship'. It was not without difficulty, however: while my co-trainer worked with me to establish a more equal relationship, it was clear that his first responsibility was to the group and at times I had to look after myself. Over time, difficulties and inequalities may be reinforced if not carefully monitored and worked on. If one trainer (often the less experienced one) takes the role of nurturer and supporter, and the other trainer takes the role of challenger, how does the nurturer learn to challenge and confront? The apprentice in the co-training relationship can be compared to the passenger in a car; no matter how many miles are spent in the passenger seat, generally passengers do not learn navigator skills until they are behind the driving wheel themselves (Clark 1991). If an apprentice feels 'watched' by the other trainer, then they may find difficulty in relaxing and getting to grips with the work, becoming more stilted and less skilled rather than growing more confident (Glassman and Kates 1990). I remember clearly as a new trainer that on a couple of occasions my co-trainer was ill and I worked with the group by myself. I recall the feeling of exhilaration and a new kind of knowledge that I could 'do it'. Other new co-trainers have recounted similar experiences on such occasions.

Supervision may help to identify and reduce sources of difficulty for co-trainers, particularly if it focuses on the relationship between the trainers as well as the training process. Levine (1980) maintains that it is hard to develop a clear identity as a co-trainer if you only ever work with the same person; over the years I have worked with a growing number of co-trainers and each new partnership brings its own challenges and rewards, and each new partner broadens my knowledge and understanding of working in groups. One criterion for a successful partnership is active choice of one's co-trainer (Friedman 1973). Selection should explore the similarity or compatibility of theoretical orientation as well as agreement on more practical issues such as how active or inactive each trainer believes they should be, and ways of identifying and handling problems (Paulson et al. 1976).

Clark (1991) outlines the groundwork needed to establish an equal working partnership: shared understanding of aims and objectives, a common style or approach when working with the group, and a relationship based on professional respect. Although there may be disparities in terms of knowledge, experience, skills, models or beliefs, there needs to be a willingness to respect and accept each other as people and to value the differences between them in order to make an effective team. What impedes the development of this personal respect, he argues, is a failure to recognise that training is a 'narcissistic' profession, that is that the product 'sold' by the trainer is him or herself, and this product is explicitly and regularly assessed by others. Many trainers find it difficult to cope with this continuing process of being 'accepted' or 'rejected' by groups. By its nature, he argues, the co-training relationship lends itself to repressed and unacknowledged feelings of inadequacy and envy.

In order to manage some of these potential problems, a thorough planning schedule was drawn up for intending co-trainers by Hodge (1985) to help them systematically work through issues and circumstances that might affect the co-training relationship; this includes theoretical orientation, issues related to the setting of the work and to authority, theoretical and practical considerations, the co-training relationship itself, defining the aims and objectives of the group, establishing how goals are going to be achieved, leadership styles and the management of meetings. When the co-training relationship works well, the trainers are in tune with each other's intended direction, thoughts and feelings, and are able to interject with appropriate additional material in a manner which complements and does not disrupt the other's work (Hobbs 1992).

A high level of skill, co-operation and commitment indeed!

The co-training relationship revisited

After some years of experience as a counselling trainer, I found in the M.Sc. Counselling (Supervision and Training) course the opportunity to research one particular aspect of the training process: the co-training partnership. The resulting study lives in me as a major achievement in my training life; it allowed me to explore and improve my training practice, and explore and learn more about me. The focus of my study was the co-training relationships of colleagues working on the Royal Society of Arts (RSA) Counselling Skills in the Development of Learning courses. The RSA sees the presence of two trainers working jointly throughout the course as an essential training requirement; the model of this course is to mirror the counselling process. As the relationship in counselling is accepted as a fundamental part of the process, so the co-training relationship is crucial. For many of the participants on the course this is their first substantial introduction to counselling training and their relationship with and experience of the trainers is particularly significant.

To find out how other trainers experienced the co-training relationship and some of the difficulties they had met, I interviewed eight co-trainers who had all worked on RSA courses. I was also interested in exploring with them the idea of paradox – that is the self-contradictory yet true concepts and forces that provide dynamic tension within groups and so account for some of the excitement and danger in the work.

During in-depth interviews about their experience of co-training my colleagues echoed and extended many of the advantages and disadvantages outlined above. Anne, Beth, Cath, Dave, Evie, Faye and Glyn either worked together in the same training team that I was in or worked in other local training providers on RSA courses. It seems fitting that, as they contributed so much to my research, their voices should also be heard in this chapter.

Advantages

The clearest benefits come from shared responsibility for selection, coping with the consequences of poor selection, as well as for input and the running of the sessions. Co-training was also felt to relieve pressure at times.

Dave: When the chips are down, you can't pull out an overhead projector and blind them with science. That's when you need your co-trainer with you. Even when it's midnight on the residential weekend, I can let my hair down and have fun, but I never lose sight of my role as trainer. My responsibility to the group never fades away.

Some felt that sessions were likely to be less trainer-centred and less trainer-directed if there were two trainers. One could keep a check on the other; for example, opening things up to the group, breaking up a question and answer exchange and getting the whole group working.

Faye: We have a clear plan of where we might go but we are now more able to dump that and respond to immediate needs; we are modelling immediacy.

It was also seen as helpful for group members to hear from the trainers different perceptions of what was going on within the group with perhaps a differing feel of whether to move on or not. This helped individuals in the group to express their own perception and broadened negotiation. If there is conflict or collusion developing between trainer and group member, the other trainer can observe and give feedback. Faye had observed what seemed like a 'seduction' process between student and single trainer on an introductory course and felt this was less likely to happen if there were two trainers, and that if it did there was someone else to monitor what was happening.

Within the co-training partnership, one trainer can put self on hold and give the other the opportunity to risk a more challenging response or intervention, and, obversely, one trainer can use more of self with a co-trainer present. Glyn described a situation when he felt able to step into a group and challenge some extreme dysfunctional behaviour from one member of the group (who later withdrew from the course). He felt able to be himself and confront in a more real, genuine way because his co-trainer was still there to monitor the process and to offer appropriate feedback and support. Co-training also gives immediate access to peer supervision which can operate within and between sessions for the length of the whole learning experience.

Overall, it was felt that co-training generates more ideas and creative ways of working and the available pool of energy is greater. Faye felt that apart from generating more ideas, co-training encouraged trainers to experiment and try new ideas. These were likely to evolve between two trainers working together, as each bounced ideas off the other.

Difficulties

The difficulties experienced were connected with the relationship and echoed the work of Yalom and the other writers mentioned earlier. Spontaneity within the group was seen as difficult to achieve unless the relationship was good; sometimes group members got confused by contradictory messages, information or opinions. Faye spoke feelingly about the need for trainers to keep both positive and negative transference from group members in perspective, and to avoid any vying for power between the trainers. This theme was expanded by Evie.

Evie: We let group members know that we consult about things which have a bearing on the progress of individuals through the course, and about things which relate to the group as a whole. We try to keep everything as open as possible and to avoid one trainer being played against another.

All the trainers acknowledged that making the relationship work required commitment, negotiation and a shared philosophy of learning; planning and debriefing time was essential. Where two more experienced trainers were working together, less time was needed for planning and there was more willingness to abandon structure and follow the group. Even so, time was an issue for all the trainers.

In the main, difficulties within the co-training relationship seemed to occur where there were variations in experience and confidence between the trainers. The imbalance of experience caused tensions which sometimes spilled over into the group. It became clear that there were frustrations for both co-trainers. The feelings and frustrations that new co-trainers experienced from time to time in the first years of working with a more experienced colleague were graphically described. These included feeling more like a group member than a trainer, not knowing how to be in the group, as well as feeling impotent and deskilled.

Evie: There was a tension for me because I didn't want to be just an observer, or one of the group. But I felt I hadn't won my wings, so I couldn't behave like a trainer.

Faye: The experienced trainers can make mistakes and still draw out the learning and it all comes together, while I sit there thinking 'what's going on?'.

Beth: In the previous training that I had done, I was very confident and felt I knew what I was doing – coming into co-training was like taking a step back. I had to learn how to do it again.

Several newer trainers talked of giving away their power in the training role.

Beth: Power lies with Dave because I put it there, he has more experience.

Cath: When I started there was a lot of my stuff going on about being an apprentice.

One of the strongest comments came from Evie about how she had felt during her first year as a co-trainer:

Evie: I used to think of myself as the magician's assistant, not having the skill and the power to be another magician, which was frustrating and demeaning. The omnipotent bit of me couldn't stand being the assistant, the minion.

While several trainers were aware of their own inexperience as they came into co-training, Cath had also had experience of the effect of such disparity from the point of view of group members.

Cath: I've been in a group where there was a new and an experienced tutor. It was rather unnerving as a student. We tended to ignore the new one, the apprentice, and go to the experienced tutor who was then invested with a lot of power over the group, and over the co-tutor, who even started making jibes about the co-tutor in front of the group.

One new trainer saw it from the perspective of the more experienced trainer.

Beth: It probably puts a strain on them. When can they make mistakes?

What also became clear was the frustration that the more experienced trainers felt from time to time. For Dave, this included working at times in contradiction to his preferred style.

Dave: I can't always be open and immediate in the group. If there is friction between myself and my colleague, I can't always bring this in to the group. It's not appropriate, but sometimes it makes me dysfunctional.

Whatever the level of training, the more experienced co-trainers at times felt unsupported by their partners and resentful.

Dave: At times I've felt unsupported. My colleague sometimes disappears when the chips are down. ... Why should I have to look after my co-tutor? It's hard enough looking after myself at times.

Juggling with different priorities – group, co-trainer and self – was also experienced as difficult at times.

Faye: No matter how much planning and preparation you do with a newer trainer, you can't ensure that everything works as you want it to. A couple of times I've felt that I've had the ground cut away under my feet by a new trainer in the middle of a session, and then I've had to keep the learning and the safety of the group uppermost, try not to undermine the other tutor, and hang on to my own stuff! The group comes first, the co-trainers can sort their issues out later.

Another outcome of the difficulties experienced was the imbalance between the progress of the group and that of one of the trainers.

Dave: I've felt as if I was running the course by myself at times, my co-tutor was there but not there; and the group moved on but the tutor didn't.

For Dave it was difficult to break out of the existing pattern; he felt he was the one to initiate discussion about the difficulties in the co-training relationship, and, by this very fact was reinforcing the inequality.

Dave: I'm the one who says we need to work on this, and by the very fact that I do it, it's perpetuating the status quo.

Glyn, who had worked with a number of co-trainers, commented:

Glyn: In most of my co-tutoring partnerships, I've been the more experienced one, and had to handle the misunderstanding, lack of understanding, the naivety of the tutor, and at the same time help that tutor to be as equal as they can. I'm conscious of being the more experienced one and try not to let that inhibit me or the other person too much.

He described some of the difficulties he had found being the more experienced trainer working with a less experienced female trainer in a predominantly female group:

Glyn: It can be difficult in two ways. A few students will have had a bad experience of abuse of power and project that onto me, and I find myself holding something that's not mine, but it clearly is to them. Others defer to me and think that tutors aren't there to be challenged or equal. So for some I'm a challenge, for others I'm a disappointment. It's a bit like being given star billing, and then they find you're only a mere mortal after all.

Sometimes the newer tutor can evoke protectiveness from some group members. So then there's a contrast between the 'good' and the 'bad' tutor.

While most inexperienced trainers felt their lack of confidence or lack of clarity about their role more keenly in large groups, all were happy about their contributions in subgroups. They all also felt that some of their participation in the large group was competent, so that feelings of difficulty did not extend over all course activities or for unbroken periods of time. Although talking over difficulties with co-trainers helped to lessen lack of confidence and they could work out strategies to take more of an equal share, it was not always easy to sustain their contribution.

Evie: We talked it through and I found ways of taking a more equal share, but then I handed power back again; to a certain extent this has continued with a change of tutor.

Unlike Evie, once Anne began to feel her power in the co-training role, it was a reinforcing process.

Anne: It was too easy to sit back and let my partner do the work, then I felt pressure to make my own contribution and was only aware of feeling inadequate. When I began to realize that *I* could do something about this, that there were contributions that I could make that were my own, then I relaxed enough to start learning.

Anne and Faye were both able to identify a critical experience that was a watershed in their development as co-trainers.

Anne: The change came when I was running the group myself, my co-tutor was ill. They were challenging me hard about something that had happened the previous week. I held and dealt with the challenge, and was quite challenging myself. They said later that they probably would not have challenged had the other tutor been there. I was less formidable!

Faye: I was thrown in at the deep end when my co-trainer was taken ill suddenly during a residential weekend. I was left by myself with two half groups who had had very different experiences of the same exercise. The group I had worked with had been 'storming', while the other group, which my co-trainer had worked with, had been beautifully 'performing'. I was left to integrate the two half groups, process the learning, and move on. It really did feel as if I was left in the deep end – but I did swim.

Accepting and working to each other's strengths also helped Cath:

Cath: We worked to become more equal, now we're more interchangeable, although we also work to each other's strengths – she's
great on theory and likes more structure. I like leaving things to
rise, I'm more prepared to go with the group, I find it exciting …
and terrifying.

There was recognition by experienced trainers that at times they need to
draw back and give more space to newer colleagues.

Glyn: I have had a lot of experience, but I don't want to feel responsible for everything and be a ringmaster dominating everything
that happens around me. I often prefer to withdraw into the background because it's too easy to take over myself. So I stand back
and let the other tutor take over, and then I'm free to respond and
come in at any time because I know I can.

Moving forward

Training supervision gave a forum for perceived differences in experience to be explored. In supervision for one training team, one trainer
said that she felt like her co-trainer's little sister; once this was expressed,
both trainers worked towards a more equal partnership. All the trainers
stated that their continuing professional development with further counselling and groupwork courses helped them to feel more at ease in the
co-training role. The possibility of changing co-trainers was limited for
some, but for others was put into practice when the opportunity arose so
that trainers gained a wider experience by working with a number of
different partners.

There was a common approach to working out differences in co-
training. Personality clashes between trainers, sitting on difficult
feelings or tension between trainers were not helpful, but these should
be expressed and worked on outside the group preferably in supervision.
On the other hand, differences of perception or opinion between trainers
could usefully be looked at within the group.

Faye: It gets away from the idea that some group members have that
there is a 'right' way to do things, and helps them to develop a
sense of what's appropriate for themselves.

It can be difficult for individual co-trainers to take their own power,
and it may take some time. Each must confront his/her own issues

around power and each must realise his/her own 'power-from-within' (the awakening of potential for the individual) in order to realise his/her own 'power-with' (social influence and responsibility), and each needs to monitor his/her 'power-over' (authority and control) (Starhawk 1990), both within the whole group and within the co-training partnership. The new co-trainer learns to take his/her own personal power appropriately and not wait for it to be given. In this situation, there is a parallel process: the new trainer is learning to take personal power within the co-training relationship, as the members of the group are learning to do the same within the learning community. All of the trainers were very aware of the power in the training process, the potential power in the role of trainer, the power invested in trainers by some group members in the trainer role, and the potential for abuse of power if not carefully monitored.

Even if both co-trainers strive to make the relationship as equal as possible, it could be argued that it can never be equal, because of different knowledge, skill and experience. A paradox for co-trainers is that they are not in competition and yet will be seen differently. Equal but different is an ideal perception; and human nature prompts comparison between the two.

As the training partnerships developed and as 'right relations' were established, more flexibility and fluidity in the training process were experienced.

Beth: We're increasingly trying to balance our roles, they are separate only in terms of organisation and co-ordinating.

Dave: We're able to slip in and out of different roles.

Evie: When we're working well together, there's unspoken communication between us.

Glyn: Ideally co-trainers should work interchangeably. Each should be in tune with the other, so that there's a complementary style, an easiness with each other and a developmental flow rather than a rigid 'your turn, my turn' approach.

Dave: It's like free-wheeling downhill, it's lovely; either of us can pick up the ball and run. There is a resonance between us which is symbiotic, organic, intuitive.

Faye: Like two amoebas, we're complementary, we change shapes to suit each other and the group.

Beth echoed the thoughts of other trainers when she said:

Beth: The co-training relationship is a developing one; it is often intimate and therapeutic. We learn and develop and become more
aware of each other, and this leads me to more of my own personal work.

Conclusion

Bringing to awareness some of the issues in this key relationship in counselling training proved useful at the time of the research and as new team
members have entered our training team. Revisiting these issues now
has also given me a sense of how far we have moved since then in some
respects, but also reminds me that issues around power are never far
from the surface. The ethical framework and boundaries of all counselling work are paramount; co-training gives added support for holding
the boundaries clearly and tightly within the training process.

New questions emerge constantly. This research was based on the experiences of a number of co-training partners, while the experiences and
perceptions of group members were not elicited. Ironically and paradoxically, the 'group' has been almost invisible in this study. The effect
of gender was also not addressed. Both these issues are worthy of further
exploration.

As I reflect upon the co-training relationship, what has been confirmed
for me is the safety it offers not just to the trainers themselves but to
those course members who enter the 'white water rapids' with them. I
have been fortunate to work on a course whose examining body requires
two trainers, and within an organisation which in spite of financial restrictions recognises and supports the need for co-training within counselling training programmes. Counselling training is powerful and at times
difficult, if not dangerous; co-training increases the level of support which
then allows all involved to take risks, learn together and go forward.

References

Assagioli, R. (1980) *Psychosynthesis: A Collection of Basic Writings*,
    Wellingborough: Turnstone Books.
Benson, J.F. (1987) *Working More Creatively in Groups*, London: Routledge.
Clark, N. (1991) *Managing Personal Learning and Change*, London: McGraw-
    Hill.
Dies, R.R., Mallett, J. and Johnson, F. (1979) 'Openness in the Coleader rela-
    tionship'. *Small Group Behaviour*, 10(4), 523–45.
Douglas, T. (1991) *Common Groupwork Problems*, London: Routledge.

Dryden, W. and Feltham, C. (1994) *Developing Counsellor Training,* London: Sage.

Friedman, B. (1973) 'Co-therapy: A growth experience for therapists'. *Internal Journal of Group Psychotherapy,* 23, 211–34.

Glassman, U. and Kates, L. (1990) *Group Work,* Newbury Park, California: Sage.

Henderson, P. and Foster, G. (1991) *Groupwork,* N.E.C., Cambridge.

Hobbs, T. (ed.) (1992) *Experiential Training,* London: Tavistock/Routledge.

Hodge, J. (1985) *Planning for Co-Leadership,* Newcastle upon Tyne: Groupvine.

Levine, B. (1980) 'Co-leadership approaches to learning groupwork'. *Social Work with Groups,* 3(4).

Paulson, I. *et al.* (1976) 'Cotherapy: what is the crux of the relationship?'. *International Journal of Group Psychotherapy,* 26, 213–24.

Rabin, H.M. (1987) 'How does co-therapy compare with regular group therapy?'. *American Journal of Psychotherapy,* 21, 245–55.

Starhawk (1990) *Truth or Dare,* San Francisco: Harper & Row.

Yalom, I.D. (1985) *The Theory and Practice of Group Psychotherapy,* New York: Basic Books.

Part II

Aspects of counselling training

Juggling or fire-eating?

The six chapters in this section explore a variety of *training* issues, all of which necessitate the balancing of needs, responsibilities, skills, awareness and values in a range of settings.

The first three contributors outline some passions and paradoxes to do with professional counselling or counselling skills training. In such contexts, students commit themselves to a course in some depth over a substantial period of time, will undertake assessment and face, with tutors, all the fascination and rigours of being in groups as a central part of the training process. These chapters consider appropriate and innovative kinds of learning, the needs and potential of adult, mature students, the complex issues of creative methods of assessment and some aspects of group experience in counselling training.

The second three chapters tackle some of the 'juggling' demands of counselling training in the voluntary field. Here, participants are choosing to commit their own time to acquire counselling skills in the service of others – and, of course, in pursuit of their own self-development. Training in this context has some of the same balancing acts described above – course design, the place and purpose of group activity, the relevance of different kinds of learning opportunities. Many of the current developments in the wider world of counselling, however, have particular implications for volunteer counselling agencies – some of them more dangerously like 'fire-eating' than the relaxation of juggling. The contributors explore the effects and unintended consequences of professionalisation, the challenge of offering counselling skills training in organisations whose primary purpose is something other and the fascination of adapting counselling training techniques to telephone contact rather than the more traditional face-to-face meeting.

Chapter 5

Reflective learning

Celia Levy

For me, becoming a counselling trainer was serendipitous. At the time I was asked to be the third facilitator on a recently established Foundation Course in Counselling Skills, I was already practising as a counsellor, but had not contemplated becoming a trainer. Nothing could have prepared me for what was to come, neither the rewards nor the complex challenges. My novice years were terrifying and yet, at the same time, magically transforming. I applied for the M.Sc. in Counselling Supervision and Training at the University of Bristol in 1992 in order to create a context for myself in which I could reflect on and learn more about the training process. My research project arose out of my curiosity to discover and uncover how students change during counselling training. It will already be apparent that while I was busily engaged in exploring changes in my students' lives, I was seeking some way of explaining my own transformation: hence the title that emerged for my study was 'The Parallel Journey' (Levy 1994).

In this chapter, I offer some highlights from the study in which I evolved one way of facilitating reflective learning for a group of students during the thirty weeks of a Foundation Course in Counselling Skills. Throughout the study, I kept my own journal in the interests of reflexivity, a key concept in qualitative research in the counselling field. As a researcher, I had to take responsibility for constructing that which I claim to have discovered. Reflecting on the research process enabled me to tell my story and explain how my presence as both a participant and an observer influenced the meanings I attributed to the body of data collected during the study. Some extracts from my research journal are included below.

As I reflect here on the multitude of reflections from all the participants in this project, you are invited to join me in this hall of mirrors.

The reflective practitioner

The counsellor's use of self is one of the most important products of counselling training and stems more from growing awareness of self than from learning the techniques or skills of counselling. The capacity to be-in-relationship with another person (client) requires an investment in the self of the counsellor both during and after training. Mearns and Thorne (1988) stress the importance of facilitating intra-personal channels of communication in training in order to enhance the quality of the counsellor's being. This includes the capacity for self-love, the ability to listen to the self and self-acceptance. In course outlines, such objectives are usually couched in terms such as 'personal growth and development', 'increasing self-awareness' or 'self-exploration'.

To achieve this, counselling training involves experiential learning, facilitated 'through an active and aware involvement of the whole person – as a spiritual, thinking, feeling, choosing, energetically and physically embodied being' (Heron 1989: 11). Perhaps the best known account of experiential learning is Kolb's (1984), which describes a cycle of learning activities that include concrete experience (the learner actively explores an experience and tests out ideas and assumptions), reflective observation (the learner critically reviews this experience), abstract conceptualisation (the integration of theory and practice), and active experimentation (the learner puts into practice what has been learned and receives feedback). Thus the endless learning spiral involves a *doing* component and a *reflective* component, the synthesis of which results in what Schon (1983) has labelled 'the reflective practitioner'.

One of the more challenging issues for trainers is how to assess the quality of trainees' reflections on their learning. What is acceptable and what is not? On many training courses, some form of learning record is required from students to demonstrate evidence of learning, for example 'statements about the self, ideas, reflections, observations, statements from peers and tutors as well as score sheets from exercises or instruments that form part of the course' (Wheeler 1996: 76). Little guidance on assessment of learning records exists in the literature or in documentation for validation of counselling courses. Wheeler emphasises the fact that students need to learn how to bring the impact of their experiences into conscious awareness and record these meaningfully.

Reflexivity: notes from my research journal
It has begun. The question is here. I will explore the nature and process of personal change. I notice at once that my eagerness to observe change

is other-directed. And yet, in that private space where the researcher and I communicate, I tell the researcher that I, too, am in the process of change. I am on a course as well, different from the one you want to study. See the spirals coiling round and round, holding each other in never-ending revolution. There is no exit, no clear space for this research. I am there alongside you, inevitably and inexorably. I feel your urgency: your need to enquire. I will try to give you what you want and in return I require that you take account of me.

The search for an answer

The central question to be addressed in this study was: what impact does a Foundation Course in Counselling Skills have on its participants? Apart from my overtly declared interests in exploring change, I had another motive for undertaking this particular study. This was to demonstrate that the growing trend towards assessment of competencies was insufficient on its own as a measure of change. In a recent article, Mearns (1997) criticises NVQs (national vocational qualifications) as measuring only '*surface relational competencies*', whereas the extent of personal development work required on person-centred training courses enables students to work at relational depth. I wanted to tell this more profound story, not with the aim of establishing standards for counsellors, but in order to understand more about the process of personal development itself.

My next task was to find a means of enabling students to reflect on their learning experiences. I needed to collect a body of data that had some structure so that I could present meaningful findings. If the task were too open-ended, for example writing a learning journal, I would not be able to provide any evidence of trends; if too directed, the students might only reflect on what was asked and be denied the pleasure of discovering meaning for themselves. This tension was ever-present throughout the project.

Context of the study

The Foundation Course in Counselling Skills (ninety hours) took place in an adult education establishment, the City Literary Institute, in London. The core philosophy of the course was humanistic, focusing mainly on the approach to counselling put forward by Carl Rogers (1961). In line with this, the facilitation style was student-centred. The course was not accredited, but many students attended with a view to pursuing further training and a career in counselling. At the start of the course a group contract and a group agenda (content) were negotiated with the students. The trainers (of whom I was one) undertook to present the agreed content in a meaningful order.

The research group initially comprised twenty-six students and three trainers. Students came from a variety of different backgrounds which included differences in class, sexuality, ethnicity, nationality, age, parental role, health, educational and employment status. The trainers were all women, of varying ages between 42 and 60 years.

The structure of each weekly three-hour session involved a brief opening round, followed by the tutors introducing the topic for the session, experiential exercises and time for feedback and discussion (ninety minutes). After the half-hour coffee break, the group divided into three personal development groups, each with a trainer, and worked together for fifty minutes. Then the whole group reassembled in the base room for a closing round.

Reflexivity: notes from my research journal
Hear this: I am your trainer and I want to be a resource for you, to enable you to learn what you choose to learn. I am here for you (and for me because I find the process fascinating).

Hear this: I am a researcher and I want to find out how you change and what contributes to your development over the next thirty weeks. I want you to join me, please, in this enquiry, but if you don't want to, that's OK (I think).

Hear this: I am a trainee too and feel myself changing from week to week. I can't always make sense of it. Perhaps you will teach me what I need to know for myself.

Finding a framework

I chose to use a qualitative research methodology because its underpinning philosophy accords with the humanistic values which are central to my counselling and training practice. For example, qualitative research is interested in 'meanings' rather than 'causes' and is based on involvement, empathy and experience (Munn-Giddings 1993). I was not aiming to conduct research *on* the students, but rather to do research *with* them as co-researchers in a more equal relationship. Their views and meanings would have central priority.

This is precisely what an action research framework aims to achieve. A definition pertinent to this study, was formulated by Carr and Kemmis (1986):

> Action research is a form of self-reflective enquiry undertaken by participants (teachers, students or principals, for example) in social (including educational) situations in order to improve the rationality and justice of (a) their own social or educational practices, (b) their understanding of these practices, and (c) the situations (and institutions) in which these practices are carried out.

Action research is an on-the-spot procedure for dealing with a specific issue in an immediate situation. Its aim is to bring lasting benefit to the current process rather than to some future occasion. It is flexible and adaptable and therefore more useful to educational research than scientific methods based on logical positivism. The action researcher 'has made a decision to understand the world from her own point of view as an individual claiming originality and exercising her own judgment, intending her understandings to be used by others if they wish' (McNiff 1988: 124).

In order to explore the impact of the course on its students and trainers and discover a meaningful way of facilitating reflective learning, participants were given five sets of trigger questions at regular intervals over the thirty weeks of the course (sessions one, seven, fourteen, twenty-two and twenty-eight). The sets of questions were not planned in advance of the course, except for the very first set which was given out at the end of the first session. Each subsequent set of questions emerged from hypotheses arising from our (my co-trainers' and my own) understanding of events as the course progressed. The questions were open-ended and aimed to provide participants with the opportunity of reflecting in writing on their learning and experiences on the course (see table 1). Individual experience was a central concern.

Participation in the research project was voluntary. The trainees were invited to become co-researchers by contributing questions of their own.

The research design aimed to illuminate our shared experiences as they happened. It was felt to be important that participants' responses to questions did not disappear into a 'black hole' only to reappear in the form of a dissertation at a later stage, without having been discussed, confirmed or challenged. After each set of responses had been collected, I presented a verbal report of the general trends to the course group the following week. The aim of the report-back was to bring individual experiences into group awareness: to allow material that was discovered through the research to inform the group process. This was one way in which the research was reflexive. Another was to explore the impact of the research on the students. In each set of questions, students were asked

Table 1 Examples of trigger questions from each set

Set	Trigger questions
1 (week one)	What were your first impressions of the tutors? What were your first impressions of the group? (Feel free to draw pictures, use metaphors or other images.) How did you feel in relation to the group? Did any people stand out? If so, write a bit about each person. What struck you about them?
2 (week seven)	Are there any comments you want to make arising from the last set of questions and the report back to the group? How do you see (or feel about) the group as a whole? How do you see (or feel about) yourself in the large group? Have your impressions of others in the group changed? If so, please elaborate.
3 (week fourteen)	In the process of choosing your small group, did you get what you wanted? If so, how? If you didn't get what you wanted, can you say why? Were you aware of taking any risks during the session today? Please expand. How have you found answering these questions?
4 (week twenty-two)	How do you see yourself now as compared to the start of the course? Have you changed? Please say how. Have your perceptions of others on the course changed? If so, how? Are you aware of any projections you have made on to others in the group? Have your perceptions of the trainers changed? If so, how? What has the impact of this course been on you and your relationships outside the course? What feedback have you been given about this?
5 (week twenty-eight)	What are the most important things you've learned about yourself over the duration of this course? What are the most important things you've learned about other people? What has challenged you most on this course? What has the impact of these trigger questions (including this set) been on you and on the course?

to comment on how they had found answering the questions, and from the second set onwards, if they had any comments on the report-back to the group.

Issues of confidentiality were very important as the research process unfolded. Initially students gave permission for their responses to be included in the report-back, provided no one was singled out by name. Consent was later extended to allow me to present the findings in the form of a dissertation or a published document such as this chapter. But anonymity created other problems for the course group and left students wondering who had authored particular comments. This also presented problems for us as trainers: the research data formed a sub-text that could not be alluded to in sessions. It was up to the students themselves to raise points they wished to make in the group.

Reflexivity: notes from my research journal
The action is over: one process ends and another begins. The ending is tender and loving in places, hot and angry in others and distinctly absent of feeling for some. Today you are there as trainer, occupying your space. Alongside your co-trainers you help to bring the course to a close. As researcher, you are grateful and humbled by all that has been shared, and delighted that the process has been so meaningful to participants. Now you have to take it away from the group and make sense of it all; the arduous and lonely walk of the researcher. I notice your reluctance and awareness that this part of the research raises uncomfortable feelings. The participants have entrusted you with their personal stories. How will you do justice to them all and yet remain true to the purposes of the research?

Telling the story

> An old Rabbi spoke to his son who was copying a passage from the Torah and said, 'My son, be careful in your work and do not change one title or word, for in so doing you would change the whole world.'
> (Gersie and King 1990: 30)

As stated earlier, participation in the research was voluntary. Over the thirty weeks of the course, the participation rate increased from 69 to 80 per cent, indicating that students could see the value for themselves and others of responding to the trigger questions. Altogether, their responses generated around 100,000 words. The story presented below can only draw on a small sample of their detailed and often passionate responses. I have based my selection on some of the central aspects of person-centred counselling which reflect the development of use of self with respect to the core conditions (Rogers 1961). I have also included a section which explores the impact of the research on the course and the students. I have omitted much that is fascinating and of value: for example, how students adapted to the student-centred approach to learning; the impact of their experiences in the personal development groups; how they dealt with life events that occurred during the course and how they related to and felt about the trainers.

(Notation: In order to preserve anonymity, each of the twenty-two students who participated in the project was identified by a number prefixed by the letter 'S'. For example, student no.1 becomes S1.)

1   *The development of acceptance and empathy: self in relation to other*
In the first set of questions, students were asked if any people stood out. Their responses indicate the baseline from which they developed. The most striking feature of their initial responses was the attention paid to differences. Eleven people noted that one student stammered: however, this student presented an enigma because she seemed so articulate and confident, and it was possible to observe students grappling with a stereotype that had been invalidated. *She appears to be (although she says she isn't) so confident and assertive* (S1). *I was filled with admiration at the way she handles her problem. She seems in control* (S4). *She stuck out in my mind initially because of her stammer then for her intelligence and humour* (S5). One student made an empathic observation: *I wonder if it cuts her when no one dares to interrupt her?* (S2).

The next most important difference to be noted was the gender split: the group was predominantly female. *As usual there were many more women than men* (S5). *As one of the few men, I felt rather conspicuous* (S14).

Age differences were noticed in a variety of ways: *I was pleased to find that there were some older women around my age* (S1), as compared with, *My first impression of the group was how young, in most cases, everyone was and that they were more like students of life than participants who wished to stamp their personality on life* (S18). *The group appeared to be a mixed bunch ranging from early twenties to late fifties* (S15).

The fact that the group members were mostly white was commented upon: *it was overwhelmingly female and white* (S14). Others made similar remarks about the white, middle-class nature of the group. One student wrote, *I felt a 'foreigner' as usual* (S9). Other differences were mentioned by only a few: *Again, as expected, I thought the majority of the group were straight* (S14). One student was noticed by a few others because she was *beautiful* (S2); *very pretty and bubbly* (S18). However, this evoked a different reaction too: *She is someone I feel difficult about already. I feel like I don't like her and yet I haven't met her. Perhaps her accent makes me scared of her attractiveness* (S11).

In a later set of questions, students were asked if their impressions of others in the group had changed, in order to see how they were beginning to elaborate their views of others as they became more aware of themselves. This might throw light on emerging empathy or the ability of students to see events through the eyes of another. Awareness of judging versus acceptance continued apace.

I am clearly moving from the 'impressions' stage to the stage of 'knowing and understanding' others more. I don't feel I've had any surprises though (S1). Others wrote about how they were confronting their assumptions or stereotypical thinking. *I have had quite a lot of assumptions challenged and I am looking forward to many more* (S9). *I am less dismissive of some people. I see them as more human and real rather than a set of assumptions. I see more similarities between myself and others now in terms of feelings and some experiences* (S14). One student appeared to judge others without including herself: *The initial feeling was one of warmth and stability and now I feel most people are very vulnerable and a lot of the group are battling with their own emotions* (S15).

By the fourth set of trigger questions, changing perceptions of others were very much in evidence. What was most interesting was how discovery about others reflected back an insight into self: *I'm aware of how safe I feel/felt when I perceive people as having a need for me. I now know X doesn't need rescuing, she is strong, independent, a watcher, contained and a great laugh* (S2). *People I imagined to be very self-assured and confident now appear to share similar anxieties and doubts to myself* (S4). *Through my interactions with her, I have realised how I project this need to protect 'gentle folk' onto people (especially women, but not exclusively) who remind me of my mother* (S5).

Some of the developing interactions in the group seemed to evoke strong and difficult feelings: *I saw X as a hostile person, very eager for attention, and always playing the 'drama queen', the one who knows better about suffering. All of this could apply to me ... hence a projection. But again, I am much more able to detect jealousy in all that, than I am able to see a projection* (S9). *I have assumed that some people have been jealous of me like D, but I know this to be true. I have also been jealous of her* (S22). Other reactions indicated movement towards greater intimacy: *As I've got to know people better I've grown to respect and care for them and this is especially true of people I wasn't drawn to in the beginning* (S12). *I feel closer to W, quite an affinity with X, and less wary of Y* (S14).

In the final set of questions, students were asked what were the most important things they had learned about other people. The responses to this question stand in contrast to opinions expressed in the first set of questions. One student noted that *people are complex, surprising, and it could be easy to dismiss someone or be judgmental and not give people a chance* (S1). In a similar vein: *everybody is full of surprises, everyone has a story to tell. And when I take time to listen everyone becomes worth knowing and/or worth understanding and/or worth loving* (S3).

Some students ended the course struck by how similar people are: *No matter what sort of packaging we come in, we are all essentially the same*, which helped this student to realise that he *can view others as more human and less threatening than twelve months ago* (S5). *Although people have different backgrounds and stories, our concerns seem remarkably similar, i.e. the need for love, respect and acceptance* (S12). Others found a different balance: *I've learned that as humans, we share a lot of similar emotions, fears and experiences but that we are all essentially unique too* (S14). One student learned *that other people can really be responsible for themselves, that I can't change people, and it's okay that others work at their own pace and they will help themselves only if they want to and not if I want, so I am really powerless over other people and their actions* (S17).

One student, who had been noted earlier for seeming to be judgmental, ended the course with a comment which tended to confirm that she saw herself as different from the rest of the group. *I have learned that many people on the course are full of hang-ups, insecurity and low self-esteem and they have had difficult childhoods that have left their mark. I have learned that my mother must have been very caring and never doubted my abilities and never put me down and gave me confidence* (S15).

What was very remarkable in following this development of perceptions of others across time is how students began to notice more about each other than the presenting differences. Labels became less and less useful as a way of knowing each other. For example, after the first set of trigger questions, the subject of stammering never featured again. Others did, such as age, sexuality or class, but in so doing, students demonstrated that they had changed and no longer saw these differences as barriers: *I don't feel as afraid of people with different social backgrounds* (S17). *I am also aware of the cultural differences I have to face on an everyday basis. While they seem wider and bigger than ever, I feel much less powerless towards them. I now think it is up to me to deal with them, and challenge them if they are in the way of my life and emotions* (S9). *I have learned more about my differences from other people but more strikingly, the similarities between myself and others* (S14).

Kelly (1955) believes that our view of ourselves develops in tandem with our developing understanding of others. The fact that students were now more able to be accepting and respecting of differences should be mirrored by greater acceptance and regard for self. 'For the person-centred counsellor the ability to love herself is, in fact, the cornerstone for her therapeutic practice, and in its absence the usefulness of the helping relationship will be grossly impaired' (Mearns and Thorne 1988: 23). To illustrate this very point, one student wrote a very moving account of change: *My self-worth was so downtrodden, I thought of myself as bad news ('a victim'). I believed that my lot was bad lot and that was my life and always would be. I now know my life experiences do not cheapen me, my opinion does count and maybe I can feel in control of my life instead of the other way around. I have changed … I like myself* (S2). And: *I feel more confident, I like myself more and I'm more willing to take risks* (S5).

2   *The development of congruence: self in relation to self*
The development of congruence was an aim that was evident from responses to the first set of questions. *I hope that by the end of the course I will feel more confident to say how I feel* (S1). Others noticed their difficulties about expressing feelings in the group over time (S1, S12). Towards the middle of the course some students already felt differently: *More open about myself even where that feels risky and I'm afraid of the consequences* (S1). *I have opened up a bit, I'm more trusting and less dismissive of others* (S14). *The way I have changed is that I am much more comfortable talking openly about feelings and emotional needs* (S18).

In week fourteen of the course, students were taken through a facilitated process to enable them to divide into three personal development groups. Until this stage, students were free to form groups in different combinations and work with different trainers each week. The third set of trigger questions was given out after this session to enable students to reflect on the process that they had been through.

The process of small group formation faced students with the challenge of choice. Important learning was to be gained by reflecting on how they had got what they wanted, and, if they had not got what they wanted, why this might be so. Those who did not get what they wanted explained it thus: *I wasn't clear about which tutor I wanted, feelings of rejection, a tendency to step aside rather than confront or challenge* (S1). *I was unassertive and felt afraid to ask for what I wanted, firstly, it felt too risky since the chances of rejection seemed great and I also find it difficult to ask for what I want anyway – something I know I need to change* (S4). Two students remarked: *I didn't receive the group that I wanted but in saying that I feel that I have got what I need* (S5, S12).

Those who did get what they wanted did so as follows: *It was hard but I had to be very honest with people* (S3). *I felt quite proud of myself for going with the feeling* (S16). *I got it by saying that was what I wanted and why* (S18). For one student, getting what she wanted left her charged up with nowhere to go: *The fact that I didn't have to fight to get it left me with an unspent dose of aggressiveness. It was as though I had gathered all my forces to launch a heavy stone very far, and instead, I was forced to drop it, effortlessly, at my feet* (S9).

In describing the 'seventh stage' in his process conception of psychotherapy, Rogers (1961: 151) states: 'New feelings are experienced with immediacy and richness of detail.... The experience of such feelings is used as a clear referent.' 'In the moment when a person experiences feelings, she is coming to be what she is: she becomes herself' (113). The task of choosing groups provided students with an opportunity of noticing their feelings, trusting their organismic self and taking responsibility for themselves. Whether this was expressed or not, the process was important in the development of both self-awareness and congruence.

3   *The impact of the research on the course and its participants*
Students' reactions to the research project were monitored in three ways: first, by asking students to say how they had felt answering each set of questions; second, by asking students to comment on my report to the group a week after they had handed in their responses; and, third, by asking students to comment in the last set of questions on the impact of the project on themselves and on the course.

Comments on answering the questions varied, but some themes stand out. Many students found the questions *quite difficult to answer: a lot of hard work* (Ss1, 2, 5, 10, 13, 14, 18, 19, 21). However, many of the same students observed that answering the questions had been *useful, helpful, therapeutic, healing and helped to monitor change* (Ss1, 3, 5, 9, 14, 16, 17).

Initially the feedback process seemed to evoke anxiety for some that somehow they would stand out. *I got nervous when it came to how other people stood out. I was afraid I would hear that the group was happy except there was one pain and it would be me* (S11). *I think I was feeling anxiety about some of my responses being identifiable and them being judged* (S14). Others found the process reassuring: *I felt a sense of relief because others had similar experiences and feelings* (S1, S15).

Later reactions to the report-back indicated some problems. *I felt very uneasy. I found it difficult having my voice mixed up with those of others. I felt lost and under-represented* (S9). *The feedback was a little disappointing – I wanted to know more, and what was reported back only skimmed the surface. I also wanted to know who felt what – my inquisitive side – and consequently the feedback is frustrating* (S16). One student noticed that the group now had *access to a sort of subtext, i.e. what was not said openly* (S1). *I do wonder about using them as a way of channelling my thoughts, feelings and uncertainties not directly back to the others in the group, but to the trainers* (S14).

As a researcher I was very moved by the response to the question on the impact of the research on the students and on the course. *I think the questions gave this group a whole other dimension which for me has been extremely important. Often been my way of 'making sense' of how things had gone for me ... thanks* (S1). *The impact of the trigger questions has been extremely beneficial. Writing the journal has been like walking along a fairly straight road and the trigger questions have been sudden crossroads* (S3). *The trigger questions have been a very important part of this course for me. They have allowed me to stop and look at my development at what have felt like appropriate times during the year* (S5). *It's rather like someone feeding you the right question to really make you feel and think about the most important aspects of what you are feeling and doing* (S18).

Reflexivity: notes from my research journal

The work is almost done. The process of collating the findings has presented anxious moments: awareness of what has been included and what left out; awareness of having to express opinions on material that was given to me in good faith, not to be judged; awareness of exposing the participants; knowing that participants would select differently. Trainer values clashing with researcher values and the compelling need to tell the story.

You the researcher, are like a giant now, holding all the knowing of the course, rendering but one version of the truth for others to share. Tomorrow you will be ordinary and less visible again.

Conclusion

It is now three years since the ending of the course described above. You may be wondering if I have continued to use trigger questions as a way of promoting reflective learning. The answer is no, not in the same way. With hindsight, I have learned some of the limitations of my study. First, it entailed an enormous amount of work for one trainer (myself), yet the task would be difficult to share between all three trainers. This created an inequality in the relationship of the trainers to the course group. Second, in setting up the feedback to the group, I agreed not to identify students. This meant that my report was aimed into the 'middle distance' of the group, which created difficulties of its own and left participants wondering who had said what. If I had the time over again, I would not agree to preserving students' anonymity. Part of the ethos of counselling training is learning to take responsibility for feedback, and I was unhappy that comments to others could be channelled through the research without ownership being known. The third problem was that, unlike journal writing, students were directed to look at particular aspects of the course, and other experiences might have got lost in the process.

The successes of the project were evident. Students wanted to join in and their increased participation as the course unfolded underwrites the perceived value of the part played by the research on this course. Although the questions directed students' attention to particular aspects of the course, the questions were planned with the students in mind in a very immediate way as a means of facilitating reflective learning. It is evident from students' responses that the questions were not just a way of exploring personal development, but became a way of promoting it.

This course was not assessed. However, had the responses to the questions been an assessment tool, they would have differentiated those students who were making progress in incorporating the core conditions into their way of being from those who were not. This has led me to use similar trigger questions as a self-assessment tool in my current training practice.

If experiential learning is to be taken seriously, students need to be given different learning activities that include both a doing and a reflecting component. I believe that the aim of counselling training at this level should be to produce neophyte counsellors who are able to use themselves resourcefully, and are not merely skilled technicians.

Having made a discovery, I shall never the see the world again as before. My eyes have become different: I have made myself into a person, seeing and thinking differently. I have crossed a gap, the heuristic gap which lies between problem and discovery.

(Polanyi 1958: 143)

References

Carr, W. and Kemmis, S. (1986) *Becoming Critical: Education, Knowledge and Action Research*, London, Falmer Press.

Gersie, A. and King, N. (1990) *Storymaking in Education and Therapy*, London, Jessica Kingsley Publishers.

Heron, J. (1989) *The Facilitator's Handbook*, London, Kogan Page.

Kelly, G.A. (1955) *The Psychology of Personal Constructs*, New York, W.W. Norton & Company.

Kolb, D.A. (1984) *Experiential Learning: Experience as the Source of Learning and Development*, Englewood Cliffs, Prentice-Hall.

Levy, C. (1994) 'The Parallel Journey: The Impact of a Counselling Skills Course on its Students and Trainers', unpublished M.Sc. thesis, University of Bristol.

McNiff, J. (1988) *Action Research: Principles and Practice*, London, Routledge.

Mearns, D. (1997) 'Achieving the Personal Development Dimension in Professional Counsellor Training', *Counselling*, 8(2): 113–20.

Mearns, D. and Thorne, B. (1988) *Person-Centred Counselling in Action*, London, Sage.

Munn-Giddings, C. (1993) 'A Different Way of Knowing: Social Care Values, Practitioner Research and Action Research', *Educational Action Research*, 1(2): 275–85.

Polanyi, M. (1958) *Personal Knowledge*, London, Routledge and Kegan Paul.

Rogers, C. (1961) *On Becoming a Person*, London, Constable.

Schon, D.A. (1983) *The Reflective Practitioner*, London, Temple Smith.

Wheeler, S. (1996) *Training Counsellors: The Assessment of Competence*, London, Cassell.

Chapter 6

Negotiated learning and assessment

Jane Speedy

As I set out for the first time in my life to write a chapter in a book, I am feeling very anxious. I have spent several months avoiding this moment and now my heart is racing. The anxiety is not about writing, which I do all the time in my work, and generally do well. It is a fear of exposure; a fear of unknown criticisms from unknown readers, all of whom will find me out and find me wanting.

In my most trusting self, I have a sense of shared purpose and a desire to enter into a dialogue with readers. In my least trusting self, I am frightened of letting our counselling assessment practices and processes at the University of Bristol be known. I am worried that by writing about them I will somehow destroy the sense of dynamism and movement that continues to enrich them and that they, like these words, will be stuck forever on a dry and dusty page. My fear is not only about being judged, but is also a fear of 'tablets of stone'. I am afraid that I and the work that I value will be judged, and found wanting, not just in this moment, but FOREVER. Powerful and primitive feelings.

Context

The tensions and fears that I have described above seem to mirror absolutely the dilemmas that tutors and students experience when they are faced with the opportunity (or crisis) of assessment. The crucial task of separating assessment of the evidence from any implied criticism of the person is at best a delicate operation and often seems impossible to achieve in a profession wherein the 'person' of the counsellor is central to the success of his or her work. Rowntree (1987) describes a mismatch in the purposes ascribed to assessment between course providers, the gatekeepers of standards, and course goers, the hurdle jumpers who may or may not 'make it'. In the counselling field much has been written (Connor 1994;

Dryden and Feltham 1994; BAC 1990 and 1995) about the need for assessment to be an integral part of the learning process, and, wherever possible, an activity shared between tutors and students. In practice, this shared ownership and responsibility for assessment and, implicitly, for course standards, applies mainly to ongoing, formative assessment practices, often for practical work. It is the summative assessment procedures, the final judgements on academic excellence and professional competence, which seem to cause the counselling field so much dis-ease. It is in these that I have a particular interest.

In this chapter I would like to explore some of these issues, in the context of the M.Sc. in Counselling Supervision and Training at the University of Bristol. Assessment, or, at least, evaluation of each other takes place all the time 'in counselling as in life' (Johns 1996). I am interested in exploring the more formal aspects of assessment. I want to examine the summative, academic and graded assessments that are university requirements and the competency- and congruency-based assessments that are required by the counselling profession (of which more later). Our M.Sc. course is unusual because it provides a climate of negotiated learning. A core feature of that climate is the model of self, peer and tutor assessment that has developed and become integral to all aspects of assessment. It is this model that I want to explore, describe and define.

The M.Sc. course exists not only within a university but within the context of a large programme of courses in counselling and counselling skills, all of which are based on core humanistic and person-centred values. There are enormous advantages to operating in a university setting. Frameworks and facilities for teaching and learning, and structures for safeguarding and moderating assessment processes through academic boards and external examiners are already established. The alliance, however unholy, between the university and its 'microbubble', the person-centred counselling education and training unit, has worked creatively to produce useful parameters around assessment processes. These include the right to submit 'work in progress' for feedback; the right to resubmit work that has not met the required standard and the requirement that all work should be, at least, double marked. At other times the apparent mismatch between the person-centred values we place at the core of our work and the lack of trust of students endemic in the atmosphere of a very traditional university seems unworkable. The less compatible and less tangible 'counselling' values, such as establishing the university as a place of emotional as well as intellectual curiosity, are part of a quieter revolution. The significance of personal experience as a contributing factor in the pursuit of academic excellence is embedded, quietly, in all our assessment criteria, but not upheld elsewhere in the university's statutes. Like Carl Rogers (1978) we tread determinedly, but softly.

There can be a tendency, in these circumstances, for counselling trainers to diminish the values of their 'host institution' and consider themselves caught in a conflict, rather than a combination, of values. Dryden and Thorne (1991) bemoan the lot of counselling courses in university environments which are 'saddled with' academic requirements and regulations. Proctor (1991) talks wistfully of the disappearing play-space and freedoms, as counselling becomes addicted to the 'sugar in the diet' of assessments and qualifications. It can be tempting for tutors to relinquish responsibility for the more challenging and uncomfortable aspects of summative assessment and place this on the doorstep of 'university requirements', while themselves keeping ownership with students of the more supportive, developmental process of shared formative assessments.

Counselling, however, is coming of age in Britain. Alongside the development of the standards of competence and even excellence that we seek as a profession come qualifications with their accompanying assessments and requirements. The staff and students at the University of Bristol's Counselling Education and Training Unit are undoubtedly interested in gaining professional and academic recognition for their courses. They also have to uphold the core person-centred values of the courses, acknowledge a legitimate and genuine desire for academic credibility and accountability, and explicitly recognise their gatekeeper role with regard to professional standards. A complex, but by no means impossible or even incompatible, juggling act.

The nature of the course

The M.Sc. course, in particular, is not about counselling, but rather, about counselling training and supervision. This is a course in which assessment forms a crucial part of the curricular content as well as the teaching and learning processes and outcomes of the course. In this respect, the course has a different emphasis from most initial counsellor training. It is substantially *about* assessment and a great deal of time and energy is legitimately given to explicitly considering the 'necessary and sufficient' conditions needed to create assessment procedures congruent with some core values of counselling training. These explorations also raise issues and ask questions that have relevance for initial counsellor training, although time constraints alone might prevent initial training courses from adopting some of our procedures. The course is designed for experienced counselling practitioners and its *content* and *process* are negotiated within a structure agreed by the university. So are its assessment procedures. Professional practice as a trainer and a supervisor is assessed 'live', and there are also six written assignments exploring various aspects of counselling supervision and training, followed by a substantial dissertation on a subject of the student's choice. The course and assessment structure is non-negotiable. The content and process are negotiable: they are designed by each course community as an integral and ongoing aspect of the teaching and learning process. Curriculum development and design and corresponding assessment processes are, therefore, not so much taught as experienced (albeit sometimes painfully) as the course progresses.

The course has been in existence since 1990, and consequently has a history of previous curricula and assessment processes that are made available to course members, via the staff group, who have become the keepers of the 'back catalogue' of course experience. The course membership is made up of practitioners from a range of theoretical backgrounds, tutored by person-centred trainers. It is, perhaps, this juxtaposition of consistency of approach among the trainers and immense diversity among the trainees that makes the whole process workable and particularly worthwhile.

Negotiated, experiential learning and self-assessment are not the exclusive property of person-centred training. Indeed, Wheeler (1996) has recently described some very innovative models for the self-assessment of personal development on a psychodynamically orientated initial counsellor training programme. None the less, it is the core person-centred emphasis on expertise and experience, rather than 'expertness' within the trainer role, that allows a unique and different curriculum and interlinked assessment procedures to emerge for each course cohort. The course tutors do not know the 'right' answers, but they do have a commitment to providing the climate, more experience of the process, and initially, may have more understanding of the 'useful' questions.

The development of assessment practices

It seems impossible to write about these assessment processes without referring to the course history and, to a certain extent, my own. I was, initially, a student on the first M.Sc. course, and subsequently a staff member. During the first cohort the principle of self, peer and tutor assessment was established, after a painful process of negotiation. The continuum of thoughts, feelings, dynamics, tensions and projections around assessment, ranged in that initial pilot scheme (Speedy 1992) from:

> 'I did not come all this way and pay all this money to have the tutors delegate all their jobs to me ... I'm quite happy to have them take responsibility'

to:

> 'this should be a pass/fail course, with no exams, and self and peer assessment only'.

Versions of these views and their underlying assumptions continue to be aired, quite rightly, on every cohort, but the shared responsibility for assessment and the university requirement to grade students' work at M.Sc. level have been maintained as part of the structure ever since. As the course has developed, paralleled by a developing professionalism within the counselling world at large, the assessment process has evolved into a complex and varied web of competency-based and criterion-referenced assessments. The self, peer and tutor assessment triad and the grading of these assessments have become central.

A commitment to self and peer assessment (as opposed to evaluation) is certainly not the norm at the University of Bristol, but it is in the key words *'and tutor'* that this process differs so greatly from its predecessors within the self-managed and self-directed counselling training communities that developed in London (Charlton 1996). My own initial training took place within the self-managed courses at South West London College, where the formal task of assessment was delegated to the student body, facilitated by staff. This seemed a very useful parallel with counsellor/client relationships. Having experienced the process, I remain convinced of its immense value, not least in healing the deep-seated and disabling wounds of years of traditional education. It does not, however, allow for the necessary modelling of assessment expertise by tutors on a 'training the trainers' course, nor does it allow the student body to grapple with the very real issue of 'systemic' trainer power, influence and authority. Gaie Houston (1984) commented:

> The whole experience was intensely educational, often in quite unlooked for ways ... [but] we did not to my mind ever work the authority issue, which is another way of saying, deal with our notions of magic around leadership.

From my own perspective, removing the tutors entirely from the summative assessment process somehow imbued them implicitly with supernatural powers, as if, by implication, their involvement in the final assessment process would have been completely overwhelming.

A model of assessment

Shared responsibility for assessment on the Bristol M.Sc. course has not resulted in an immediate sense of equality. What does seem to have emerged is a developmental model, not unlike developmental models of supervisor development (Hawkins and Shohet 1989) for the transfer of this expertise from tutor to peer and ultimately to self. As time has gone on, and more has been understood about this developmental process, it has been made more explicit within the course community. As a result, students have been able to anticipate a developing confidence and competence in assessing their peers, themselves and ultimately this, and other assessment practices. The tutors, on the whole, have more initial experience, skill, and influence in assessing, particularly the academic work produced. In the initial stages, as in *infancy*, assessors have in general relied more on the tutors, feeling unable or unwilling to 'grade' their peers, or give themselves accurate feedback, as these comments from a peer- and a self-assessor show:

> 'the essay is written from a psychodynamic perspective, which I know nothing about.' ... 'I haven't given myself any feedback, I just hope it passes. Over to you lot.'

Later on, in *childhood*, assessors feel more competent as criterion-referenced assessors, and more able to grade, as well as evaluate, the written work of their peers, and give themselves well-balanced feedback. Subsequently, in *adolescence*, there has been a tendency to challenge the role of the tutors and for self and peer assessors to unite against the staff group. My own version of this was, as a student, to try to award myself, in collusion with my peer, an A* for an essay which, I was later persuaded, deserved no more than a 'scrape' into the 'A' category, when measured against the course criteria. By the end of the course, an *adult* equilibrium has, for the most part, been reached, and staff and students, alike, have been able to evaluate and assess work, each participant in the process, including self-assessors, giving equal depth and weight to their input. A self-assessor from the first cohort (Speedy 1992) commented:

'this essay was not nearly as polished as the last one. I simply ran out of time. There is not enough in it about my personal influences, and it doesn't have an ending. It falls off the page. The theory is sound. I think it is interesting and highly original in parts, and good enough – a solid "B".'

Like all models, these four stages are useful only if they are seen as a notional construct, rather than 'the truth'. Course participants do not necessarily enter the course at the same stage, course tutors do not always behave in an impeccably adult fashion. I have, in my tutor role, been reduced to infancy at least once, and have also indulged in several adolescent sulks. Most significantly, the course of the transfer of 'power' rarely runs smoothly. Perceptions and avenues of power in counselling training have been written about more extensively elsewhere (see Chapter 3 for my own contribution). Nowhere is the systemic, professional and personal power triangle more acutely evident than in the summative assessment arena. These issues of power, within the group and within the university as a system, become all the more explicit, and transparent, when in self, peer and tutor assessment groups. Each group member may be at a different developmental stage as assessee or assessor. This can be acknowledged and worked with as part of the process, and content, of the assessment group. We have developed a model of assessee leadership during assessment groups. This changes the power balance of assessment groups. It allows for an overt and visible role-shift to take place when the assessee becomes his or her own assessor. It also acknowledges the limitations, strengths, and experience of assessors as well as assessees.

The courses continue to experiment with different ways of assessing within the self, peer and tutor triad, providing themselves with a rich seam of choices, styles of networking, uses of power, authority and professional integrity. Should assessors, for example, be allocated at random, or chosen, and if chosen, should they be similar or different? Should assessment groups take place in front of the course community as a whole, or not? What difference does this make to the experience? Should all assessments take place on a specific named day, or 'as and when' the individual assessment group members are able to meet? Are these experiences different, and if so, in what way?

Each course community has added to the collective wisdom about assessment practices. For example, the majority of cohorts have elected to work in three person (self, peer and tutor) assessment groups, but one community decided to include two peers. This even number of group members allowed 'stalemate' to be reached, in terms of feedback and grades, very early on in the assessment history of the group and well before most of the community had begun to feel confident as assessors or assessees. This was a painful and useful learning experience for all, but particularly for the staff, who have subsequently been even more careful about making safeguards and appeals procedures concrete, explicit and legitimate from the very beginning.

Graded assignments

Perhaps one of the most startling ways in which the courses have differed from much that is written about counselling training or adult and continuing education has been their allegiance to, and even enthusiasm for, the grading process. Current writers on counselling training advocate 'pass/fail' assessment procedures (Dryden, Horton and Mearns 1996) and a leading British adult educator maintains that:

> the crowning instance of incongruity between educational practice and the adult's self-concept of self-directivity is the act of a teacher giving a grade to a student. Nothing makes an adult more childlike than being judged by another adult.
>
> (Knowles 1990)

But what if you are awarded this grade by a fellow student, or by yourself?

The written assignments at Bristol are assessed against criteria that include a balance of theoretical understanding and critical analysis, evidence of personal experience and development, and examples of professional practice and expertise. The criteria evolve all the time, the range of 'pass' grades moving from demonstrating competence to excellence in these areas. An external examiner for the course recently argued that these would be excellent criteria for giving feedback to students on a 'pass/fail' basis. He was challenged by some of the course participants, who maintained that:

> 'The process, and experience of "grading" had been one of the most valuable aspects of the course.... [It had provoked] debate about the extent to which assessment could, or should, ever be objective, and had highlighted a whole range of issues around individual progress versus overall standards.'

From my own perspective, as tutor, I found myself surprisingly resistant to dispensing with grades. I realised that I also have an additional agenda, in relation to the university and its values. This focuses on the opportunity of achieving academic excellence, as well as professional competence, within counselling. I have come to regard counselling as a discipline in its own right that offers an emotional as well as intellectual meaning to the word 'academic' and an experiential as well as experimental research paradigm. I no longer seek to challenge, but rather to broaden the scope of 'academic' horizons and notions of excellence.

Assessing 'good-enough' practice

Our academic assessment criteria differ from current counselling training orthodoxies in their alliance with 'traditional' university standards of excellence. In contrast, our increasingly competency-based assessments of supervision and training practice are more in line with professional and vocational trainings found outside university settings. When the M.Sc. course started, the practical assessments took place within the whole course community, whose members demonstrated a supportive and challenging feedback climate, but were more ambivalent about being able to pass or fail their peers during what was an 'in the moment' live demonstration of supervisor, or trainer, practice. There has subsequently been much discussion about the possibility of 'grading' the practical assignments, in light of the issues outlined above. For the moment the consensus has been, and rightly so to this author's mind, that grading is inappropriate. Evidence of practice can only open a window on a passing moment, can only catch a glimpse that can never be reworked, more finely tuned or resubmitted (resubmission being the snapshot of a different fleeting moment). It is possible to make judgements about 'good enough' standards, but perhaps unwise to try to make further claims for our powers and parameters of assessment.

Our gatekeeper role as assessors of 'good enough' practice in counselling, supervision and training owes a great debt to the advent of competency-based assessment. The competency-based revolution, like much of the counselling revolution, is an import from the United States. It was first introduced as an attempt to improve the standards of teacher education by returning to assessments of outcomes within the workplace, rather than knowledge acquired within training institutions (Wolf 1995). In Britain, competence-based learning has been embraced by advocates of open and work-based learning. They have challenged the adult learning 'monopoly' of institutions such as universities, hide-bound by their commitment to specific qualifications. In particular, the National Council for Vocational Qualifications has worked with a vast range of professional and work-based organisations to develop schedules of recordable and achievable competence-based standards. The lead body for advice, guidance, counselling and psychotherapy has worked with our own professional organisations, such as the British Association for Counselling, to produce schedules for counselling, training and supervision practices in Britain. The BAC also continues to provide its own accreditation schemes for good practice in the counselling field and to promote not only competency- but also congruency-based assessment criteria. In order to gain BAC accreditation as practitioners, counsellors, supervisors, and more recently trainers, not only have to demonstrate their professional competence but also the congruence of this practice with their stated theoretical and philosophical orientation.

The self, peer and tutor assessment groups on our M.Sc. course continually adjust their practical assessment criteria to take account of developments in the competency- and congruency-based schedules outlined above. For the moment, the course remains purely a university award, separate and distinct from professional and vocational qualifications. I have no doubt that in time, just as our postgraduate Diploma in Counselling is linked to professional accreditation from the BAC, accreditation of prior learning and prior experiential learning, validated by the NCVQ and the BAC, will form part of this degree's assessment portfolio.

Community-based assessment

It would seem that there is no conflict between the role of the professional organisations and the 'qualifications monopoly' of the educational institutions. Indeed, all the courses at Bristol have developed in tandem with the BAC and with nationally agreed standards of professional practice and intend to continue to do so. I notice, however, that as a tutor I regard the increasing predominance of competency- and congruency-based standards with some caution, and some regret. This wariness might be accounted for by a vested interest, as a university lecturer, in maintaining my own pre-eminence as a gatekeeper of awards and standards. I have a stronger sense that it comes from a commitment to community-based learning and 'live' acknowledgement of that learning. The most stimulating assessments of supervision and training practice on our courses have centred around those moments when practitioners have acted in ways that are not easily quantified, and that may not even obviously fit with their stated ways of working. Competence and congruence are important components of good practice, but it is hard to legislate, in advance, at a national level, for that which is unknown.

Practitioners working live and in the moment may well experience key 'moments of psychological contact' with individuals or groups in unexpected and uncharted ways. It is in this witnessing, challenging, and perhaps celebrating of the unexpected, that a climate of community-based assessment seems irreplaceable. It is surely in the shared recording, challenging and analysing of these moments that the leading edges of our work are expanded. Looking to the future of assessment, perhaps it is here that the differences between competence and excellence in our practice are to be found. No doubt an experienced and competent self-evaluator can witness much of this for himself or herself, but, in a profession that is by definition interactive and interconnected to its very core, the loss of 'community' either in learning or in assessment of that learning would seem very great indeed. As one such community member pointed out:

> 'My greatest learning was making a mess of the supervision practice (as I saw it) and then getting such astonishing feedback on what I had done well. I don't think we have a clue what we are up to half the time. I'm up to a great deal more, and a great deal less, than I think.'

It is, of course, equally important to get feedback from peers at a national or even international level; hence accreditation, external moderation, and even this chapter. This is likely to be of a very different nature and at a very different level from that afforded by your peers in a community which has existed for two years. Such a community will, at best, have developed an intimate and unique atmosphere of support and challenge and is, at the very least, there with you in the moment.

A person-centred ethos

I have no desire to claim any higher ground for my own preferred approach, but it does seem to be in this particular arena, of community-based learning and assessment, that 'person-centredness' really comes into its own. Our M.Sc. course is not a 'person-centred training', but rather, relies on a person-centred approach on the part of the trainers. The diverse nature of the course communities may change in the future, as more qualifications in supervision and training develop in Britain. For the moment, however, it remains one of the few such trainings in Britain, and attracts a wide range of practitioners, from a variety of counselling and psychotherapy approaches. The person-centred style and ethos of the course facilitators allow for and overtly attempt to foster a climate of mutual respect and interest, perhaps a welcome antidote to the current notions of 'schoolism', or trends towards complex models of integration that dominate initial counsellor training. The course advocates neither integration nor purism, but rather, attempts to provide a community climate, whereby a psychosynthesis counsellor feels confident and competent to assess the supervision practices of, for example, a solution-focused brief therapist, and perhaps even able to acknowledge his or her own 'inner' solution-focused therapist. The course of such co-operation does not always run smoothly and often leaves groups with much to struggle with. Perhaps one of the unforeseen consequences of these multi-denominational' self, peer and tutor assessment groups is the necessary development, within each community, of a differentiated assessment curriculum. In other words, distinctions emerge, and are different each time, between 'universal' assessment criteria (congruent with all therapeutic practices), discipline-specific assessment criteria (supervision or training specific), approach-specific criteria (for example, integrative or psychodynamic) and criteria specific to individual course members (as people with different learning styles and personality types). If nothing else, the course provides a fertile training ground for future assessors at a national level. As a recent graduate commented:

'It was more like an ongoing two-year conference than a training course.'

Conclusions

As I glance back to the beginning of this chapter I realise that much has been left out, but I also feel relieved that I have managed, within the constraints of the time and space allowed, to record enough of the climate and practice of assessment on this particular course. In so doing, I have described some of the dimensions and differences between criterion referenced assessment for academic purposes and the competency- and congruency-based assessment of our professional practice. I hope, too, that I have challenged current tendencies to play down the significance of academic excellence to our profession and highlighted some of the advantages and pitfalls of self/peer/tutor and, above all, community-based assessment processes. Our experiment with 'experiential' assessing at the University of Bristol continues to evolve and this chapter would, no doubt, be very different, if written in six months' time. For the moment, however, I am done. The primitive fears that I acknowledged at the outset have been channelled into an adrenalin rush of ideas, thoughts and feverish activity. My desire to communicate and make connections has overridden my desire to hide from criticism. According to Rowntree (1987):

> If we wish to discover the truth about an educational system, we must look into its assessment procedures.

I hope that I have enabled more than a passing glance to be given to our assessment procedures, our educational system and perhaps our core values and 'truth' in Bristol. I am also aware that in describing this, I have allowed something of myself and my own truth, as a learner, as a teacher, and as a person, to be seen. In one short chapter, I have come a long way!

References

BAC (1990) *The Recognition of Counsellor Training Courses*. Rugby, British Association for Counselling.

BAC (1995) *Code of Ethics and Practice for Trainers*. Rugby, British Association for Counselling.

Charlton, M. (1996) *Self-directed Learning in Counsellor Training*. London, Cassell.

Connor, M. (1994) *Training the Counsellor*. London, Routledge.

Dryden, W. and Thorne, B. (eds) (1991) *Training and Supervision for Counselling in Action*. London, Sage.

Dryden, W. and Feltham, C. (1994) *Developing Counsellor Training*. London, Sage.

Dryden, W., Horton, I. and Mearns, D. (1996) *Issues in Professional Counsellor Training*. London, Cassell.

Hawkins, P. and Shohet, R. (1989) *Supervision in the Helping Professions*. Buckingham, Open University Press.

Houston, G. (1984) *The Red Book of Groups*. London, Rochester Foundation.

Johns, H. (1996) *Personal Development in Counsellor Training*. London, Cassell.

Knowles, M. (1990) 'Androgogy', in M. Tight (ed.) *Adult Learning and Education*. London, Routledge.

Proctor, B. (1991) 'On Being a Trainer', in W. Dryden and B. Thorne (eds) *Training and Supervision for Counselling in Action*. London, Sage.

Rogers, C. (1978) *On Personal Power*. London, Constable.

Rowntree, D. (1987) *Assessing Students: How Shall We Know Them?* London, Kogan Page.

Speedy, J. (1992) 'Streemin' '. An Exploration of Assessment on the M.Sc. in

Counselling Supervision and Training, University of Bristol, 1990–92. Unpublished paper.

Wheeler, S. (1996) *Training Counsellors: The Assessment of Competence*. London, Cassell.

Wolf, A. (1995) *Competence-based Assessment*. Buckingham, Open University Press.

Chapter 7

Groups in counselling training

Alyss Thomas

Counselling training happens in the context of a group: this is both a simple fact and a highly complex reality. As Mair writes, 'we know more than we can say and have to learn sometimes to say what we do not know' (1989). Such an attitude to learning reflects the depth and subtlety of this type of learning situation, in which we as trainers are usually learning at least as much as our students. None of this may be comfortable.

A counselling training group is composed of people who have agreed to come together in a shared and structured task, and who meet regularly over an agreed period of time to achieve a standard of training, sometimes with a qualification attached. In the literature of counselling training, there is not always enough attention paid to the nature of working with this large group *as a group*, and with the very specific group processes that evolve in this special setting. This is partly because the task and administrative requirements of counselling training are demanding and consuming of the facilitators' time and thinking; and partly because such training has traditionally held the individual student as its main focus. I believe the experience of both trainers and trainees can be conceptualised and understood more fully through the inherent dynamics of the group. In this chapter I offer some ways of exploring this view, based both on my experience as a trainer and on the conversations, reading, further training and research I have enlisted to help me. I take an integrative approach, making use of material from both humanistic and psychodynamic sources. This discussion does not refer to the specific content of counselling training – which forms the group task – but attempts to find doorways into the rich and multi-layered network of interpersonal communications which form the environment within which the group task occurs. This is referred to as the group process.

A new counselling group

Imagine yourself as the facilitator of a new group of counselling students who have been meeting for the first few weeks of a two-year course. They indicate in various ways that they are terrified, bemused, confused, bored, anxious, critical, excited, helpless and uncertain. Several of them express feelings that they have bitten off more than they can chew. A few express doubts about the validity of the core theoretical model of the course, and someone says that the facilitators are not doing enough to help them. Someone says he or she does not like one of the facilitators, the one who is not present at this session. One person complains how uncomfortable the chairs are, and makes a request for floor cushions to be provided. Another student says, 'If it were me, I'd completely rewrite the course. It's not fair we should be expected to do all this extra work outside course hours. I don't have time to do the assignments before Christmas. And I can't afford to pay for all this extra supervision, why can't we do our supervision hours during course time?' Other students chip in and say they cannot afford to do any personal counselling at present, and they want to negotiate for more time in the personal development groups and less time spent on skills training which they do not feel is as useful at present. You know that the students, before accepting a place on the course, were informed about the course requirements, and agreed they would fit them in to their schedules.

Any experienced counselling trainer will find this scenario familiar. How any of us as facilitators would respond to this example of counselling group life depends on how we would see and understand what was happening. How we would feel, what some theoretical approaches call our countertransference to the group, would also depend on our personal, biographical response to being under pressure in a group. For example, a trainer might feel provoked and want to defend the integrity of the course; or another could sympathise with rebellious and anxious students and suggest to them that the course requirements were indeed rather tough. Neither of these approaches would be helpful to the group's development, because neither response recognises what is actually taking place. In addition, careful introduction of the course requirements and sensitive, supportive handling of these issues by the staff do not always reduce the feeling of panic. What exactly is going on here is a fascinating question and of course open to many different interpretations. For example, the anxiety can also be understood and worked with as a more basic insecurity about whether or not individuals feel they will be accepted in the group or whether they will be 'good enough'. This anxiety and vulnerability are hard to admit to or deal with, and blaming the course requirements for one's anxiety can provide a way of making the tension feel more manageable. Another aspect of this is that students could feel insecure because they were not being taught in the same way as they were at school.

Towards a typology of counselling group life

Rowan (1993), in referring to the transpersonal dimension of group work, writes that we can get a much more accurate sense of what we are doing in groups by recognising that we are working on many different levels all the time. Each of us has a finite capacity for awareness, and in any group there is a wide range of different levels of awareness. A group is complex, alive, paradoxical, full of contradictions, a collection of disparate individuals and yet still a human unit with its own unique atmosphere and energy. Experienced group workers in many fields tend to relate both to groups as entities in their own right and to the individuals within them. Humans are born into pre-existing groups: family groups are the crucible of both our potential and our limitations. We inherit and learn an aptitude and a need for group activities and group emotional involvement. Participating in a well-functioning group can give us essential supplies of emotional energy, feedback, a renewed sense of individual identity, and a refreshed self-concept. It also allows us to express our love and care for others in individual ways. At the same time, groups are places where astonishingly destructive and damaging interactions can take place, which the group members feel are outside their control (Nitsun 1996).

Our responses when in a group may be embedded in our cultural assumptions about groups. These are often based on pairs of opposites, such as individual versus group, psychological versus social, professional versus personal, democratic versus authoritarian, or constructive versus destructive. It is often possible as a group member or leader to find oneself lost in any one of these contradictions, rather than holding both of the possibilities open. Indeed, these concepts may not actually exist within the group, but only in our concept of the group. In group analysis, one theoretical approach to working with groups – the concepts of network and matrix – underlies an appreciation of how groups function: people exist in relation to each other in the group, not as separate entities. The group is something that all the members, present and implied, create and are part of together. Everyone is part of the whole. Through identifying with or opposing others in the group, a member can see and understand her own characteristics more clearly. On this basis, 'identity is defined as

something closely woven into the transpersonal matrix of one's own primary group' (LoVerso 1995). Meeting new people in a potentially
transformative setting like this offers opportunities for re-creating the
self. In counselling training, this is what many members value in personal development groups.

People can be said to bring a pre-existing group along with them. Eric
Berne's concept of the group 'imago' is 'any mental picture, conscious,
pre-conscious or unconscious, of what the group is or should be like'
(Berne 1963). This is either reinforced or challenged by the behaviour of
the actual group and the experience of being in it over time. It is thus
useful, in terms of encouraging the development of both the group and
individuals, for a trainer to reflect back when individual group members
are construing the group in a particular way, or inducing the group or its
facilitators to enact a particular group imago. In the example above of the
anxious new group, the facilitator might point out that members were
perceiving the group as critical, demanding, impatient and excluding.

Clarkson (1992) expands Tuckman's (1965) well-known four-phase
model of group life (forming, storming, norming and performing) in a
useful and insightful way in relation to counselling training groups. She
includes extensive lists of constructive and destructive trainer behaviours at each of these phases, related to an understanding of the specific
leadership tasks at each stage. The *forming* stage is one of establishing
boundaries and dependencies. The facilitator's function is to create a
bounded, dependable space within which the group's work can take place.
If the facilitators handle this badly, the group members can feel that the
boundaries are designed to exclude them and make the tutors unavail-
able, or else they can feel anxious and structureless. Facilitators may
tend either to over-control or to be over-zealous caretakers at this stage.
The *storming* stage is noticeable for its interpersonal conflicts, and disagreement or rebellion towards a leader is common. Clarkson shows that
it is important to understand that, although the group may appear to be
complaining about the course tasks, in fact, on a psychological level its
members are really testing the strength of the leader. The task of the
norming stage is to establish a constructive and cohesive group, in which
new rules and behaviours evolve, and the leaders can facilitate this by
encouraging healthy, self-actualising aspects of the group and the individuals. At the *performing* stage, the group has established an interpersonal structure that enables the group tasks to be carried out without
disabling distractions. At this stage, trainers can encourage students to
take increased responsibility for their tasks. A final stage can be added to
this typology, that of *mourning*, in which members work through, or

deny, feelings of grief and anger about the impending loss and separation as the group ends.

Personal development or personal therapy?

The group processes that occur on many counselling courses are a product of the combination of consistent opportunities for personal development, group work, self-reflection and so forth, combined with the tensions of a professional training course. Hazel Johns (1996) argues that the traditional personal development component of counselling courses – delivered in the form of various kinds of focused small group sessions – should not make a counselling course into a therapy group. In her view, therapeutic issues will inevitably be stirred by the intense interpersonal contact and the material that emerges in counselling practice sessions; this personal material may be identified and explored in group sessions, but the training group is not the place to continue to work on this in depth. Time devoted to group process is mainly intended to help facilitate the group to maintain itself as a learning community. The trainees are to be encouraged to take unresolved personal issues to individual counselling for more in-depth therapeutic work, which in turn feeds back more constructively into the training group. On the other hand, Clarkson (1992) takes the view that in-depth personal therapy on courses 'is considered ethical and responsible as well as a primary avenue of learning "the inner map" '. She says that through using the training group in this way, students can develop a deeper level of awareness and skills which they can then apply in different settings. In my experience, individuals' intense personal issues demand space and attention in the group, and keep coming back in various forms until they are attended to. This can be seen as disruptive and difficult if the facilitator sees her main job as being a counselling trainer rather than a group facilitator, since the pressure of individual therapeutic issues emerging in the group effectively turns it, at times, into a therapy group.

The primary purpose of counselling training courses is not to provide therapy for their members, but they will inevitably be therapeutic in process. Since (a) counselling students are asked to disclose personal information in the interests of the group and their own professional development, and (b) courses are usually run by experienced counsellors and psychotherapists who offer an empathic, accepting and contained space, a counselling course will include members who are facing their own previously unprocessed distress. It is unrealistic and unethical to ignore or deny the therapeutic aspects of training. However, the balance of such therapeutic work, and the use and focus of group time, then become key questions. How individual members deal with their own needs depends partly on their own cultural background and emotional history. If they have been emotionally deprived, they may be unable to *refrain* from taking the opportunity that is apparently presented. For example, a student on a diploma course on which I was a core tutor discovered a disturbing aspect of her personal history while doing a practice exercise. She then revealed this in her personal development group, as her preoccupation with the problem was affecting her ability to listen or take anything in. This set off a wave of similar disclosures by others, and the room was full of tears and grief as this group of people decided to deal with old issues that many of them had had in common but had never dared to open up before. It would have been impossible to continue with the course as if nothing had happened. At the same time, I knew it was essential to contain this material so that it did not take over the entire course.

Mearns (1994) makes the point that the personal development group component on a course can provide richer and more challenging opportunities for growth and change than personal therapy alone. He goes so far as to say that personal development in counselling training is so important that 'it cannot be left to the vagaries of individual therapy'. In the group, 'the public perception of the trainee becomes part of the agenda'. Issues which may simply not arise in one-to-one work, in which the counsellor mainly follows the client's lead, are brought to the surface in the group. Examples I have experienced include a male student's critical and defensive reaction to another student because she was a lesbian; a man who believed he had excellent relationships with women outside the course but who got involved in conflicts with all the women on the course (his view that this was nothing to do with him was, he believed, confirmed by his male therapist) and major conflicts in belief systems such as between a fundamentalist Christian student and another student who was grieving for an abortion. Students can refuse to participate when difficult or emotive issues are being discussed, and demonstrate behaviour such as yawning and being bored or sleepy, not hearing, or trying to talk about something else. These situations reveal areas where the students' acceptance, pliancy, empathy and congruence may possibly need further development. The students themselves can see this, and point this out for each other, with or without the intervention of a facilitator.

The central dilemma for counselling trainers and group members is how to balance training requirements, the therapeutic or developmental needs of individuals, and the wellbeing of the group. I think this dilemma gives counselling courses a specific tone and atmosphere. Whatever you decide to focus on is to some extent at the expense of giving time to something else. Some members can experience the personal development groups as tantalising and frustrating, and feel that their needs are never fully met, while others find them stressful and intrusive or consider that they are being forced to expose their inner workings.

Therapeutic groupwork

For these reasons, I find it appropriate to use some of the principles of therapeutic groupwork to aid my own understanding of counselling training groups. Although this has been looked at in the context of social work training (Douglas 1976) or in the training of psychotherapists (Clarkson 1992), there has not been so much attention paid in the literature of counselling training so far to the *therapeutic* dynamics of the group. Part of the reason may be that much of the accumulated knowledge and approaches from therapeutic groupwork have evolved in entirely different, equally specialised, contexts and therapeutic traditions. These areas of knowledge can seem hermetically sealed from each other, which means that insights from, say, group analysis or from person-centred residential group work do not usually enter the arena of counselling training, and vice versa. Counselling courses sit somewhere between the traditions of adult education, professional training and one-to-one counselling. Some group therapeutic insight and experience can be successfully transferred to the counselling training group, if we accept the premise that at times this performs the function of a specialised therapy group, with its own specific and limited intentions.

I'm a mouse and I want to be a dolphin

It is the second day of a certificate course. The facilitator is using a pack of cards printed with pictures of different animals as the focus of a structured group activity. The trainees are asked to choose two cards, one representing the way they are now, and one showing where they would like to be at the end of the course. They talk about the cards they have chosen in the group. One trainee says, 'I'm a mouse and I want to be a dolphin'. Forgetting about her 'counsellor' self, she talks about her life and how she is using the course as a vehicle for her personal growth. She has been raising children and living in a rather dull and suffocating marriage in a small town. The course is opening up new possibilities in her life, and she cannot wait to arrive each week.

This vignette illustrates that there is more than the desire to acquire a set of skills or a professional training involved in the decision to come on a counselling course. Our culture is significantly lacking in opportunities which this woman can take to help her develop and express herself. There are precious few opportunities for empathic, authentic relationships, in which truthful, painful and deeply personal topics can be discussed without judgement, indifference or negative reactions. She knew – perhaps without realising it – that the course would provide the kind of environment she desperately needed in order for her to begin to look at what was going on inside her and in her interpersonal world. This does not negate her clear instrumental reasons for coming on the course – such as wanting to be a better listener, wanting to develop latent skills, or wanting some training and part-time work. She talked about these at the interview stage, feeling that they would be more acceptable to the interview panel. These were also the reasons she gave her husband, her colleagues, her family, and possibly herself. Self-development may be considered selfish, indulgent or too expensive. Clarkson (1992) points out the 'apparently' in the external shared purpose that people have in coming together in training. As she says, while there are commonly held views of the purpose of the group at a social level, 'there may be very many conflicting, confluent or complementary ulterior-level agendas at the psychological level of the group'. This 'private structure' of the group is complex and volatile, and requires skilful handling if it is not to subvert the group's development. For example, the student who comes in order to reconnect with his ability to rebel and his enthusiasm for being an outsider, and who eventually leaves the course without completing it, can make it difficult for others to treat their work seriously. They can identify with his point of view, and start to use the course as an opportunity to assert their own individuality, for example by opting out of work.

Smith (1994), in an article on the experience of facilitating psychodynamic process groups on a counselling course, describes how he works directly with a set of pre-identified group – rather than individual – hidden agendas. He assumes that these are present, and that they are understandable, predictable and follow a recognisable sequence. The groups are structured with activities, such as sculpts – a drama exercise in which members take up physical positions to express their interrelationships – to take account of the themes that he believes are present each term, beginning in the first term with encouraging the group to get involved and share on a deep personal level, moving on later in the course to the group's relationship to the authority of the course, and closing with issues of disillusionment, loss and separation.

This would be a different kind of group experience from one in which the group is encouraged to discover and explore the nature of its own agendas, as in the person-centred approach.

These various personal and psychological agendas also take place within the sociological–emotional contexts of adult education. Most British adults have painful memories of how their childhood experiences of education failed them. They were not taught in a way that involved them or was relevant to their own lives, and they were humiliated or made to feel a failure. Many people coming onto counselling courses (which increasingly emphasise student-centred or negotiated learning) have not done much systematic study since they left school or college, and bring with them many unresolved feelings from those earlier experiences. They often expect to be treated like passive children, and, to begin with, may resist the expectation to become self-directed learners. They are confused by the facilitator's attempts to share power with them and are new to the practice of formalised experiential learning. Rogers (1986) distinguishes between intrinsic and extrinsic motivation in students. He emphasises the importance of facilitating students to engage with their own inner motivation for meaningful self-actualisation. This is often a strongly emotional process, as trainees discover more of who and what they can be, which inevitably influences the climate, process and focus of the training group.

On the positive side, the sharing of oneself in a group brings unforeseeable rewards. Often a strong sense of community grows out of the members of the group living through difficult issues together or sharing in each others' struggles and distress. This makes the experience of belonging to and participating in the entire course much more rich and meaningful, and suggests that learning and reflection are taking place on deeper, more emotional levels. It grounds the theory and skills practice in real experience. This encourages the individuals to take more risks, use each other for support, and become stronger by acknowledging thoughts and feelings for which they had previously not had an appropriate context.

However, this deep emotional learning is also risky and difficult, and raises complex issues about selection for courses. Students have come for a professional training; many do not realise at the beginning what deep water they are stepping into. Hutten (1996) suggests that students should be made aware of the experiential nature of the training at the outset so that they can make an informed assent to it. They can experience this growth as dangerous, painful and victimising. They can experience facilitators, who may apparently sit back and allow all this to happen, as neglectful or absent or as failing to do their job properly. They want solutions to the pain that being on the course has brought them. If the trainers are also the facilitators of the personal development or community groups, their dual roles can be confusing, both to themselves and to the students. Dickinson (1996) says that her research 'consistently revealed that students experience group facilitators as uncaring, cold and distant'. She suggests this may have to do with the differences in style that staff may adopt when in training role (more active) or when in group therapist mode (passive). Students can misinterpret or misunderstand staff roles, and can take a silent response to a personal disclosure as a lack of acceptance or involvement. Whatever the reasons, strong transference issues arise when therapeutic material is being evoked. On courses run in a person-centred style, facilitators will be more open and responsive, using immediacy and self-disclosure. Students can then struggle with seeing trainers as human or weak, rather than authoritarian and strong (Johns 1996).

Groups, assessment and transference

On a counselling course, transference issues can have a particular, recognisable flavour. In addition to the material that individuals are confronting and processing in order to make themselves more available and effective as counsellors, there are specific transference issues that are fostered by the context. These are to do with power, judgement, authority and the educational context. The staff may also feel uncomfortable about these issues. Staff on a counselling course are involved in the assessment and validation of the students' work, and make judgements about the trainees' suitability to graduate or practise. However skilfully and tactfully they perform these functions, and even on courses where peer assessments carry equal weight, students have feelings about this. They want to be accepted, they want to make a favourable impression – or they may feel rebellious and want to assert their individuality by not handing in assignments on time or in some way declining to meet course requirements. This can be complicated by any transference issues with the course or module leaders concerned. The emotional tensions surrounding writing essays, completing case studies or making videos become more visible and take up more space than on more narrowly academic courses. Underlying any discussions about the course work, assessments and expectations are fears and anxieties and, often, low self-esteem, stemming from previous educational experiences. Trainees facing these issues again as adults are likely to regress at times into dependent child states, and both request and resent firm guidance from their tutors. Original class-room situations can be replicated, with anxious students and a teacher who feels barely in control and believes that she must cope by being firm and assertive. Or the trainer/teacher may feel apologetic, and on the side of the students, and try to abrogate her authority and role by sympathis-ing with the students' position. It is often difficult for less experienced trainers in these circumstances to hold on to their legitimate authority and be clear about boundaries, expectations and contracts. This can often be confused with authoritarianism; trainers who particularly value a non-hierarchical, equal relationship with their trainees can forget that their role is also necessarily different. Heron (1993) refers to three types of facilitator authority: tutelary, political and charismatic. Tutelary refers to the passing on of knowledge; political authority is the taking of decisions which affect the whole course; and charismatic refers to the way in which tutors affect the course members, or empower them, by their way of being and behaving. A balance of all these types of authority needs to be confidently present for a course to be well facilitated. Heron reminds us that 'old-style teaching confuses the three kinds of authority in the crud-est possible way'. Because teachers have knowledge, they are then ex-pected to be directive, controlling and make educational decisions for their students. Counselling students often have to deal with their semi-processed expectations that their tutors will behave in this way, and in so doing they are battling with the idea of taking responsibility for their learning, and are confused when they are not told what to do. The theoretical model of the course will govern and colour the ways in which tutors and the training organisation itself handle and respond to these issues.

Course tutors can also have various personality characteristics ascribed to them because of their role in relation to the students. These can be seen on a spectrum of indulgent and caring versus aloof and reserved (Hilpert 1995). Through general agreement, the strong transference of one or two students, or a more general process of projective identification, both tutors and students can come to occupy particular transferential posi-tions in the group. Groups appear to need certain role positions to be occupied, such as caretaker, absentee, spokesperson, judge, scapegoat, or person in need of looking after. The way in which these roles come to be occupied seems to be a feature of group life in many different contexts. They can be described and explored through a range of con-ceptual frameworks, from the parent, adult and child of transactional analysis to the unfinished business of gestalt approaches (Clarkson 1992), depending on the core model of the course.

In counselling training it is generally assumed that individual learning takes place when individuals immerse themselves in the interactive, experiential learning environment, which consists of the interactions of all the persons present. A mixture of therapeutic and professional learning is specifically provided for in personal development or group process modules. Yet there are some commentators (such as Irving and Williams 1996) who question the usefulness for everyone of personal development groups in counsellor training. They say that the reasons for including personal development modules are often less well thought through than the provision of counselling practice and theory, and that vague ideas of 'personal growth' are not satisfactory. Irving and Williams argue that trainers are often not clear or specific enough about the intentions of personal development or process groups. They insist that without a clear model and systematic guidelines the learning can be haphazard, and even negative, and that it is naive to think that the provision of a group space in itself enables a constructive learning experience. However, I feel it is also naive to think that in-depth learning can occur without considerable chaos, and that any 'clear and systematic' guidelines are likely to be superficial in the face of what actually happens in groups where people begin to be honest with each other. The BAC in its guidelines for good practice states that there should be 'regular and systematic approaches to self-awareness work'. It is important that the model offered to the group for processing its own life and experience is consistent, theoretically and experientially, with the core counselling model of the course, and that the tutors are in agreement about its aims.

In a letter to the BAC journal *Counselling*, Joy Dickinson (1996) says that her extensive research into the way personal development groups are run in organisations throughout the world has led her to conclude that '*how* a group is facilitated is by far the most important factor' and that this requires careful and extensive planning and thought. Important points to consider, she says, include decisions about which model of group work to use, and how this model interfaces with the core model of the course. It is also important that the manifest purpose of the group is defined and agreed upon, and that there is a way of perceiving, reflecting on and responding to the *latent* group process. It is assumed that counselling tutors should have the resources and the necessary understanding and experience to be able to facilitate personal development groups and deal with the big process issues and the unpredictable but inevitable chaos that come up on every course. Many trainers handle this well, through an intuitive ability to apply therapeutic principles in different contexts. They can make effective use of countertransference feelings, as well as their core counselling skills, to help them respond. However, what is required of them in this context is far more complex than in one-to-one work and some form of groupwork training is also important.

In addition, trainers have to mediate between individuals and organisations outside the course and beyond the circle of the course members. The position of the trainers, between the students and the host institution, can be complex and unstable. Even when trainers feel supported by the institution and are in good communication across its various levels, it is easy for communications to fail and for irritations to surface. The needs of counselling courses, and the needs of bodies such as universities or colleges, can appear incompatible and require the presence of staff throughout the organisation with goodwill and an understanding of the special needs of a counselling learning community. Often when administrative or managerial staff do not share the culture and values of counselling, students can feel they are being handled insensitively, and this can contribute to a general feeling on the course and in the groups that they are not being taken care of properly. This can become destructive, and it is important that administrative and course staff are in contact.

In conclusion I wish to reinforce the point that the groupwork aspect of any counselling training should not – and need not – be left to follow its own devices, but needs careful thought. Facilitating a group effectively is a complex and sophisticated skill which takes many years to learn; this has been neglected or underestimated in much literature on counselling training. If the nature and appropriate handling of counselling training groups are given more systematic attention, and if counselling trainers can get effective consultancy and training for themselves, counselling training groups can become less mysterious, the learning opportunities they provide can be exploited more directly, the inevitable difficulties can be understood and worked through more easily, and relevant knowledge and understanding from other traditions of groupwork can be applied. There are rich opportunities here for further development and discussion.

References

Berne, E. (1963) *Games People Play*. New York: Grove.

Clarkson, P. (1992) 'Transactional analysis and group therapy' and 'The psychotherapist in training, supervision and at work' in P. Clarkson (ed.) *Transactional Analysis Psychotherapy: An Integrated Approach*. London: Routledge.

Dickinson, J. (1996) 'Group work in counsellor training', letter in *Counselling, The Journal of the British Association for Counselling*, 7(4), November.

Douglas, T. (1976) *Groupwork Practice*, London: Tavistock/Routledge.

Heron, J. (1993) *Group Facilitation: Theories and Models for Practice*, London: Kogan Page.

Hilpert, H. (1995) 'The place of the training group analyst and the problem of personal group analysis in block training', *The Journal of Group Analytic Psychotherapy*, 28(3).

Hutten, J. (1996) 'The use of experiential groups in the training of counsellors and psychotherapists', *Psychodynamic Counselling*, 2(2).

Irving, J. and Williams, D. (1996)'The role of group work in counsellor training', *Counselling, The Journal of the British Association for Counselling*, 7(2), May.

Johns, H. (1996) *Personal Development in Counsellor Training*. London: Cassell.

LoVerso, G. (1995) 'The individual and the transpersonal', *Group Analysis, The Journal of Group Analytic Psychotherapy*, 28(2), June.

Mair, M. (1989) *Between Psychology and Psychotherapy: A Poetics of Experience*. London: Routledge.

Mearns, D. (1994) *Developing Person-Centred Counselling*. London, Sage.

Nitsun, M. (1996) *The Anti-Group: Destructive Forces in the Group and Their Creative Potential*. London: Routledge.

Rogers, A. (1986) *Teaching Adults*. Milton Keynes: Open University Press.

Rowan, J. (1993) *The Transpersonal: Psychotherapy and Counselling*. London: Routledge.

Smith, B. (1994) 'Training student counsellors: the hidden agenda', *Group Analysis, The Journal of Group Analytic Psychotherapy*, 27(2), June.

Tuckman, B.W. (1965) 'Developmental sequence in small groups', *Psychological Bulletin*, 63(6): 384–99.

Chapter 8

Volunteers, professionalisation and training

Arthur Musgrave

I worked for sixteen years for a service for young people which employed volunteer counsellors. During this time the number of counselling sessions we undertook rose fivefold. It was clear that young people very much valued what we provided, yet despite all we did we could only make counselling available to about half those seeking it.

We were forced to think hard about how to increase our output while giving priority to the quality of work we did. Our solution was to demand more of our volunteer counsellors, but only after carefully considering what we could provide in return. We knew they particularly valued the support and supervision they received and over time, therefore, we gradually increased what we made available. As we did this, we noticed our volunteer counsellors growing in confidence and the work of the organisation gaining in cohesion.

For me all this was exhilarating and deeply satisfying, though it was work that was undertaken in the teeth of major funding difficulties. Each year, because of the reputation we had locally, we scraped together enough money to survive. In the end, however, this success proved our undoing. We achieved so much with relatively limited resources that everyone took our continuation for granted. When local government reorganisation hit our area the key decision makers were so preoccupied that they were unable to respond to the particular difficulties we faced. As a result all the paid staff were laid off and the organisation was shut down.

While events like these are relatively uncommon, many counselling organisations struggle to respond to increasing workloads and an increasingly hostile funding environment. Many more people are seeking help from those that offer a free or low-cost service. They are bringing more serious problems: multiple difficulties that include breakdown, sexual abuse, addiction problems, eating disorders, self-harming and so on. Services with a good reputation for the work they do are forced to keep waiting lists or, in effect, turn people away. At the same time public authorities face one restructuring after another, cut their spending, spell out their priorities and focus on the services they are required by law to provide. Funding for many voluntary sector counselling agencies is often at risk, even though the work done may represent remarkable value for money and be highly regarded by professionals of all kinds.

Just as interest in counselling has exploded, so counsellor training courses at all levels have multiplied; counselling organisations in the vicinity are besieged by individuals on these courses offering their services as volunteers. The support that a well-established organisational setting can offer to these counsellors is clearly valued. Not only are such placements able to guarantee a steady flow of counselling experience, but they offer management and professional expertise that is invaluable to the fledgling counsellor. They provide supervision and opportunities for support and networking. Many volunteers make a weekly commitment over several years before they are ready to consider starting in private practice or applying for posts as paid counsellors in organisations. A substantial number maintain their commitment beyond this point, finding that their voluntary work provides a stimulating contrast to the work they do with those who pay them.

Why volunteers?

If new counsellors have much to gain from volunteering their services, the same is true for organisations that employ them. The successful use of volunteer counsellors hinges on establishing an exchange which is seen to be fair by all involved and which allows for the development of the individual alongside the development of the work of the agency. While individual volunteers make an input of their time and commitment, the organisation will be providing opportunities for them to undertake counselling and gain experience within a safe, structured setting.

A number of studies have suggested that volunteer counsellors with limited training are as effective as professionals who have had many years of counselling training (Durlak 1979, 1981; Hattie *et al.* 1984; Christensen and Jacobson 1994). Moreover, a team of volunteer counsellors can provide a rich organisational culture based on diversity of background and life experience. This means more choice for service users, while the larger pool of people involved gives managers greater flexibility when allocating work.

Counselling services with well-established structures for using volunteers can also be particularly cost effective. There is a powerful argument that volunteer counsellors who are well managed and supervised make better use of limited resources than teams of paid counsellors. But funders need to understand the importance of adequate, stable funding if they are to reap the benefits of using volunteers in this way. Limited resources will be deployed most effectively if continuity of funding is guaranteed for a given level of service provision. There is a delicate balance to be maintained. When this guarantee of funding breaks down, the results can be catastrophic for individual service users while at an organisational level established routines may well collapse, on occasion to the extent that the counselling service ceases to exist.

To work under pressures of this kind is debilitating. Each year plans have to take account of the possibility of imminent redundancy and closure, while enormous amounts of time and energy go into contingency planning. Raising funds to sustain an existing operation is more difficult than raising money for new initiatives and the commitment of management committee members, paid staff and volunteers is tested to an unreasonable degree. The result is that developments are held back and existing or potential service users suffer.

Volunteer counsellors and marginalisation

These changes in the context in which counselling services operate are taking place alongside the developing professionalisation of the interconnected fields of counselling and psychotherapy. As the professional groupings become more clearly delineated it is increasingly difficult to define volunteer competence except by reference to the norms used to define professional competence. These norms may be inappropriate; the result is that volunteer counsellors risk being marginalised and finding their inferior status reinforced.

Yet if the research evidence is right, standards are being set which are over and above the minimum needed for competent practice. The rapidly evolving process of professionalisation is a complex phenomenon and one which can be viewed in very different ways. BAC itself has traditionally been inclusive in its ethos and has provided a forum for a diversity of views. Setting standards is only one aspect of its work, but it is one which is leading BAC inexorably down the path towards professionalisation and an inevitably less inclusive stance. There has been strong support from within the membership for increased rigour. Professionalisation is generally seen as a benign process that benefits the public as well as practitioners. It is assumed that novice counsellors will benefit too as they use the agreed norms to help them steer a pathway through the various stages of their development.

The most compelling evidence for the adverse impact of regulation on counselling and psychotherapy comes from abroad. Hogan (1979) has written in detail about the American experience and argues that the harmful side-effects of regulation usually outweigh the supposed benefits. The supply of practitioners has been restricted; their geographical mobility decreased; costs have been inflated; the difficulties paraprofessionals face in performing effectively have grown; innovation has been stifled; and discrimination against women, the poor, the aged and minorities has increased. Although events in this country have so far been to do with non-compulsory rather than statutory regulation, the difference between the two is more usefully seen as one of degree than of kind. Mowbray (1995, 1997) has looked in detail at the arguments from a UK perspective and has concluded, first, that the regulation of counselling and related occupations 'cannot be justified on the grounds of client protection and would actually be detrimental rather than beneficial'.

Moves towards professionalisation are to a considerable extent fuelled by a widespread but understandable yearning both within BAC and outside it for absolute guarantees. The hope is that proper professional standards and a properly organised profession will protect the public from the incompetent, the delinquent and charlatans. Unfortunately the evidence both from abroad and from other professions suggests that claims to have been able to do this effectively are exaggerated.

At the same time, pressure from the media insists that the major representative bodies such as BAC must do all they can to make sure that these expectations are met. For instance, in early 1996 the BBC *Watchdog* programme criticised BAC for not protecting the public from those using BAC membership as a qualification to practise. BAC has no statutory basis and cannot stop individuals from making this claim; nor is BAC a professional association: it has charitable objectives which are exclusively to do with advancing the education of the public. *Watchdog* justified its report by claiming that the public has a right to expect BAC to act to protect the public, irrespective of its actual aims and objectives. In the face of attacks of this kind the pressures towards professionalisation are likely to prove irresistible.

The emerging pattern of professionalisation

BAC was set up in 1965 as a charity with broad educational purposes. Although the impetus towards professionalisation has been less single-minded than in the parallel organisation UKCP, BAC can now accredit counsellors, supervisors, trainers and training courses. Indeed, Courtland

Lee, as President Elect of the American Counselling Association, gave a warning at the 1996 BAC Annual Training Conference that issues connected with professionalisation are absorbing so much time and attention that counsellors may be losing sight of what drew them into membership in the first place.

Yet, training for volunteer counsellors has to take account of national developments. If counselling organisations do not pay close attention to what is unfolding, in the longer term they run the risk of losing their ability to attract and retain the volunteers they need. By keeping themselves informed, counselling organisations will be able to give their volunteers guidance about opportunities for professional development both within the agency and outside it. It is in everyone's interest that this information is available at the point of recruitment.

A key strand in BAC counsellor accreditation is the requirement for 450 hours of formal training. This benchmark underpins all the other accreditation schemes and seems to be founded on a somewhat arbitrary consensus among experienced practitioners rather than on sound evidence of what is needed for effective practice. To date BAC has not succeeded in extending counsellor accreditation beyond 11 per cent of its membership, while supervisor accreditation is held by well under 1 per cent. The schemes are not seen by volunteers as being accessible (Bond 1993). In 1995, BAC set up reviews of its counsellor and supervision accreditation schemes with the twin aims of making them more rigorous and more widely accessible to practitioners. It is hard to see how both will be met.

At first sight NVQs might appear to offer volunteer counsellors a useful alternative, since they quite explicitly set out to assess competence within work settings. However, both UKCP and BAC are major players in the development of NVQs and it is difficult to see the established standards being seriously challenged. In view of the widespread scepticism about them, NVQs cannot afford to be seen as a soft option or they will rapidly lose credibility as a route to qualification. Yet the more rigorous they are, the higher the fees are likely to be and, if they are to be accessible, the costs involved will be crucial to counsellors in training and to voluntary organisations.

The UK Register of Counsellors (UKRC)

In view of all this, it is encouraging that BAC has taken a further initiative designed to address the needs of counselling organisations alongside those of individual counsellors working in private practice or occupational settings. The creation of the UK Register of Counsellors has opened up a route for recognition both for counsellors working independently and for those working within organisations. While individuals with BAC counsellor accreditation can now go on the Register in their own right, those working in organisations are able to have their competence acknowledged within a given setting. The Register requirements for individuals working in an organisational setting are lower than those for individual counsellor accreditation; the rationale for this is that the counselling organisation will hold responsibility for a range of professional matters.

There is a balance to be struck between the fees that will have to be levied and the importance of establishing a strong, adequately resourced, public, professional presence. It is clear that significant costs will be involved. Register Sponsoring Organisations will have to pay an initial registration fee as well as an annual subscription. In addition it is likely that each counsellor entered on the Register will have to be an individual member of BAC or COSCA (Confederation of Scottish Counselling Agencies) and pay an annual fee. What remains far from clear is whether all those working in counselling organisations will agree that having their names on the UK Register will benefit them as opposed to benefiting the organisations to which they belong. Even among those who think it will, many may not be able to afford the fees involved. Many counselling organisations, therefore, may have to think carefully about whether or not to pay the annual fee for each individual in addition to the organisational charge. They may do this if they decide that the importance of having a vibrant professional infrastructure and the benefits of public recognition outweigh the additional tensions in managing a service with a mixture of registered and unregistered counsellors.

The underlying question is whether registration will provide a necessary yardstick for measuring the professionalism of a counselling service. If it does, the requirements of the Register will act as a spur to counselling organisations. Many will be keen for public acknowledgement that they offer a competent service, while funders will be encouraged by having a further guarantee of quality. If, for any reason, including uncertainties about funding, organisations are not able to join the Register, they will face additional obstacles in establishing their credentials with the public. The success of the Register from the point of view of voluntary counselling organisations may rest on whether or not funders are prepared to accept the additional costs.

Even if these are acceptable, there are further problems with the pool of applicants keen to work as volunteer counsellors. At present, relatively few potential volunteers already have enough counselling experience to be eligible for the Register. This means that in many counselling organisations a substantial proportion of the service will be provided by volunteers who are still undergoing training. Furthermore, counselling organisations wishing to promote their status in relation to the Register as a mark of quality assurance may need to select and retain only those volunteers who are working towards inclusion on the Register.

There are equal opportunity implications for counselling organisations contemplating this route. Most counsellors are white, middle-class women. Those on counselling diploma courses are largely drawn from the same population and it is likely that, in comparison with other caring professions such as social work or community and youth work, this is at least partly connected with the lack of LEA grants and the relatively small number of paid jobs available for those who qualify.

If counselling organisations wish to redress this imbalance in their workforce by recruiting and training a wider range of volunteers, they face considerable difficulties. There is a risk that any introductory counselling training they provide will be seen as limited. Counselling organisations cannot hope to offer substantial ongoing, in-house professional development. If the profession of counselling is to be representative of the diversity of cultural backgrounds within society, all those interested in working as volunteer counsellors must have equal access to opportunities for further training and development. These opportunities invariably carry with them hidden costs over and above the outlay on fees, personal counselling, supervision and so on. Those, for example, on low incomes or with substantial childcare responsibilities are undoubtedly disadvantaged and it is noticeable that minority ethnic communities are poorly represented within the field. Some initiatives have been taken, but there is clearly much to be done before these concerns are fully addressed.

In summary, then, whatever else it does, in the short term the Register is likely to add to the range of problems that managers of counselling organisations face. It will certainly benefit those in private practice, but it is likely to prove a mixed blessing for many of those in organisational settings. It may well force a divide between the better resourced services and the rest. If anything, there is the risk that it will exacerbate inequalities of access to the emerging profession. Set against all this is the opportunity that the Register offers. Above all, it provides a new benchmark for voluntary counselling organisations: if those which become involved can overcome the difficulties outlined, there is the possibility that they will not only give their volunteers added confidence but also receive substantially increased recognition from the public at large.

Volunteers and competence

The UK Register has set each counselling organisation the challenge of defining competence for the purposes of its own setting within the framework provided by the BAC *Code of Ethics and Practice for Counsellors* (BAC 1997). The UK Register Executive Committee (UKREC) merely insists that the training of those sponsored for inclusion on the Register must be in counselling and 'sufficient for the task of the organisation'. The rationale for setting the Register up in this way is not only that there is such a variety of organisational settings in which volunteer counselling takes place, but also that the Register recognises volunteer counsellors' competence solely in relation to their work within a given workplace. Entry on the Register cannot, therefore, be used by registered counsellors as a qualification when advertising their services elsewhere.

McLeod (1996) has reminded us that the definition of competence in counselling is socially constructed. It 'ranges along a continuum that stretches from creative mastery through to damaging abuse' and must include a developmental perspective. Different ways of defining competence in counselling are at present being clarified and becoming more widely understood. Thorne and Dryden (1991), for example, have argued that a professional training needs to be broadly based if the aim is to train counsellors who can communicate well across professional boundaries. Research suggests that what are needed are practitioners who are flexible enough to be able to adjust their responses to the differing needs of each individual client, while the project of becoming a well-trained integrative practitioner may well span a professional lifetime.

Some definitions are less ambitious. Inskipp (1996) has offered detailed ways of measuring competence in counsellor skills training, while Wheeler (1996) has written about the assessment of competence with particular reference to counselling certificate and diploma courses. McLeod (1996), by way of contrast, has made an interesting distinction between generic competencies and technical ones. Lay counsellors are seen as relying on 'broad-based personal qualities and attributes', while professionals have, in addition, 'a repertoire of technical skills and knowledge', which can be both an asset and, on occasion, a liability.

Once there is a better understanding of what NVQ Counselling Standards mean in practice, it is likely that the various viewpoints within the debate about competence will be more fully articulated. Qualifications and training in counselling and psychotherapy will be available at different levels and there will be pressure to make the distinctions between them intelligible. In the meantime, attempts to identify what makes for competent practice by counsellors are, relatively speaking, still in their infancy.

There have so far been few attempts to define minimum levels of competence and yet these are what those responsible for training volunteer counsellors most need. Bond (1993) has written in the following terms:

> Probably the minimum standard every counsellor should aspire to is:
>
> (a) Know why you are doing or saying something to your client;
> (b) Be sure you are saying or doing what you intend;
> (c) Know what the effect is likely to be;
> (d) Adjust your interventions according to the client's actual response;
> (e) Review your counselling practice regularly in counselling supervision;
> (f) Assess whether your level of skill is the same or better than other counsellors offering counselling on similar terms or holding similar posts.

While these are fine as aspirations, they are not wholly satisfactory as standards against which to measure competence. It could, for instance, be argued that it is more realistic to expect counsellors to notice accurately the extent to which what they say or do deviates from their intentions than for them to be sure that they actually say or do exactly what they intend. The ability to notice what happens, learn from it and respond appropriately might be closer to the heart of competent practice.

Apart from this, it is essential that counsellors know where their limitations lie and are able to work within them. Being able to communicate these clearly and succinctly is an important skill in itself; as far as volunteer counsellors are concerned, it may even be vital for competent practice.

Skills for effective volunteer counselling

Existing definitions of competence, then, take us only part of the way towards planning training programmes for volunteer counsellors. The research evidence moves us on one step further by giving an indication of what to incorporate. In each case what is also needed is a relatively simple overarching theoretical framework whose working principles can be accurately conveyed to trainees quickly and easily.

The time available for volunteer counsellor training is limited and some approaches have been more useful than others: in particular person-centred counselling and the Egan skilled helper framework. This framework for counsellor skills training has proved influential in the development of counselling in this country and is broad-based enough to allow for the integration of other approaches.

We know that effectiveness in counselling appears to correlate positively with a number of different factors (Russell 1981, 1993, 1994). Among these are the personal qualities of the counsellor, in particular genuineness (or congruence) and the capacity for demonstrating acceptance, warmth, trust, understanding and empathy (Mowbray 1995). This suggests that counsellor training should help trainees learn to release empathic sensitivity (Mearns and Thorne 1988) and show through their behaviour that they have heard and understood what their clients are communicating to them both verbally and non-verbally.

Even more important is the congruent matching of client and practitioner. Luborsky (in Russell 1981) suggests encouraging clients to try several different counsellors and make a selection based on their feelings. This in turn indicates that volunteer counsellors need to be skilled in accurately communicating their strengths and weaknesses as counsellors, and in helping clients clarify what they want. In addition counsellor and client need to be able to identify shared values and reach agreement on the aims of the work they will do together. A strong working alliance, as judged by the client, may well prove to be the most powerful factor in effective counselling (Russell 1994).

Effectiveness also appears to correlate with the practitioner's ability to perceive accurately what is happening. Smail (1983) suggests that this has more to do with effective counsellor selection than formal training. Trainees can, however, be helped to become better at noticing subtle changes in the way the client looks and sounds as well as becoming more sensitive to minute shifts in feeling (Bandler and MacDonald 1988). They can learn to become more flexible in their practice by paying close attention to these changes and by matching congruently the behaviour they observe.

Two other factors linked to effective counselling are the motivation of the client to change and the client's ability to engage in a working partnership. This suggests that trainees need to be adept at putting together clear contracts. The ability to identify well-formed outcomes is crucial and so are negotiation skills (O'Connor and Seymour 1993).

The length of experience of the counsellor is a further factor associated with effective counselling, suggesting that counsellors do learn from experience. They can be helped in doing this in a number of ways. Supervision is important, as is peer support. Counsellors can also take steps to learn more quickly by, for example, keeping a counselling journal. There are specific techniques to do with learning from experience that can be taught in counsellor training. The giving and receiving of feedback must be done with precision if useful learning is to be achieved. This means tracking back, in detail, the sequence of events in interactions in practice sessions. The skills involved in doing this can then also be applied in the course of counselling so that the practitioner develops the skills of testing out with the client the efficacy of the work being undertaken while it is still in progress.

Interestingly, there is no correlation between the length of training counsellors receive and their effectiveness as practitioners. Yet, in my own experience over a period of years, trainees' evaluative comments suggest that, whatever training is provided, more is wanted. Partly as a consequence, the length of volunteer counselling training has gradually been extended. It could be argued that this is no bad thing: after all, to have awakened a hunger for further learning might be an excellent indication that an introductory training has achieved one of its key goals.

Continuing professional development

It is important that this hunger is not frustrated. One of the core values of counselling organisations is a commitment to continuing personal and professional development. This principle has to underpin the work if there is to be organisational cohesion and the contribution of volunteers is to be tapped to the full. The challenge for managers is to keep their own priorities in mind so that this commitment and enthusiasm can all be channelled in a positive direction.

Counselling organisations usually have limited budgets and have to plan carefully in order to make best use of what is available. Volunteer training programmes must be seen within the wider context of recruitment, induction, support, supervision and personal development. Planners and decision makers have to decide to what extent they want to seek out volunteers who have already received counselling training. Some counselling organisations use only volunteers with counselling diplomas. Others recruit those with much less experience. Some organisations take on volunteers with no prior training in counselling at all, particularly in parts of the country where there are few accessible courses locally or where minority ethnic communities or others are identified as being under-represented within the volunteer counsellor team.

Whatever decision is made about whom to recruit, volunteers' continuing professional development must make the most of relevant training opportunities available outside the organisation. It may be that all trainees will benefit from help in thinking about their options, particularly as the routes to professional qualification become more varied and better defined. Appraisal systems can be worth considering for volunteer counsellors, since every activity undertaken by volunteer counsellors has a potential impact on longer term professional development. Because of this, portfolios are important as a record of training and experience gained (Aspinall 1993).

Identifying service needs

When planning volunteer counsellor training, the extent of the need for the service must be established as precisely as possible. This means estimating the number of hours of counselling that will be required by service users. Sometimes there will be a record of the numbers being turned away or kept on a waiting list, but very often the best data will come from equivalent services elsewhere.

Each agency has to decide what commitment it wants from each of its volunteers. Counsellors who undertake three or more counselling sessions a week are more likely to get a good range of experience than those doing less. The target agreed on will often be influenced by other factors, such as the number of hours of counselling needed for BAC counsellor accreditation or entry on the UKRC. When the number of counselling appointments per week is calculated, account must be taken of holidays, the amount of supervision the agency can provide, the planned ratio of paid staff to volunteers and the number of sessions it is anticipated that clients will not attend. In order to complete 150 hours of counselling a year, it is wise to think in terms of allocating four sessions a week.

Once these two calculations have been done it will be possible to work out how many volunteers need to be recruited. Some contingency planning is necessary, in order to allow for some of those selected not completing the training. There are problems with having too few volunteer counsellors just as there are with having too many. When there is not enough counselling available, managers have to ensure that volunteers retain their motivation or face the prospect that they may leave. Without careful planning it is easy for scarce training resources to be squandered.

Identifying resources

Good counselling training is expensive. BAC recommends a ratio of one trainer to twelve trainees and many argue that trainers should work in pairs so that trainees have more than one person on whom to model their practice. Unfortunately relatively few organisations can easily absorb large intakes of new counsellors, even if enough suitable recruits can be found.

Too small an intake can make for difficulty when running training exercises in small groups. The same problems arise if attendance at the training is erratic. It pays for counselling organisations to be firm about this, as good planning involves making the best use of time. It is sensible to build volunteer trainings around volunteers' availability. This may mean, for example, designing training programmes around school holidays and the times traditionally allocated to evening classes. The span of weeks over which training takes place can play an important part in shaping the training.

All of this planning will be affected by the resources that are available. This is only partly a question of the size of the training budget. Sometimes there are paid staff with the skills and experience to deliver the training themselves. The drawback to this is that volunteers can be exposed to too narrow a range of counselling practice, but the advantage is that it can be easier to achieve greater cohesion in the training programme as a whole.

Some small organisations find, particularly in their early stages, that training is provided either voluntarily or at a nominal rate by experienced practitioners who are keen to see the new initiative succeed. Provided this arrangement is made explicit, it can work well.

The training specification

Counselling organisations should formulate clear outcomes for training. It is likely that, taken in isolation, any good basic training for volunteer counsellors will be felt by participants to be too short. An introductory counsellor training course is therefore best seen as an integral part of a continuing programme of professional development. It can make an important but sometimes overlooked difference to morale if trainers are able to communicate congruently a belief that the initial training and the staff development programme as a whole are sufficient for the needs of the organisation.

The overall aim when providing an introductory training for volunteers is to give them an adequate range of skills and sufficient knowledge and understanding in order to begin work. A longer training gives participants opportunities to explore a much wider range of material as well as the chance to consider how this might be applied in a variety of contexts. Because time is limited, there needs to be a carefully planned balance within initial volunteer counsellor training of a range of different elements. Some of these, such as most of trainees' personal development needs, will have to be met outside the training. However, volunteers should be selected who already have a relatively high degree of self-awareness, whether or not they have already undertaken personal therapy themselves. The training can also quite deliberately set out to stimulate experiential learning and make appropriate use of personal material. Trainees can be encouraged to keep a reflective journal.

Because there is so little agreement about standards of competence for volunteers, each counselling organisation has to decide for itself the training objectives required for its particular setting. Wheeler has suggested five broad headings – self-presentation, preservation and professionalism; other-centredness; the therapeutic relationship; the therapeutic frame; and the social, cultural, economic and geographic environment (Wheeler 1996). According to Johns (1996):

> The key question, whatever voluntary organisation, client group or training model is involved, is one of *balance*, appropriate proportioning of self, skills and theory work according to the needs of the client group concerned and the counsellors being trained.

An important indicator of success will be the degree to which each trainee's initial enthusiasm has been developed and maintained while he/she is grounded in a growing appreciation of good practice.

Training objectives should be drawn up in enough detail to allow for proper evaluation afterwards. If the training is provided in-house, trainers themselves need to have enough of a record to be able to interpret trainees' evaluative comments. If the counselling organisation wants to commission training, it is important to provide outside trainers with clear guidance as to what is required. The discipline involved in specifying what training is required will, over time, enable systematic improvements to be made.

Evaluation should incorporate the views of trainees, trainers and managers. This cycle of identifying needs and evaluating afterwards can be done by focusing primarily on the learning needs of trainers, or it can be done as part of a process of organisational development. An important strand in this chapter has been the argument that counselling organisations need to strengthen their identity if they are to prove resilient in the face of increasing threats and challenges. One important way of doing this is to evolve tried and tested training programmes that exist independently of the personal expertise of key people within the organisation.

Volunteer recruitment

Counselling organisations need to be proactive in extending good equal opportunities. The selection of volunteers should be as scrupulous as the selection of paid staff. Job descriptions and person specifications are essential. When drawing up a person specification for volunteer counsellors, it is particularly important to be clear what skills and qualities applicants are expected to have at the time of selection and what skills, knowledge and understanding will be covered in the initial training. It is, for instance, important to select applicants with a commitment to personal growth and development, who are open to others and open to change and development.

Advertising for volunteers needs to be done imaginatively and may have to go beyond the use of printed posters and leaflets. Since the pattern of use made of a service is influenced by perceptions, the volunteer counsellor team has to be seen to be representative of the local community. Good practice, therefore, includes addressing any difficulties in retaining volunteers from groups traditionally poorly represented within the field of counselling, for example those from minority ethnic communities.

Selection can usefully be undertaken in stages, thereby allowing many less appropriate applicants to drop out early on. In an established counselling organisation, potential applicants can be sent printed material before meeting an existing volunteer to talk over what the commitment involves in practice. If application forms are only handed out after this, the number of completed forms can be cut by perhaps half. Many counselling organisations hold a group interview to test how potential volunteers operate as part of a team. For the individual interview, applicants can be asked to bring a tape and a transcript of the counselling session with commentary on their interventions. The selectors then look for accurate self-appraisal as well as the degree of counselling competence displayed.

Selection along these lines is rigorous and can provide an accurate indication of how volunteers might make use of training and how they are likely to perform in the work setting. Selection has been called the most crucial phase of counsellor assessment. If it is done well, the first component of a successful staff development programme is in place.

Supervision and continuing training

Given that the initial training is likely to be brief, supervision plays a central role in helping new counsellors perform well as they start counselling. New counsellors who are eager to learn can make particularly good use of supervision. Contracts between the counselling organisation and its volunteers need to be made explicit and must be seen to be fair. This is best done by making sure that volunteer counsellors understand what is required of them and have clear structures available that offer them what they need for their professional development. There needs to be flexibility so that volunteers can discuss any concerns that they have as soon as possible. Managers need to be vigilant and accessible. Ideally, they should be able to identify potential difficulties at an early stage.

There must be a strong framework of supervision. As well as meeting the BAC requirement of at least an hour and a half's counselling supervision a month, new counsellors need a minimum of one hour of supervision for every eight hours of counselling. Good supervision can be crucial to the development of volunteer counsellors who have completed a relatively short introductory training programme. Volunteers can be allocated an individual supervisor, or instead encouraged to negotiate in much the same way as they would if they were seeking a supervisor for themselves when working independently. Supervision groups can help new volunteer counsellors to learn about different ways of using supervision. There is a strong argument for having a supervision group for new volunteers to serve as part of the induction into the organisation's values and ethos. Peer support structures can offer an additional channel and give all volunteers the chance to clarify concerns that they are reluctant to raise from the outset with their managers or supervisors. Organisational meetings can provide a further useful channel of communication within the agency.

Good equal opportunities practice includes developing cross-cultural counselling (d'Ardenne and Mahtani 1989; Eleftheriadou 1994; Lago 1996). Counselling organisations have a responsibility to the wider community to ensure their services are seen to be accessible. Volunteer counsellors are likely to be exposed to a diverse population of service users and they must be sensitive to the needs of all their clients, taking steps to challenge their own prejudices and assumptions. This includes gaining skills and knowledge which give them a deeper understanding of oppression and what they can do within the work setting to combat it.

Volunteer commitment and empowerment

When using volunteer counsellors, managers need to have a sharp eye for organisational dynamics. If they are to make the most of volunteers' enthusiasm and commitment, their management style must be in keeping with the values and ethos they seek to inculcate within the volunteer counsellor team. Many volunteers want to make an impact on the organisation they have joined. They make a big commitment of their time and are inspired by the rewards they find. Very often they tap levels in themselves that have been dormant for years and become keen to make an even greater contribution. This can be a powerful force for organisational development or it can be immensely destructive if it gets out of balance.

Existing volunteers can have a powerful impact on new ones. Those sharing a rota slot will use each other for immediate support in assimilating and making sense of their work, but sometimes the time spent together will be less productive. Many different kinds of collusions are possible in the life of organisations. Sometimes what happens can be more to do with meeting the social or other needs of the volunteers than addressing the needs of service users. Managers have to be ready and able to intervene to maintain good practice; training is clearly a key part of their armoury.

Counselling organisations often ask volunteers to talk with each other about concerns that they have. While the intention may be to encourage direct negotiation and mirror the values promoted in counselling, the effect can be to stir up fears and anxieties. One result of this can be the exacerbation of an intergroup dynamic. This can be countered by developing opportunities for direct communication, for instance support groups and other meetings that provide reflection time. Managers themselves can benefit greatly from good consultant supervision.

Many have commented on the need for professionals to learn to be reflective practitioners. It is important to be able to think clearly not only about work undertaken with members of the public, but also about every aspect of professional activity. Managers have a duty to facilitate this process through the structures and procedures they establish. If practitioners are to respond creatively to this rapidly changing environment they must be in a position to plan proactively. They need mental space to be able to do this.

Professionalisation can be seen as a fundamentally irrational process. It arouses fierce emotions and the dynamics are sometimes more akin to those of a large intergroup event than anything else. It is vital therefore that managers are able to create mental space within which reflection can take place. If they can do this for the volunteer counsellors and for the organisation as a whole, the interface with the outside world will be managed more successfully. They will create an environment conducive to good counselling and those working within the organisation will feel proud of the work they do.

Implications for training volunteers in organisational settings

Good training programmes for volunteer counsellors are not just scaled down professional trainings. I hope I have shown in this chapter that it is more useful to think of them quite separately. Volunteer counsellor training programmes are almost always constrained by a lack of time or funding, if not by both. They need, therefore, to be carefully shaped in order to meet quite specific outcomes. Very often they are designed to supplement training that volunteer counsellors are undergoing elsewhere and so are best seen as one element in the continuing professional development of a staff team.

Sometimes, however, those who identify the need for a counselling service have to choose between offering a service using volunteer counsellors and offering nothing at all. Because of the absence of good counsellor training courses locally they may have to rely on in-house provision. In these circumstances the decision about going ahead and offering a service may hinge on a judgement as to whether volunteers can be trained to a level of competence at which they will be able to undertake good quality work.

Irrespective of the circumstances they find themselves in, those designing training programmes for volunteer counsellors need to pay attention to the research that is available. Although this does not offer definitive answers, it does suggest, as I have outlined in this chapter, what some of the key elements of a volunteer counsellor training might be.

Conclusion

This is an exciting time to be working in counselling organisations. Workloads have always been somewhat different from private practice, but this has become particularly apparent as more people from disadvantaged backgrounds have come for help. Counselling has become much more sought after in recent years and there are important demands that counsellors become more rigorous in delivering high quality services. Counselling organisations using volunteers can make a very real response to public need, but they require sensitive, creative management if they are to address the quite considerable challenges they face.

References

Aspinall, E. (1993) *Creative Appraisal; or Crime and Punishment? A study of the design, implementation and evaluation of annual appraisal for volunteer counsellors*, unpublished M.Sc. dissertation, University of Bristol.

Bandler, R. and MacDonald, W. (1988) *An Insider's Guide to Submodalities*, Cupertino, California: Meta Publications.

Bond, T. (1993) *Standards and Ethics for Counselling in Action*, London: Sage.

British Association for Counselling (1997) *Code of Ethics and Practice for Counsellors*, Rugby: BAC.

Christensen, A. and Jacobson, N. (1994) 'Who (or what) can do psychotherapy: the status and challenge of non-professional therapies', *Psychological Science*, 5: 8–14.

d'Ardenne, P. and Mahtani, A. (1989) *Transcultural Counselling in Action*, London: Sage.

Durlak, J. (1979) 'Comparative effectiveness of paraprofessionals and professional helpers', *Psychological Bulletin*, 86(1): 89–92.

—— (1981) 'Evaluating comparative studies of paraprofessionals and professional helpers: a reply to Nietzel and Fisher', *Psychological Bulletin*, 89(3): 566–9.

Eleftheriadou, Z. (1994) *Transcultural Counselling*, London, Central Book Publishing.

Hattie, J., Sharpley, C. and Rogers, H. (1984) 'Comparative effectiveness of professional and paraprofessional helpers', *Psychological Bulletin*, 95(3): 534–41.

Hogan, D. (1979) *The Regulation of Psychotherapists*, 4 vols, Cambridge, Massachusetts: Ballinger.

Inskipp, F. (1996) *Skills Training for Counselling*, London: Cassell.

Johns, H. (1996) *Personal Development in Counsellor Training*, London: Cassell.

Lago, C. in collaboration with Thompson, J. (1996) *Race, Culture and Counselling*, Buckingham: Open University Press.

McLeod, J. (1996) 'Counsellor competence', in R. Bayne, I. Horton and J. Bimrose (eds) *New Directions in Counselling*, London: Routledge.

Mearns, D. and Thorne, B. (1988) *Person-Centred Counselling in Action*, London: Sage.

Mowbray, R. (1995) *The Case against Psychotherapy Registration*, London: Trans Marginal Press.

—— (1997) 'A case to answer', in R. House and N. Totton (eds) *Implausible Professions: arguments for pluralism and autonomy in psychotherapy and counselling*, Ross on Wye: PCCS Books.

O'Connor, J. and Seymour, J. (1993) *Introducing Neuro-Linguistic Programming: psychological skills for understanding and influencing people*, London: Aquarian Press.

Russell, R. (1981, updated 1993 and 1994) *Report on Effective Psychotherapy: legislative testimony*, Lake Placid, New York: Hilgarth Press.

Smail, D. (1983) 'Psychotherapy and psychology', in D. Pilgrim (ed.) *Psychology and Psychotherapy: current trends and issues*, London: Routledge.

Thorne, B. and Dryden, W. (1991) 'Key issues in the training of counsellors', in W. Dryden and B. Thorne (eds) *Training and Supervision for Counselling in Action*, London: Sage.

Wheeler, S. (1996) *Training Counsellors: the assessment of competence*, London: Cassell.

Chapter 9

Training volunteers in a non-counselling setting

Anne Stokes

Doing voluntary work is a little like falling in love. You make an initial commitment which you hope is going to work, but you can never be completely sure.

(Ford and Merriman 1990)

This sentiment applies to the training of volunteers in counselling skills and also to writing about such a scheme. How can I know that you will understand that this is simply one person's experience as a trainer? Will you read between the lines and know that this is not the whole truth, or even the whole experience? Can I be faithful to the people I worked with and do them justice, while still recording our problems? If we were starting again, with our current knowledge, would we do some things very differently? I have written very specifically about one support scheme, and have tried to draw out of it some of the issues which might concern others involved in doing something similar.

The background

A comprehensive school, with which I already had very close connections, wished to establish a one-to-one support service run by parents for the benefit of other parents who were experiencing personal difficulties in some area of their family life. The school is a voluntary aided Church of England establishment with an overtly Christian culture and an underlying philosophy of care and concern not solely for the pupils, but also for their families. There was already a prayer chain scheme for pupils, parents and staff. This works on the principle of a request being made to one of several central telephone numbers, and then passed through a network of parents giving prayer support for as long a period as necessary. The organisers began to find that they were not only receiving prayer requests but that concerns, problems and difficulties were being off-loaded on to them over the telephone. This was not a function of the prayer chain, yet there was an apparent need for a different type of support. A parent-governor, who was a founder member of the prayer chain, felt that it was worth exploring ways of meeting this need. At the same time, the school's pastoral staff were offering considerable interpersonal support to parents. It was agreed that it would be helpful to train a group of parents, and possibly some staff, in counselling skills so that they were in a position to be able to offer support. As an experienced teacher and counselling trainer, I was asked to set up the scheme and devise the training.

There were some initial questions. Is it possible to set up a one-to-one counselling service in a non-counselling organisation? What would its limitations be? What are the issues in running it? And how ought the ongoing supervision and training needs be met? A key issue in this particular project was the integration of a Christian context and a secular scheme: others setting up a support scheme within an institution might not have this specific issue, yet they will always be faced with matching the culture and values of the host organisation with that of counselling provision (Carroll 1996).

Planning and preparation

There was no clear initial plan about what form the support system would take. This can be both the strength and a weakness of such a scheme. The work was free from earlier decisions, yet some boundaries and issues were not clear, which caused tensions later on. It was important to consider from the outset who needed to know what was happening: in this case, no formal 'permissions' had to be obtained, but as I wanted to work co-operatively, it was important that the governing body of the school and the staff were aware of what was being planned. If formal or informal permissions are needed, organisers should be aware of the length of time which this may take – other people are not necessarily concerned with your time limitations and do not necessarily share your view of priorities! At the information-giving meetings, it was also useful, even if embarrassing, to be asked questions which I had not considered about some of the logistics: I felt I ought to have thought of them first! It was important to try and keep an open mind and not be defensive. I discovered that those who were basically on my side could raise problems, while those who believed that I had no business meddling in areas best left to the 'professionals' found even more. One major mistake was made: everything should have been documented and the outcomes of the consultations communicated. For example, it became obvious as the scheme progressed that some people were unclear as to the extent of my involvement once the training of the volunteers and the initial implementation had taken place, and had not understood that I would be withdrawing gradually.

The nature and amount of training offered to the volunteers was dependent on what the scheme itself was hoping to offer. In consultation with the head teacher, the parent-governor and a small group of interested parents, it was decided that at the outset all that would be offered to parents using the scheme would be a maximum of four sessions, with a system for referral on to other counselling agencies if appropriate. This enabled the training to be planned from a basis of necessary learning outcomes: the ability to use counselling skills with clients for four sessions required volunteers to be equipped with a basic level of skills training, and also to have an awareness of the limits to the service being offered.

Recruitment

Hatch (1983) claims that the majority of volunteers become involved because they were asked to come to a meeting and certainly the experience of Parentlink – the name eventually given to our scheme – seems to bear this out. Although information was given out in a variety of ways, most volunteers came from an initial meeting to which they had been invited through the school and Parent Teacher Association channels. This brought in enough suitable people to begin the initial training, but also raised the question of exclusion. How can people be reached who are not already within the formal systems? If ways can be found to do this, then more of the target client population is also likely to be reached when the scheme actually starts, as there will be 'moles', i.e. the trainee volunteers, who will spread the word in the informal networks of the institution.

Organisers of a voluntary counselling scheme within an institution have to consider whether it will include the paid staff or 'professionals' among its possible recruits. Will this help to break down barriers within the organization – or will it create too many tensions within the scheme, particularly during training? In Parentlink, teaching staff were included, to cement relationships and help to counter any adverse reactions within the staffroom. Sometimes it is not enough to have the blessing of senior management; grassroots institutional support can be vital. However, balance is also a consideration in establishing who 'owns' the group and so it was decided that not more than one-third of the group would be from the teaching staff.

Recruitment will be affected by the pattern of training offered. The pattern at first proposed of fifteen weekly sessions of three hours each was a non-starter for everyone except the trainer! This immediately raised the question of whose needs are given priority – the volunteers', the institution's or the trainer's. The group of parents felt that whole days would suit their needs better, the institution could not afford to release staff for five working days, and as trainer, I was concerned about excluding working parents and my greater loss of income by setting aside five whole days rather than evenings in which I would not normally be undertaking paid work. In practice, the employed parents appeared willing to take leave or rearrange their working schedules. Three Saturdays were used and two weekdays, which also went some way to meeting their other commitments, as well as mine. This was an acceptable compromise for everyone, and the sessions were spaced over a period of three months. There were some advantages in using whole days, such as group cohesion and depth of work, but also disadvantages: the gaps between sessions were substantial, while volunteers who missed even one would lose one-fifth of the training.

When a volunteer scheme is set up within an institutional setting, it may have no financial backing. How are initial costs to be met? The obvious way is for those involved to raise funds or find a sponsor to cover start-up costs, which can also have the side-effect of drawing people's attention to the scheme. Fund-raising may instead deflect from the purpose of the scheme and become the focus of all the energy. Those involved in conceiving Parentlink wanted it to begin without fund-raising, so there were implications for how the training could be provided. Even though I was prepared to offer the actual training free, there were other costs involved.

One group of trainees felt that if participants paid for the course, they would be more committed to it, while others thought that it was inappropriate to expect volunteers to pay for their own training in order to set up a free scheme for others to use. Yet another compromise was reached whereby the cost was set at £25 to cover hiring rooms for three days – free rooms were found for two – course materials and basic refreshments. Compared with the true cost of the training, this was only a token, but it is possible that it excluded unemployed or low income parents. In some institutions, rooms and photocopying facilities might have been made available, but under the funding arrangements within the school, the rooms would have had to be paid for at weekends, and it was cheaper to hire a church hall. It could also be argued that outside venues provide a more neutral environment for volunteers.

In writing about it now, I am reminded of all my impatience and frustration at the slow pace of even getting to the stage of recruiting volunteers, but I tried to bear in mind Richardson's (1984) words that 'a few months spent in preparation, perhaps using a small steering group, is not wasted'.

Selection

There are various views on recruiting participants for the training stage of a volunteer counselling scheme (Tyndall 1993): some argue that all applicants should be taken on and a final selection made at the end of the training, while others believe that there should be a more rigorous initial selection, in the expectation that those people will automatically proceed to working with clients. As each scheme will be different and its values represent its particular culture, there is no 'right' way. Parentlink interviewed all applicants who came forward from the initial publicity and information-giving meetings. The selection interviews were conducted by the trainer and centred around reasons for wishing to be involved, current understanding of the counselling process, emotional support available, and the ability to commit time and energy to the training, and to the scheme when it got under way. As this was a pilot scheme, it was a relief that there was only one applicant about whom there were reservations and she decided not to proceed. It was therefore virtually a self-selected group. For the trainer to be the sole interviewer when the recruitment process was also about working in the voluntary scheme after training, was poor practice. It happened because anyone else who was sufficiently aware of the proposed scheme was actually an applicant. With the magic gift of hindsight, it is possible to think of others who could have been involved such as another counsellor trainer, a supervisor, or a volunteer organiser from elsewhere. They may not need to be involved in the scheme as long as they have been well briefed.

Since this was a new scheme, it was vital to ensure that the trainees were likely to be able to cope not only with the training, but also with the pressures of teething problems. They would help to shape the future of the support scheme, so rigour in selection was important. Balanced against this was the desire to be inclusive and represent the various groupings within the institution they would service.

Philosophically, it was hoped that the group would be balanced:

> an ideal mix is rare, so care must be taken that there is no one isolated – one man amongst women (or vice versa), one old person amongst youngsters, one black amongst white, one Catholic amongst Anglicans. Two of any one type is preferable.
>
> (Jacobs 1985)

There were imbalances in the twelve volunteers who accepted places for the five days' training. There were a further three applicants who wished to join the course, but who could not be present for the first day. This caused a dilemma as ideally the training group size would have been more than twelve to allow for dropouts: there needed to be enough volunteers at the end of the training to get the scheme up and running. In the original group, there was only one man, and he was a member of staff. After much thought about the ramifications, it was decided to incorporate the extra three applicants on the second day of training, providing they had also undergone a separate first day equivalent. There were also qualms about including a married couple as trainees, but because of the context – a parents' group – it was decided to go ahead. The mixture of parents and staff, men and women, older and younger, married and not married, worked well.

Over half of the group had stated on their application forms that they wanted to do the course partly to enhance their paid work. This matches the findings of other volunteer groups (Hatch 1983). Trainers and organisers of voluntary groups might have some concerns about this – are people seeking training on the cheap? The optimistic view is that it is an advantage for participants to be able to achieve something tangible for themselves, as they are more likely to be wholehearted and committed to it. A quarter of them had received counselling themselves, which was significant in bringing reality about the counselling process into the training, though it was also a watchpoint: are trainees seeking a substitute therapeutic experience?

McCurley and Lynch (1994) emphasise that there is a difference between employment and volunteer interviewing: employment is concerned with 'who can do this job?' and volunteering focuses on 'who will want to do this job?' Perhaps it is not quite so straightforward, since volunteers have to be able as well as willing, but it helps selectors to remember that the scheme is dependent on people being prepared to come forward and give freely of their time and energy.

The training experience

The initial feelings of the trainees are encapsulated in this extract from one reflective journal:

> Before I came to the first session, I had a mixture of thoughts and feelings: who would be there; would there be a 'them and us' situation with parent and teacher working together; what would we do; would I be up to it? I felt excited, expectant, but also nervous about the unknown.

Other reflections included not being seen as a good enough Christian, which demonstrates how the culture of the institution is present overtly or covertly within the training of the volunteers in a support system. At the end of the first day, feedback suggested that there had been a dramatic shift in relationships between teaching staff and parents.

The philosophy behind the design of the course was that training involves offering ideas and encouraging people to develop skills and experience through sharing their discoveries with each other. Parentline (Organisations for Parents under Stress) emphasises in its *Training Manual* (1991) that if people are to become skilled listeners they need to be able to hear the distress of a client, encourage the difficulties to be talked about and acknowledge their own need of support.

The Parentlink training aims to:

- introduce trainees to basic counselling skills and give an opportunity for practising those skills;
- differentiate counselling from other activities such as advice giving;
- provide a safe group setting which enables open communication, self awareness and the sharing of experiences;
- help trainees reflect on how they would use their skills in a voluntary setting to help other parents;
- consider the place of the counsellor's personal faith and belief systems when working as a volunteer;
- introduce some of the concerns which parents may present to volunteers (e.g. family issues, loss, substance misuse);
- generate an awareness of the limitations of using a counselling approach with other parents.

In broad outline, each day was made up of skills training and, apart from the first day, an experiential workshop relevant to the nature of the group, e.g. loss and bereavement, Christian issues, 'drugs 'n' sex 'n' rock 'n' roll'. The framework for the skills training was Egan's (1998) three-stage model, which also provides a solid structure both for brief training and for time-limited counselling. New volunteers need a model which they can grasp effectively and use safely, which will continue to be valid if counsellors undertake further training and work with different client groups.

The balance between experiential and knowledge-based learning had been considered in the training design. In pre-training discussion, most participants had said that they wanted to be told how to do things; they wanted the apparent security of instruction, while my fundamental training belief is in the value of experiential learning. Since most of the time I would be working as a sole trainer, the resolution was to facilitate the experiential sessions within a structured framework.

The workshop on families illustrated the difference in learning experience from that expected. Trainees commented that they had anticipated being 'taught' about families. 'Dealing with families turned out to be different from what I had thought it might have been. I guess I had not actually analysed the feelings I looked at before today.'

Co-training is the ideal, but small voluntary groups may not be able to afford this, so it is worth looking at flexible ways of meeting your own need for support as a trainer. Debriefing with a fellow trainer, even by telephone, can be useful, or finding ways of using other trainers for part of the time. Parentlink training achieved this to some degree by using the former school chaplain, who is also a counsellor and trained teacher, to work with me for part of the last two days. Because of his past involvement with the school he was prepared to donate his time and was particularly helpful in the Christian issues and counselling workshop. His involvement also provided a male counsellor role model. With hindsight, trainee trainers might have been approached to see if they would be interested in gaining the experience of co-facilitating a course. This would have avoided some of the difficulties which arose from the contrast between working by myself with the group and working with the chaplain. He and I had thought about our own process in doing this, but that did not prevent some fairly strong group reaction when an 'outsider', albeit someone known to most of them, joined us.

Where a volunteer group is working within a specific institutional setting, time has to be spent exploring the context. In this case, that involved the distinctions between a counselling skills approach which is appropriate for parents to use in their support of other parents of children within the same school, and the 'Christian counselling' approach which might be appropriate in a church setting. The former, though rooted in Christian beliefs, is not necessarily overtly Christian within the counselling session. At times this was a fairly contentious issue, but absolutely necessary in formulating the principles and practice of the support scheme. The day on families in particular was formative in the bonding of the group and it was from this point onwards that participants took ownership of the scheme and were not simply trainees. This was vital as they were the ones who would take the scheme forward. If trainees were being inducted into an existing or larger volunteer setting, problems might have arisen at this point, with the need to value their new perspectives, but also to hold in check some of the enthusiasm for a drastic reorganisation of everything which had been previously set up.

At the beginning of training, it is difficult to know who leans towards which of Honey and Mumford's (1986) learning styles, and how to maximise these. For that reason, it is important to provide a variety of activities and learning experiences to try to ensure that everyone is catered for. Thus for the activist there will be new experiences, involvement with others and 'here and now' activities. For the reflector, there will be time to think before activities and time to review what is happening by standing back from it. The theorist will benefit from knowing how what is being offered fits into systems, models and theories and will welcome structure and being intellectually stretched. The pragmatist will seek links between the subject matter and the situation in which it will be used – the practical application of any given model. The support scheme benefited from having volunteers from all four styles, not simply in the training but also in the setting up and running of the project.

In evaluating the first training programme, it became clear that there were concerns about referring clients on to other agencies. Although this had been included, some of the volunteers still felt unsure about how and to where they could refer. This may have been due in part to the fact that these trainees were the pioneers with no well-trodden paths to follow, and were anxious about their competence, needing to be very sure that they knew the limitations and boundaries. Evaluation at the end of initial training was useful in highlighting some of the areas for follow-up work.

Accreditation

Organisers and trainers of volunteer counsellors have to consider the value of an external accreditation of their work. While volunteers are giving freely of their time, it may be useful for them to be able to add such accreditation to their personal career portfolios. The disadvantages are that when training is geared to a specific situation and is small scale, there may be no suitable validation, or it may involve an extra level of work which will put people off volunteering. At that time I was a counsellor trainer at a nearby institute of higher education and we managed to design the course to fit the criteria of a module from one of the professional diplomas, which could also be taken as a stand-alone course. Volunteers were not required to put themselves forward for formal assessment, but could do so if they wished. If the scheme was being set up now, it would almost certainly have involved NVQ competences, which would have probably been more appropriate and transferable into other areas of the volunteers' lives.

This raises the question of whether it should be left up to participants to decide if they wish to achieve external recognition. In terms of accountability, there is a case to be made for it being mandatory. Certainly, a competence-based model, such as NVQs, has much to offer in this respect, as it obviates the need for written work which may not be relevant. On the other hand, the amount of work, and indeed the cost, may take formal recognition out of reach for very small idiosyncratic schemes. Participants on our training course were strongly encouraged to keep a reflective journal from which an assessed developmental record could be drawn at a later date. Insisting on a formal system of assessment, whether or not it is external, may help when the trainer feels that a volunteer may not be suitable, or not yet ready to work with clients; there may be evidence rather than just an instinctive judgement.

Parentlink in action

When the scheme was envisaged, there was great difficulty in finding any similar structure. This is likely to be a problem for any small community or institution support scheme, as it is based on the needs of that particular community at that moment, known only by those involved.

I looked at three different models to try to learn something from their experience. The first was a 'buddy scheme', which was also a community based organisation involving training and supervision. Although this was a befriending situation, including many practical tasks which Parentlink was not designed to do, it highlighted a number of issues. The support and supervision system had no clear structure or function, with the result that no one knew the extent of a particular volunteer's work, as she or he might be contacted directly by the friends of clients. It was also obvious that some buddies were not able to balance the needs of their clients and those of their own families. This alerted me to the possible over-involvement of some volunteers and the responsibility of the group organiser or the supervisor to confront this. The discussion on buddying also touched on where meetings took place. This raised issues of appropriateness and safety which enabled me to become much clearer about boundaries.

Parentline, a national organisation with local groups, had most in common with Parentlink, though it operates mainly as a telephone helpline, is a much larger organisation and is not constrained by the institutional setting. An interview with a local organiser gave useful leads as to how money might be obtained for training from statutory bodies or children's charities, or how existing facilities might be utilised. The discussion was also valuable in leading to a consideration of whether help was needed with non-client tasks, such as administration and publicity. This can be a good way of utilising trainees who may decide not to go on with face-to-face work, or volunteers who need to take a break.

In a loosely based support scheme which serves a very small institutional network, confidentiality is vital. After talking to other groups, a way was devised of maintaining this and recording all contacts. Names and addresses were kept separate from client notes, yet could be cross-referenced when necessary, although this was a major problem as there was no office base. In the end two distinct places were established. Volunteers were not working in a central location but records needed to be kept centrally.

It could be argued that for such a small group of volunteers working with a number of clients over very short periods, there is no need to keep records at all. Houston (1990) acknowledges that if few clients are seen, it is possible to work effectively without any writing up as counsellors can carry sessions accurately in their heads. If there is a danger of lack of confidentiality, if keeping records promotes a high degree of anxiety arising from the fear of being judged by these records, or compared unfavourably with their fellow volunteers, or if they are made after a session 'for the sake of it', and never referred to again, then the process will be counterproductive. It is therefore necessary to be sure that the reasons for keeping them are valid, and that trainees understand their purpose.

The third scheme was a parent-support programme which was run by an individual teacher in a school. This was to provide a supportive environment in which parents could meet and share their experiences and the challenges of their family life. Though this had only tenuous links with what we were working towards, we learned from it. Parentlink trainees ran a series of focused workshops for parents within the framework of the school's regular programme of meetings with parents. This served two purposes: the support scheme was brought to the attention of a wider group of potential users and it provided a way of keeping volunteers interested and committed at a time when there were very few clients.

Much of the practical organisation for setting up Parentlink was left fluid until the training was under way, in case the group decided not to proceed with the venture. In addition to the five training days, there were two sessions where participants thrashed out the fine detail of how the scheme would work and who would do what. In larger voluntary organisations, it is less likely that trainee volunteers would do this. In this type of institution-based initiative, it was not only appropriate but essential that the scheme was run by the volunteers and not by the trainer, nor solely by the parent-governor who was the originator of the idea, or the school management whose members were supportive but separate. Two of the volunteers offered to be the central co-ordinators and undertook to work out with individuals how much time they could afford to commit and when during the week this might be. This averaged out as two hours per week per person. It was decided that there would be an initial session, and then by agreement between the client and the volunteer, a maximum of four further sessions. If further support was needed, the client would be helped to move on.

Supervision took place mainly in small groups, though in the early stages this had to be augmented by extra one-to-one contact, as there were periods when only one volunteer had a client. Volunteers who do not have clients themselves do learn from being in a supervision group, but at times the sole volunteer with a client might need more supervision than it would have been reasonable to expect the whole group to participate in. Apart from supervision being a requirement for counsellors working within the BAC Code of Practice, and its normal functions of monitoring, developing and supporting, Foskett and Lyall (1988) recognise its value in the early stages of volunteers' work when they go through a period of disillusionment. 'They expect to be "doing counselling" and instead they find themselves in ordinary conversations with ordinary people.'

Where support is given to and by people within the same umbrella organisation, it is difficult to prevent overlap between the various areas of life, so measures have to be worked out to go at least some way towards establishing boundaries. When parents telephone one of the two central numbers, they are asked to give their child's class so that they will not be matched with a volunteer who has a child in the same one. They will also be asked if they attend a church and, if so, similar criteria apply.

The venue for meeting clients posed problems. While the school might have seemed the obvious place, it had a number of disadvantages. During the daytime, space is at a premium and in addition parents may be put off by the thought of being seen by their children, their children's friends, or by staff as they arrive or leave the counselling session. Although a comparatively small school, there is a very wide catchment area. Using a variety of bases seemed to make the service more accessible to parents, though it can cause occasional problems. Safety was a consideration when choosing premises, and it was felt necessary to be cautious. It was agreed that volunteers would not use their own or client's homes, and that if for any reason volunteers were likely to be on their own, there should be another person, preferably a volunteer, elsewhere in the building. At times maybe we were over cautious, but it freed the counsellor to concentrate on the process when with clients.

Key learning

Perhaps the most important lesson was that when other people need to be consulted and involved, most things take twice as long as anticipated, so this needs to be built into time schedules. On the other hand, if communication does not take place and outcomes are not clear, problems may, indeed usually do, arise.

It is imperative to consider how to keep volunteers motivated if a counselling support scheme is slow to take off. Regular on-going training sessions help to provide a supportive network, as well as monitoring the use of the newly acquired skills in other areas of volunteers' lives. While the needs of clients must always come first, beyond that there should be an equable distribution between trainees, so that even if there are only a few clients, there is an opportunity for all to begin to work in the scheme.

'If you can't hide it, make a feature of it' is an old adage: an initial period without clients can be valuable, for example in designing and producing publicity material, making contacts and ensuring that everything is in place administratively. The ongoing involvement or gradual withdrawal of the initial trainer and supervisor is a question which can vex support schemes such as Parentlink. There is a danger that if the trainer has been a key person in the creation of the support scheme within the institution, when she or he leaves, it can begin to crumble. Within this group, there was a volunteer who has since obtained a Diploma in Counselling and who is also a good facilitator. Bringing in her skills as a trainer with new volunteers would be a way forward.

The training of further volunteers was a central issue. There is little point in doing so until the scheme actually needs them, but if it is left too late, it will put extra strain on the existing volunteers. When recruiting people to join the previously trained cohort, it may be possible to address imbalances in race and gender and meet gaps in the existing provision.

Conclusion

In recent years there has been a significant growth in a wide range of small groups set up for particular needs, which have no immediate ambition beyond their own orbit. Groups come and go depending on the needs and energies of their members (Headley and Davis Smith 1992). The volunteer is often seen by professionals as 'a wishy-washy figure undermining professional standards and only possessing vague boundaries' (Perry 1991). Parentlink has tried to avoid some of the pitfalls and has inevitably made some mistakes. A guideline for the future might be to recognise that voluntary support systems within an institutional setting need to do what they do well, and not be concerned that they cannot do everything.

It is difficult to quantify the success of a support scheme: is it the number of clients seen, how long the scheme goes on, its evolution to meet changing needs, or is it simply the value which an individual client gives it?

Moreover, how might a support scheme further contribute to the institution? If, for example, a number of parents highlight a particular problem within the organisation which has troubled them, can counsellors find a way of feeding that back into the institution? Maybe that would raise the profile of the scheme, or maybe it would be seen as a threat by the professionals. Much will depend on the relationship and communication between the two.

Parentlink still exists at the time of writing, but its function is changing. I am no longer involved and three of the volunteers have become responsible for managing the scheme, one of whom provides the main interface with the school system. It seems likely that the work with clients will cease in the near future as there is now little take-up. The scheme was created for a particular need and it is important to recognise that needs change over time, rather than seeing the current lack of clients as a failure. Volunteers have been asked to train sixth formers in basic skills so that they could 'buddy' new pupils. Maybe this is the next phase of the scheme.

> It is a truism of the voluntary ethic that it does not have to be; it is not coerced or required either through social attribution or legislation.... The voluntary ethic is an impulse to do good – not to be a

'do-gooder' – within the constraints of community resources and the rather arbitrary decisions on priorities taken by individuals.

(Higginbotham 1990)

Perhaps a fitting way to end is to offer a set of guidelines on evaluating training programmes within the voluntary sector, as they will help support schemes to decide on their priorities:

- Find out what training is needed.
- Bring together advisory groups and agree the training programme.
- Agree on when, and specify what, to evaluate.
- Identify methods for collecting information.
- Design and develop the training programme.
- Implement the training.
- Evaluate it.
- Publicise the results.

(Adapted from Evans and Burridge 1992)

References

Carroll, M. (1996) *Workplace Counselling: A Systemic Approach to Employee Care*, London: Sage.

Egan, G. (1998) *The Skilled Helper: A Problem-Management Approach to Helping*, 6th edn, Pacific Grove, CA: Brooks Cole.

Evans, P. and Burridge, D. (1992) *Evaluating Training Programmes: Guidelines for Voluntary Sector Training Organizations*, London: NCVO.

Ford, J. and Merriman, P. (1990) *The Gentle Art of Listening: Counselling Skills for Volunteers*, London: Bedford Square Press.

Foskett, J. and Lyall, D. (1988) *Helping the Helpers: Supervision and Pastoral Care*, London: SPCK.

Hatch, S. (1983) *Volunteers: Patterns, Meanings and Motives*, Berkhampstead: The Volunteer Centre.

Headley, R. and Davis Smith, J. (1992) *Volunteering and Society*, London: Bedford Square Press.

Higginbotham, C. (1990) *Return to Community: The Voluntary Ethic in Community Care*, London: Bedford Square Press.

Honey, P. and Mumford, A. (1986) *Using Your Learning Styles*, Maidenhead: Peter Honey.

Houston, G. (1990) *Supervision and Counselling*, Rochester: The Rochester Foundation.

Jacobs, M. (1985) *Swift to Hear: An Introduction to Pastoral Counselling*, London: SPCK.

McCurley, S. and Lynch, R. (1994) *Essential Volunteer Management*, London: Directory of Social Work Change.

Parentline (1991) *Training Manual*, London: Organizations for Parents under Stress.

Perry, C. (1991) *Listen to the Voice Within: A Jungian Approach to Pastoral Care*, London: SPCK.

Richardson, A. (1984) *Working with Self Help Groups: A Guide for Local Professionals*, London: Bedford Square Press.

Tyndall, N. (1993) *Counselling in the Voluntary Sector*, Buckingham: Open University Press.

Chapter 10

Training by telephone

Emma Fletcher

Introduction

The role of telecommunications in the development of counselling and related activities has not received much attention in counselling literature. Telephone counselling (or, perhaps more accurately, the use of counselling skills on the telephone) is now achieving some recognition, although, as McLeod (1993) points out, this is still fairly small, considering that client contacts with telephone agencies are far more numerous than face-to-face experiences. It is rarer still to find any discussion of the telephone itself as a medium for counselling training. Where new technologies are acknowledged, their uses are little explored (Sanders 1996). My purpose therefore in writing here is to share my personal experience of running counselling skills courses entirely on the telephone. This experience was also the focus of a research study conducted for an M.Sc. dissertation (Fletcher 1994). Although the study concentrated on training for a voluntary organisation, the outcomes have wider implications.

Training by telephone is delivered via telephone conference calls. A conference call is a telephone conversation between three or more people in different locations. Winders (1984) offers a more technically precise description of this facility, but as far as the end-user is concerned, technical knowledge is not required; it is just like making (or receiving) an ordinary telephone call. The technical expertise and equipment are provided by the system operator, which may be a telephone company (for commercial conferences) or a private licensee such as Community Network (see below), which makes this service available at low cost for charitable and educational purposes.

Through the telephone conferences, all the participants can be brought on the line together and can speak to and hear one another, making it possible to hold group discussions or teaching sessions without having to get together physically. Its usage in educational settings is not new: the Open University have for many years been using such conferences to link tutor and students who may be widely scattered geographically (George 1983). This has been regarded as a back-up to class teaching or private study, rather than the principal mode of tuition (Woolfe, Murgatroyd and Rhys 1987). More advanced technology in forms such as videophone conferences and interactive computer networks is now also entering the field. These require sophisticated equipment which is not as yet found in the average home, whereas to join in a telephone conference, all you need is an ordinary telephone, without any adaptation. This means that telephone conferencing is available to small organisations, self-help groups, or individual users in their own homes. It was this accessibility which made the telephone conference facility so exciting to me in terms of counselling skills training, and which carries the potential for widespread development.

The Phobic Action training programme

The possibility of using telephone conferences for counselling skills training first occurred to me some years ago when I was given the job of setting up a national telephone helpline for a small mental health charity. Phobic Action came into being for the benefit of people with anxiety disorders and others involved with them. As a self-help organisation, part of its general aim was to help those affected by severe phobic and other anxiety-related conditions to improve their quality of life, and it was committed to involving its members as volunteer helpers. There were, however, certain obstacles to constructing a volunteer team on self-help principles. Anxiety disorders comprise a range of conditions of varying severity: the people who became sufficiently involved with Phobic Action to wish to offer their services to help others tended to be substantially disabled, often to the extent of being housebound. Membership was also small and distributed across the United Kingdom. Furthermore, the agency had very limited resources at its disposal, so the service had to be set up and run at the lowest possible cost. Indications were that there would be sufficient volunteers willing to work for a helpline, provided they could take the calls in their own homes. With only one part-time staff member to run the project, the problem was how these volunteers could be trained to the required level, and, once trained, how a communications system could be established to monitor the service and maintain the commitment of the Helpliners.

In 1989, Phobic Action made contact with Community Network, a newly formed charitable organisation seeking to promote the use of telephone conference facilities to link groups of housebound, socially isolated or geographically separated individuals. The potential benefits of this resource were evident: a common characteristic of Phobic Action's members was their isolation, in both a physical and an emotional sense. The organisation's first venture with Community Network was a pilot group to link up members who wished to talk to others similar to themselves, who could not easily attend a self-help group in their locality.

It quickly became evident that this device could also be used for volunteer training and support: through the telephone conference network we could surmount the obstacles of distance and disability to create a volunteer team which was both compatible with the agency's ethos and feasible within the budgetary and staffing constraints.

The training model

The growth of telephone helplines in the past decade has generated interest in setting standards for operation and training. The guidelines produced by the Telephone Helplines Association (endorsed by BAC) state that it is essential to have 'a programme which encourages trainees to develop their listening and responding skills ... (which) should include both theoretical and practical components, and trainees must be able to practise the skills ... through role-play and other practical exercises' (Telephone Helplines Association 1993). People working on the telephone are often handling highly sensitive situations. The guidelines stress that the more emotionally supportive helpers are expected to be, the longer the training process needed.

These listening and responding skills are an application of counselling skills more usually employed in face-to-face work. Sanders (1996) maintains that the key concept is Carl Rogers' notion of *psychological contact*, which is established through the core conditions of empathy, acceptance and genuineness (Rogers 1965). Psychological contact does not depend on physical or visual presence, but its quality may be different on the telephone. Training for telephone work has to give emphasis to particular counselling skills, and must address the effect of the telephone setting on boundaries, ethical issues and professional responsibilities.

Available research (McLeod 1993) largely endorses helpful telephone behaviours as being similar to effective face-to-face counselling – understanding, caring, listening, offering feedback, positive attitude, acceptance, keeping focus on the problem. However, there are indications of process dimensions which differ. It has been suggested, for instance, that telephone counselling increases the positive transference felt by the caller, who perceives the unseen helper as an ideal. Again, Hunt (1993) observes that even trained counsellors may need extra skills to cope with the urgency of telephone work. The key skills seem to be extra-careful listening, including awareness of voice tones and any background sounds; responding with verbal acknowledgement or 'gesturing' to encourage speaking (but not overdoing it), dealing sensitively with different kinds of silence, communicating empathy through accurate and succinct paraphrasing, and structuring a long and rambling discourse. Furthermore, telephone counsellors need the ability to decide what is appropriate to offer in a shorter time-scale, to identify hoax calls, and to terminate calls. There can be more pressure to offer something concrete, and an expectation that the caller will call only once, leading to an inner drive to come up with a complete solution.

These are special considerations which apply on the telephone. At the same time, all training in counselling skills is about teaching helpers to communicate effectively with their clients. This holds true whatever the context or level of training, whether preparing professional counsellors or volunteers for a telephone helpline. These relationships form part of the continuum of helping (Murgatroyd 1985) characterised by the use of personal qualities in the helper to increase the well-being of another person. My model of training, derived from the person-centred philosophy of Carl Rogers (1983) and the skills model of Gerard Egan (1990), assumes that the acquisition of skills and personal development go hand in hand. Important factors are the climate of trust and the balance of support and challenge under facilitative leadership. The training group provides a supportive learning environment which acts as the foundation for all counselling training, not only as the medium for conveying the practical elements, but also as the place where trainees can explore themselves in relation to others.

Evaluative study of the telephone training

I had already taught a listening skills course for Phobic Action's local self-help groups in London. Early in 1990, I set about adapting this for delivery via Community Network's telephone conferences. For the practical training in handling telephone calls, I borrowed from my experience with the Samaritans the practice of introducing 'live calls' role-played by volunteers, to be taken by the trainees in turn, and then discussed by the group as a whole. In this case the 'callers' were actually being brought on the line in the same way as the other participants, which gave added verisimilitude. It was important that these callers remained on the line to take part in the ensuing discussion as themselves in order to dispel any illusions! Another modification was for the group members to telephone one another for paired practice sessions between the weekly conference meetings. This was to compensate for the work in pairs which would normally take place within a conventional counselling training session.

Each course consisted of twelve weekly telephone conferences, after which the group continued to meet through the Community Network conferences for regular supervision and follow-up training. By the summer of 1992, the Helpline was fully staffed, though the basic training programme needed to be repeated two or three times a year to replace volunteers who left or moved into other duties.

I led courses myself as trainer/facilitator. At a later stage, I invited an experienced volunteer to act as assistant to gain experience and to strengthen the amount of facilitative attention in the group. The gains and complexities of co-tutoring are similar to those in face-to-face groups. ·

The size of the training group was determined by technical factors. When we started the programme, the maximum number possible in a telephone conference was ten (including the trainer and any 'callers'). Later, when improved equipment became available, larger groups could be accommodated, but in practice, I found that the most convenient sized group for effective participation was about six.

The training was devised as a rolling programme, with a new intake at approximately four-monthly intervals. By the time I came to prepare my M.Sc. dissertation (Fletcher 1994) there had been eleven basic training courses, involving a total of sixty-seven people. I wanted to examine two main questions: (a) how effective was the telephone network as a means of delivering counselling skills training? and (b) did it achieve the objective of enabling people with restricted mobility to gain access to opportunities for training and voluntary work? The study had two parts: a survey questionnaire and an action research project detailing the life of a telephone training group.

All past participants were invited to complete a questionnaire, asking how they came to training, their reasons for choosing a telephone-based course and their expectations; the quality of experience in the group and whether initial expectations were fulfilled; how the training was being put to use, within the agency or elsewhere; and respondents' general views of the advantages and disadvantages of telephone-based training.

Respondents included trainees from each of the eleven training groups, of whom fifteen were still working with the agency, thirteen had left the service, and ten had withdrawn during or just after training. Most of the respondents had experience of an anxiety-related condition (usually agoraphobia), either past or present, or were caring for a close family member with such a condition. More than one-third (37 per cent) had been attracted to telephone training because of difficulties in going out.

Survey responses

Initial feelings about taking a course by telephone divided approximately equally between those who welcomed the idea, and those who were uncertain or apprehensive. In retrospect, most participants felt positive about the method, even though some aspects of working on the telephone had made them uncomfortable. Trainees reported having experienced a range of feelings in their training groups, but positive feelings predominated and a climate of support and trust was created. Negative comments tended to focus on individuals who were seen as dominating the group, or who showed a lack of commitment to the other course members, for example over the 'homework' practice sessions. A major point in favour of telephone training was the opportunity to learn and practise listening skills in the setting in which they would be used. Taking the role-played calls in the group's hearing was experienced as extremely challenging, but the value of this training technique was acknowledged. Telephone training was viewed as most useful for those who were most restricted. However, the more general benefits of saving time, money and the need for child care, and the ability to bring together people from all over the country were also appreciated. The psychological, as well as practical, benefits of working on the telephone were highlighted. 'Home' is associated with safety by people with agoraphobia, while those who are socially phobic find the telephone a less risky way of communicating.

The most frequently mentioned disadvantage was the lack of visual cues and body language, which reduces information and limits relationship development. Some respondents found it difficult to contribute in the group because of this. Other limitations of the telephone mentioned were: distraction, interruption, technical problems, the fact that groups need to be small, and that time has to be well managed. There was some concern about the expense, although telephone costs were reimbursed to those who became volunteers. The friendship and supportive links formed with fellow trainees were very important, but many respondents regretted not meeting their fellow volunteers, and for some telephone contact was insufficient to maintain their involvement with Phobic Action. About a quarter of the trainees did not actually complete the training.

The main gains for trainees were the opportunity to use their experience to help others, and increasing self-confidence. The telephone was seen as important for opening up opportunities for learning and voluntary work for housebound people. More than half the respondents had left Phobic Action's service at the time of the survey, but most reported that they were still using their training in some way.

On the whole there were far more positive statements made than negative, and several respondents said the advantages outweighed any disadvantages. In general, despite some shortcomings, the survey seemed to provide a validation of training by telephone from the trainees' point of view.

Analysis of a training group

A second set of data was provided by a small action research project consisting of a telephone-based course which was planned, executed and evaluated within the framework of the enquiry. This course differed from those run previously in that it offered a more advanced training in group leadership skills. It took place through five weekly sessions of an hour and a half each in July and August 1994.

The course was to act as a pilot for a group leaders' training programme. This was in response to a need identified within the agency to extend the availability of self-treatment groups and to harmonise the work of its local branches with that offered over the telephone. Accordingly, the programme content was determined in co-operation with the participants, and each was given the opportunity to practice group leadership skills by planning and facilitating part of a session and receiving feedback. Being thus relieved of some of the responsibility for conducting sessions, I was able to pay more attention to analysing the process elements.

Four women and two men enrolled for the course, and all of them had some experience of group leadership. Three members of the group were telephone volunteers who had already led groups on the telephone as part of a project to test a distance-learning package for self-treatment of phobias (Research and Evaluation Services 1993). The other three had only led face-to-face groups and had no experience of telephone conferences. These three plus one of the telephone volunteers had also had some training and/or experience in counselling outside Phobic Action, a factor which proved significant for the development of the group. One of the female group members withdrew for personal reasons, after the first meeting; the remaining sessions were subject to fluctuating attendance. Despite these problems, the group managed to achieve a remarkable degree of trust which resulted in a deeper level of work than I had experienced in a telephone group before. Members very quickly became open about their own feelings in the group, possibly because of their prior experience and level of expectation.

Feedback from members who were new to this way of working enabled me to be more aware of some of the special characteristics of telephone group work. Though advantages and disadvantages of telephone training were commented upon in terms similar to those used in the survey, those members who had not previously trained on the telephone placed less value on the convenience or access factors as they had not personally experienced the disabling restrictions of the telephone volunteers. At first they were more inclined to have reservations, feeling that the telephone was an incomplete means of communication, and commenting on a sense of isolation through not being physically with others. However, they were able to discover that disclosing these feelings of discomfort created greater closeness. There were at least two instances where members were able to link their feelings to events in their own past, which seemed to be important pieces of personal learning. Reliance on aural communication appeared to direct attention towards inner processes and a special quality of intimacy developed. Members seemed prepared to take risks more quickly than in face-to-face groups, which in turn accelerated the creation of safety.

Telephone groupwork skills

Facilitating a telephone group calls for the same high-quality listening and responding skills as for one-to-one telephone counselling. In addition, the leader/trainer needs to adapt groupwork skills to suit the telephone environment. The leader's role at the beginning of the session is crucial, especially when participants are new to conferencing. I welcome each member individually as they are brought into the conference, and once everyone is on line, I usually start with a brief round of everyone speaking, giving each person a chance to be heard by everyone else. It is important to establish as soon as possible that members can talk to one another. In the beginning, there can be a tendency for everyone to address the leader only.

Time management, an issue for trainers in any setting, is particularly critical on the telephone. On the one hand, there is an economy of working, without the distraction of peripheral or social activity, which can be very focused and efficient. On the other hand, the necessity of speaking one at a time, with no supplementary non-verbal communication, means that exchanges really do take longer. Course content has to be slimmed down to suit the medium – attempting to include too much can make for a very rushed and leader-dominated group. My preferred method is to supply a printed teaching plan and background material by post and to use the bulk of conference time for discussion or practical exercises. Nevertheless, juggling with the teaching and management of the process, all the while keeping a careful eye on the time, is very demanding, and I have found co-leadership beneficial.

Inexperienced groups in particular work best to a fairly tight structure. The problems of balancing participation between the over-dominant and the over-reluctant are exaggerated on the telephone because of the lack of visual cues, so leadership tends to be more directive than in face-to-face groups. With experience, groups become more confident about engaging in cross-discussion, there is more spontaneity of contributions and, once the boundaries are understood, there can be more flexibility within the session.

Endings must be well managed. The operation of Community Network depends on groups clearing the lines promptly at the end of their booked time, but care has to be taken to avoid an abrupt ending, especially if emotional work has been going on. The convention used in counselling-type groups is that at about five minutes before time, the leader draws the discussion to an end, then invites each member to make a brief farewell contribution, followed by everyone saying 'goodbye' and hanging up together. All group members have the leader's telephone number and permission to call after the group or during the following week if they are left with any 'unfinished business'.

Effectiveness of telephone training

The two sets of data, from the survey described above and the group, provided a basis for assessing the quality of training on the telephone. Dainow and Bailey (1988) say 'the environment is a crucial factor in how effective the training will be. For learning skills people need to feel safe and to have opportunities for practice and feedback.' It was relatively easy to construct opportunities for practice and feedback through the conferences, complemented by the paired homework exercises. However, the effectiveness of training would really depend upon whether a safe learning environment could be created without face-to-face contact. Both the questionnaire results and the group evaluation showed that the groups were rated highly for the qualities of warmth, trust, and acceptance. Members often experienced great discomfort, especially with the role-played calls, but this is also true in face-to-face training. I am committed to the concept that a balance of support and challenge enables learning: the evidence indicated that a telephone group is capable of providing this.

The group leaders' course combined trainees who had had their basic training on the telephone with those who had been in conventional face-to-face courses. The fact that they were able to work together indicated that there had been sufficient similarity in their initial training to provide a common foundation. This does not, of course, imply that such training is equal to, or interchangeable with, that given face to face. There are many things telephone groups cannot do, and the trainer's repertoire of techniques is restricted to what can be communicated aurally. This reduces the variety of learning experiences which can be offered. In some ways it is harder work to maintain enthusiasm, without the changes of pace and energy level that are possible in face-to-face groups. From experience of training in each medium, I would agree that face-to-face training offers a fuller experience and makes for a more rounded practitioner. I would be wary of suggesting that anyone who had only trained on the telephone would be fully competent to work face to face.

However, different does not necessarily mean inferior. Where there are losses, there are also gains, and the non-visual medium may, by its very nature, present unexpected learning opportunities. Training through groups in any setting is complex, challenging and highly variable. A full assessment of the respective merits and limitations of telephone and face-to-face training might usefully be undertaken through a comparative study. For the present, nothing in the evidence contradicts the assumption that telephone-based training works. Training can be enhanced or impeded by the quality of the learning environment, so attention needs to be paid to trainees' physical well-being and personal safety, as well as to their emotional needs. Familiarity of home surroundings can provide safety and security to people who feel vulnerable.

Access issues

The second main thrust of my enquiry concerned access to training for people with restricted mobility. Agoraphobia and other anxiety disorders invariably result in a restriction in social roles, and most of those severely affected are unable to work outside the home or maintain a circle of friends. It is almost certain that a substantial number of the survey respondents would not have been willing or able to take part in face-to-face training, even if it had been available. For others, geographical factors and other considerations such as family responsibilities made telephone training highly attractive.

However, my hypothesis was that 'access' for these trainees was not simply a matter of what might be physically possible, but that there might be invisible barriers operating as well. The stigma attached to mental health problems, as well as the handicapping effects of the conditions themselves, lead to those affected feeling devalued by society. There is a consequent reduction in self-worth, and a profound feeling of isolation. Some of the survey questions were designed to ascertain how far the telephone groups succeeded in meeting trainees' personal needs. Answers revealed a variation both of awareness of their needs and degree of satisfaction among trainees, but it was clear that the groups had other functions besides training. These functions might be supportive, social, growth-related, or a mixture of these. There were reports of substantial gains in functioning and self-confidence. In some cases, this had led the individuals concerned to move on into employment or further training. Those who had continued working on the Helpline for several years did so because they had found a niche where they felt valued and achieved a sense of belonging.

Limitations of telephone training

It was apparent that a substantial number of people either did not complete the training or left the Helpline within a short time. Given the nature of the organisation, it is perhaps to be expected that trainees would experience an above-average level of anxiety in a group, whatever the setting. Possibly the initial ease of taking part failed to filter out those who were too emotionally fragile, or otherwise unable to sustain the commitment. The telephone environment itself was experienced as stressful by some. It was more difficult for me as a trainer working on the telephone to know how much support individuals were needing unless they verbalised their need. Some of the survey respondents had discovered through the course that the work was not for them. Other trainees, despite my best endeavours, simply slipped away.

Care and support for volunteers remained an issue after the training period. Long-staying volunteers were greatly outnumbered by those who moved on within a year. Although positive reasons for leaving were cited in the enquiry, there were also, inevitably, casualties of burnout, deteriorating health or other setbacks, or simply disappointment that relationships on the telephone were not enough to overcome their feelings of isolation.

A disadvantage of telephone groups is that they are very small. A high turn-over of volunteers meant that the agency had a continuing need to recruit and train replacements. In the longer term, therefore, the advantages of cost and convenience had to be weighed against the need to run more courses.

Some of the difficulties which the enquiry helped to highlight could be ascribed as much to the effects of working at a distance as to working on the telephone *per se*. In-house training cannot be considered in isolation from other aspects of work, and the programme helped to bring into focus the agency's relationship with its national membership and highlighted problems in achieving both effective management and democratic participation. Power and influence in organisations are exercised as much through informal as formal interaction, and it is this informal contact which is lost when communication is entirely by post or telephone.

Conclusions

Overall, my experience and the study confirmed that visual contact is not strictly necessary to create a supportive and challenging environment for learning counselling skills. The telephone is a suitable medium for training within a self-help setting, where constraints apply which are the result of geographical factors or individual disabilities. Telephone training was challenging for both trainees and trainers, but the benefits made it worthwhile. In the longer term, distance factors become more critical for maintaining the quality of service, because of their effects on volunteer satisfaction and agency accountability.

There are also wider implications, and perhaps three ways in which the telephone conference network could enhance training for providers of counselling services. First, it could increase the availability of counselling skills training and offer a convenient and economical way of assisting smaller voluntary organisations and self-help groups to attain a recognised level of competence. Second, telephone training could make a substantial contribution to equal opportunities in the counselling field, by enabling participation of categories of people for whom access to conventional courses is difficult. These include anyone whose mobility is limited through disability; people restricted through working as a carer, either for young children or elderly or infirm relatives; those who live in remote areas; minority language speakers; and those affected by stigmatising or embarrassing problems which make them reluctant to engage with others face to face. Apart from individual gains from improvements in well-being and self-esteem, there could be immense gains to the community from the utilisation of hidden potential. Third, as telephone communication skills are learned and practised in the medium in which they will be used, the conference network could also provide opportunities for mainstream counsellors who wished to develop telephone skills as an adjunct to their face-to-face work.

As in any training, ethical aspects must always be borne in mind. I do not believe there is anything inherently unethical about working on the telephone, but safeguards are obviously necessary. Paradoxically, the telephone's greatest benefit – accessibility – can also be a hazard, as it may attract individuals for whom training is inappropriate. Screening and support systems must have high priority, especially where training is being offered to groups likely to contain particularly vulnerable people.

Postscript 1997

Writing this chapter three years after these experiences has evoked a great many memories. They were exciting times, rich in learning experiences for me, and I am proud to have been associated with this innovative method of training. The success of the project was not diminished by the fact that the training programme came to an end within eighteen months of the study's completion. The home-based Helpline team eventually became unviable, mainly as a result of external factors, and was replaced by a smaller-scale service run from the head office of the charity. However, in essence what we created has survived and evolved: two members of one of my early training courses went on to form their own separate organisations, which are both flourishing and still making use of Community Network conferences for their training.

Training by telephone is still uncommon, but at least one step has been taken towards making it more generally available. Three years ago I was invited by Maxine Rosenfield, a manager of telephone training and consultancy services, to co-lead some open introductory courses in telephone group counselling skills, using Community Network. The first of these, which took place in the summer of 1995, brought together nine participants from a broad range of backgrounds and a wide geographical spread. Many of the issues I have covered in the discussion of my own groups are also explored in a published account of this group (Rosenfield 1997). The experience has confirmed my views about the potential of telephone groups for breaking down barriers to training, and providing an excellent opportunity for practising skills *in situ*. Courses such as these are useful to demonstrate the capabilities of the medium, which participants can feed back into their own work settings.

It is clear that the need for such opportunities is increasing. Telephone counselling is in a fast growth phase. Not only are voluntary Helplines continuing to multiply and to embrace areas of work requiring higher-level counselling skills, but counselling on the telephone is also expanding rapidly in the private sector through Employee Assistance Programmes. Telephone training offers a cheap and practical resource which could benefit both.

To end on a personal note, over the past six years I must have led or taken part in several hundreds of telephone conferences. I still find it exciting to experience the transformation of a collection of disembodied voices into a 'group'. I sit at my own desk, in my own home, seeing the familiar view from the window, hearing the clock ticking, and know that all the owners of those other voices are doing the same. Yet in establishing 'psychological contact' it is as if we are all transported by magic carpet into another place. Is it really just inside our heads, or outside the confines of time and space altogether? It is an experience I would recommend to anyone interested either in counselling on the telephone or in training counsellors for the telephone.

References

Dainow, Sheila and Bailey, Caroline (1988) *Developing Skills with People.* Chichester, John Wiley & Sons.

Egan, Gerard (1990) *The Skilled Helper.* Pacific Grove, CA, Brooks/Cole.

Fletcher, Emma (1994) 'Using Telephone Groups to Train Volunteer Counsellors in a Self-Help Setting', M.Sc. Dissertation, University of Bristol.

George, Judith (1983) *On The Line: Counselling and Teaching by Telephone.* Milton Keynes, Open University Press.

Hunt, Pat (1993) 'Relateline: An Evaluation of a Telephone Helpline Counselling Service for Marital Problems', *British Journal of Guidance and Counselling*, 3/3, 277–89.

McLeod, John (1993) *An Introduction to Counselling Skills.* Buckingham, Open University Press.

Murgatroyd, Stephen (1985) *Counselling and Helping.* London, Methuen.

Research and Evaluation Services (1993) *An Evaluation of the Distance Learning Package to Help Overcome Anxiety Disorders. Using Telephone Conferencing for Self-Help Groups.* London, Community Network.

Rogers, Carl R. (1965) *Client Centred Therapy.* Boston, Houghton Mifflin Co.

Rogers, Carl R. (1983) *Freedom to Learn for the 1980s.* Columbus, OH, Merrill.

Rosenfield, Maxine (1997) *Counselling by Telephone.* London, Sage.

Sanders, Pete (1996) *An Incomplete Guide to Using Counselling Skills on the Telephone.* (new edition) Manchester, PCCS Books.

Telephone Helplines Association (1993) *Guidelines for Good Practice in Telephone Work*. London, Telephone Helplines Group/Association.

Winders, Ray (1984) 'The Plymouth Audio-conferencing Network', *Teaching at a Distance*, 25, Autumn, 51–7.

Woolfe, Ray, Murgatroyd, Stephen and Rhys, Sylvia (1987) *Guidance and Counselling in Adult and Continuing Education*. Milton Keynes, Open University Press.

Part III

Counselling trainees

Holding the balancing-pole?

To engage in counselling training is costly in all senses. It brings rewards and undoubted growth – illustrated by all the contributors writing in these pages. It can also be painful, is certainly challenging and may even be dangerous – at least, to confidence and self-esteem; at worst, to relationships and even life.

The following chapters, powerfully personal, offer glimpses of the 'high-wire' journeys through training of three experienced counsellors and of the 'balancing-poles' which helped them survive or thrive as *trainees*. These particular accounts are in some ways extreme in the difficulties and pain they reflect, yet they are also illustrative of the range of balancing acts which trainees have to undertake. The core tensions between personal and professional, rewards and costs, risk and safety, retreat and growth are recorded here, as they are in the personal journals and tutorial explorations of any counselling trainees in any course or context.

Chapter 11

An academic invalid in a world of academic excellence

Alison Maybank

Freedom to Learn – the title alone of Rogers' (1983) book gives hope for me. The very word freedom presents such a strong image. I see a vast expanse of countryside which offers freedom to wander, to create my own picture, to walk wherever I choose, to change paths, to explore, to recreate, to find somewhere that suits, to feel comfortable, challenged, to feel myself. Freedom: to create variety, change style, colour, to dip in and out, to stay longer or to move quickly on, to choose different textures, make different things, *freedom to be me*. Freedom to be me has been at the heart of my own struggle to train and qualify as a counsellor.

Learning and being assessed

Training in the counselling world has, in general, come to grips with the facilitation of learning as described by Rogers. It hardly seems possible that less than thirty years ago Rogers was writing passionately about a classroom climate 'often greatly feared by educators' which might enable creative individuals to communicate through a variety of media, 'without fear of being squashed'. Rogers' 'mutual respect and mutual freedom of expression' are feared no longer, but are a way of life in many learning environments. Certainly many personal and professional development courses facilitate learning through writing poetry, painting pictures and finding other innovative ways to enhance learning.

What of producing the evidence of that learning, for assessment? It seems to me that all too often only traditional methods of offering evidence are used. By traditional, I mean those showing a heavy bias towards using written forms. In my experiences of training to become a counsellor, there has often been a huge discrepancy between the facilitation of learning and the assessment of learning. Dance and drama were acceptable media for learning and expression, so were painting, collage, sculpting and writing poetry. But when it came to assessment, even video evidence had to be accompanied by a written explanation. I remember arguing in vain with a visiting moderator on one course. He insisted on an essay instead of a collage coupled with a poem. I knew these spoke louder than any essay I could write. Needless to say, I was left frustrated and unaccepted.

How can the counselling world be more creative in its assessment methods when training counsellors? How can we reach a position on assessment which is congruent with the whole ethos of counselling? Counsellors are encouraged to develop the ability to 'provide different soil and a different climate' in order to help their clients 'recover from deprivation or maltreatment'. They spend hours learning how to 'create conditions for growth' and develop clients' belief in themselves so they can 'begin to flourish' as a 'unique individual' (Mearns and Thorne 1988). Then, in what seems to me a totally incongruent way, trainees have to show that ability by methods which are dictatorial or constraining. I appreciate the dilemmas which we face. It would, of course, be totally irresponsible of the professional counselling world not to ensure that evidence of learning and competency was produced and evaluated in some way. There are training centres which are creative, but such creativity is not consistently offered or even remotely usual. We should be developing creative ways to assess individuals in training.

'Trampled in the routine'

Throughout my experiences of counselling training, I have felt like a child, in the words of Rogers (1983) 'unprepossessing, weak, easily knocked down and trampled in the routine' of assessment. Like a child, too, any of my creative ideas, 'wild unusual thoughts and perceptions', can seem inadequate compared with the expectations of the established system. I did not really recognise how trampled on I felt, until I experienced something different.

Ever since I can remember, and that includes my schooldays, my difficulty in producing evidence of learning meant, as far as I was concerned, that I was 'useless', 'no good', 'couldn't have learned much', or 'can't know much'. I felt I was never allowed to shine ... and if that sounds as though I am abdicating responsibility for myself, I think I was. I have since learned that assessment, like learning, needs to be facilitated in ways that offer 'creativity, mutual respect and mutual freedom of expression' (Rogers 1983). That freedom of expression, for me, is not necessarily writing. In the past, facilitators, even though they may have appreciated my way of being, have spent time and energy telling me that I *must* convert my means of expression into some form of written assessment, if it was to be validated. That has reminded me of a frequent thought I had when I was about 8 years old. On hearing people speaking a different language, I assumed they must have to convert their language into English before making sense of it. I had no concept of them understanding their language, no concept of this being their way of communicating, their native tongue, no concept of their language being part of their 'way of being'. That links with the experience I have had on many counselling-orientated courses: I have felt as though others (mainly assessors) have expected me to talk their language. It is as though they have no concept of my language, the way I communicate, my native tongue, or my 'way of being'.

My language, my world, the university

It wasn't until I went to Bristol University, where I met and experienced the facilitation and assessments of Hazel Johns, Jane Speedy and Anne Stokes on the M.Sc. course in Counselling Supervision and Training that I learned, and it seems I had to learn, to give myself permission to acknowledge myself, and my language, my preferred way of communication – my native tongue and my 'way of being'. I think they were the first facilitators who really endeavoured not only to learn my language but to speak it and learn how to communicate with me. They showed understanding of the frustration and difficulties of being in a foreign place, they helped me to communicate in university language but always accepted that my language was a part of me. My language was acknowledged, encouraged and, most of all, validated.

It was an off-the-cuff remark by Hazel, in the initial interview for the course, that gave me hope. I had been telling her about myself, and finished by saying that I wanted to do the course because I felt I would learn so much. I didn't know if I would be capable of the academic work, but the piece of paper at the end was not an issue for me. She smiled, 'Well, you may not be what the university would be looking for, Alison, but you are exactly what we are looking for.' That phrase still brings tears to my eyes. Hazel in a brief time, heard, felt and experienced me, made the commitment to 'battle hard on my behalf', a commitment she kept to the very end. Although I did have to learn to write essays, the personal growth which followed was staggering. My final dissertation was a recognition of how an academic institution can accommodate the non-traditional. I proudly showed my beautifully bound black and gold 'book' to a Ph.D.

graduate of my local university. As she flicked through I could see her look of dismay. She saw colourful pictures of lakes and tractors overlaid with acetate, she saw writing on colourful pre-printed paper of rolling countryside, waterfalls and pools, and she saw what she described as 'a television script'. 'What is this?' she questioned, 'No university would accept this.' A smile emerged from the deepest part of me, and I quickly thought, they may send it back because I am sure there will be spelling mistakes in it, or I may have it in the wrong order, but the style is fine. 'It'll be fine,' I said, 'because it's me.'

It was as I started to think about the writing process of my dissertation, that the following paper emerged, 'When the Words in the Book Don't Mean a Lot'. I remember thinking, as the feelings poured out, this is a watershed. I offer it here as part of this chapter, as it was then in the 'here and now', with only minor amendments (such as taking out references to appendices) for the sake of clarity or brevity.

When the words in the book don't mean a lot

This essay will describe in detail some of the recent feelings, thoughts, behaviours and processes as experienced by me during the two and a half year period of study on the M.Sc. course in Counselling Supervision and Training at Bristol University. Originally I had found it very difficult to find a topic for this paper, which was to focus on adult education. I had plenty of ideas, most of which concealed 'angry' undertones. As I tried to develop some of these ideas I could hear myself saying, 'there *is* something *important* you have to say for you and other adults like yourself, Alison'. Unfortunately, true to persisting patterns, I dismissed the thoughts that my experiences, as an adult who found it extremely difficult to gain insight and new learnings from reading and writing, would be useful to others.

As a counsellor, counselling supervisor, trainer, facilitator and learner, I constantly hear the difficulties experienced by others when it comes to using traditional methods of reading, and also offering evidence via writing and recording. I often hear about, and observe, the shutting down and blocking off processes that happen to some individuals. I have come to recognise how passionately I feel about trying to alleviate those difficulties by offering or suggesting opportunities that could tap into, and develop, creative ways of absorbing, doing and offering evidence, alternative ways of showing what that person has within. How do I know that? Because when I talk to them there are patterns, difficulties and behaviours that are similar to how it is for me – there is a lot of knowledge within me, even if I can't show it in the traditional ways. So now, with the 'courage of my convictions', I wish to speak for myself. I will share the delights and difficulties of being an academic invalid in the world of academic excellence in adult education.

The content of this paper came to me while attempting to write the M.Sc. dissertation (Maybank 1995). I was experiencing so much anxiety that I did become an invalid in many ways. It was difficult to understand what was going on within me. Those who knew me believed that I was entirely competent to do all that was required for a Master's degree. I had heaps of experience, as a counsellor, counselling supervisor and trainer. I had been a counselling practitioner for many years, both in private practice and within a large organisation, I had successfully developed a Diploma in Counselling course, in an adult education setting (Diploma in Counselling, Surrey Adult and Continuing Education, 1988–94), and I was known for offering supervisees the opportunity of working with creative materials in supervision. When hearing of my interest in the M.Sc. course in Counselling Supervision and Training at Bristol, friends and colleagues made encouraging statements such as, 'You'll fly through it'; 'I couldn't do it but you can'; 'It is just what you need professionally'. So ... what was this huge discrepancy? If I gave the appearance of being competent, presumably by being professional and showing competency levels, then why was I experiencing such disability?

As I write I am aware of several objectives. First, I want to challenge traditional methods for offering evidence of knowledge. I would like to offer this paper without the usual inclusions, for example linking my work to theory by offering references and a bibliography (I have had to add personal reference in order to fulfil the assessment criteria for Bristol University). I know there will have been an academic or a writer somewhere who will have written about what I want to say. I believe (from the limited amount of reading I have done) most of what is written has been written before. What for instance, is original – first time written – in many counselling books produced by current writers, popular as they are?

Second, I want to stand up and be counted. I want to offer a paper which is 'good enough', in its own right, without having to conform to the traditional approach. I find it hard, especially in the area of counselling (although I do not believe it should only be in this area), that individuals have to be put into boxes and be told that the written word is the be-all and end-all. I want to shout from the hill tops, 'Think of those who are not as fortunate as yourselves, allow them the freedom to find alternative ways of showing what they know.' If I were brave enough, this presentation would not be in the form of an essay, but perhaps would be a visual presentation of some kind. Unfortunately the resources required for such a presentation are out of my reach. I also had to curtail my wishes as I could envisage a video presentation distracting me from the research project (Maybank 1995), since it would, of course, have been more attractive to me. Yet without piloting this method of presentation, I deny myself the knowledge of knowing whether it would be acceptable for the purpose of this degree. I do know that a video presentation would not be sufficient on its own, but I do not fully understand why.

My final objective is to illustrate what I have learnt about my own reading and writing processes during this period of time. I would like to concentrate on this section as it seems to me to be the most productive part of this essay. ** At this very point in time I have just learnt something very new and revealing. This essay was started today because ideas and images kept protruding into the work I was trying to do on my dissertation. Becoming a major distraction, it kept focusing me away from working on the task in hand. Eventually I gave in, hoping that if I managed to write this essay, I would then be totally free to concentrate on my dissertation. Thoughts and feelings flowed quickly, sometimes too quickly for me to catch, highlighting how easy it is for me to lose the ideas which seem appropriate and useful to write about. I became more and more agitated and frustrated, as I struggled to find what was disappearing so quickly. It appeared that the more I tried to access ways of retrieving the information, or ways of catching it and writing it down, the more annoyed I got.

> I have a picture in my head
> It weights me down far more than lead,
> I lay across some traitorous stones
> Sharp pieces trying to pierce my bones,
> I try to catch some slippery eel
> Which I must, to survive I feel.
> With no safe foothold I stretch and stretch
> Over a precipice to reach and fetch,
> All the time I lose my grip
> Never knowing if I'm going to slip,
> And even if I finally get a hold
> Getting back to safety remains untold.

Eventually after writing to the sign marked by ** I broke away, and went downstairs. The anger inside me got stronger and stronger, and manifested

itself by a piercing desire to do something against myself. I had been diet-
ing successfully for four weeks and had managed to lose 24 pounds in
weight. I began to push chocolate down my throat as if it were a knife.
Hurting with each piece, I could suddenly feel the 'fight' feeling. It was as
if I needed to fight the restraining experience of being made to do this
work which confined me in a reading and writing and proving box. I was
fighting myself, abusing myself, making myself hurt, after all it was *me*
that was putting *me* through this. How it hurts, but it seems as if there is no
other way to beat the system. The system is so very powerful, I either
follow it or be someone whom the system will not recognise.

So what actually happens when I try to read? The first hurdle looms at
the very thought of having to read. This first hurdle is made up of past
feelings of fear, numbness and a sort of detachment, probably arising
from earlier experiences. Being mocked at school, when, right up to the
age of 12 or 13 years, I stumbled clumsily over words and sentences
(after that age I learnt to make some excuse in order to avoid reading).
Others laughed when I couldn't pronounce words, let alone read what
they said. I would stare helplessly at the pages, but could not make sense
of them. Now, I tell myself to take things calmly, having learnt that most
writing does in fact *usually* make sense. One of the reasons why I find it
hard to make sense of writing, is that I only have a visual span of two or
three letters. This means that my brain only receives a clear picture of
parts of words, for example the word thoughtfully will be scanned in the
following format *tho ugh tfu lly*. As I have a short-term memory problem,
by the time I have reached the end of the word I am most likely to have
forgotten the beginning. In any case, as you can see by the way I have
split the word, I have not broken it up into useful syllables. Since discovering this I have worked hard at trying to track how many attempts it
takes me to read sentences accurately. Here is an illustration of what
might happen. The example used here is from the text taken from
Sanders and Liptrot 1993:

> This book does not assume that research is only done by researchers
> or students with a research-based assignment to do as part of a
> counselling course.

- I have obviously read this in order to type it, but have no idea at this
  stage what it says or even if it makes sense.
- I have read it twice to check if it sounds similar to the sounds that
  came from reading the book, but still do not understand what it is
  saying.

- Now I will read it slowly to see if I understand it.
- *Thi* – likely to be *this* – guessing
- spot the *oo* first then check the *b* and *k* to make *book*
- wonder why the words are spread out across the page and are different from the line of writing underneath
- pick up *does* straight away
- miss *not* and go straight on to *assume*
- have forgotten what has been said so far so retrace from the beginning and get confused because this time I pick up the word *not*, so have to reread it because of the discrepancy
- consolidate the *not*, by checking a third time
- start reading again at *that research is only done*, but forget what has been said so far
- start at the beginning and read straight through to *researchers*
- realise the sentence carries on, so reread *researchers* and carry on with the rest of the sentence
- recognise the word *students* at one hit
- stumble over *research-based assignment*, having to break it up seeing *sea rch* think sea search
- realise the book is about research so rethink and make a guess (more of an assumption) that the word is *research*
- lose my place, can't find it so look for 'sea search'
- progress by splitting up – *bas ed ass ign men t*, wondering what that means and checking for my own understanding
- immediately get side-tracked with thoughts of assignments that I may have done that have been research based
- wonder if I have missed the chapter on research-based assignments or would I be hearing about them in this chapter
- quickly run my eyes over the page to see if I can see the *research-based* pattern anywhere else which may give the information I am looking for
- can't see it so reread from the beginning of the page to remind myself what was being said
- finally I am ready to continue.

A long and laborious process, considering that is just one sentence. Yet it offers a clear illustration, in my view, as to why I find it difficult to gain much from reading. It takes an enormous amount of energy, which, coupled with a condition known as 'scopic sensitivity syndrome', means I get tired very quickly. With scopic sensitivity, too much light enters the eye, making everything bright and dazzling. The white of the paper 'lifts' off the page, spilling over the black print, making it difficult to see, creating white rivers and streams that stand out amid the pages, hiding the words and letters. The white background pulsates at such a pace that the black letters move and dance around the page. This can be alleviated by wearing specially tinted lenses or by using an overlay, and coloured or off-white paper. I also find it difficult to keep track of where I am on the page, my scanning ability is almost nil and I frequently lose my place. By the time I have been reading for about twenty minutes, coping with the disturbances as described, my eyes and my brain have had enough. I feel both physically and mentally tired.

Usually within seconds of stopping I cannot recall what I have read and am not likely to be able to recall it unless I have a chance to use the content in some experiential way. Thus I usually only gain benefit from reading if I am required to make a formal presentation of some kind. I may then retain the information if I am lucky. Now, this is a very different process, for I make sense of what I have read by converting it to my own experiencing language. The language of 'experiencing' is something that I find easy to 'read'. Like a deaf person who focuses on developing his or her other sensing skills, I have had to develop the skills involved in experiencing in order to make sense of the world in which I live. I believe I learnt to 'read' this way, that is by verbally checking for understanding, feelings, thoughts, actions and outcomes, in order to survive. The world is not available to me via the written word. So I ask myself what kind of world is it that is intolerant of those who cannot communicate effectively through reading and writing?

I found the world of counselling through being a client and through communicating verbally and experientially (the client/counsellor relationship). Yet to progress in that world and to gain recognition, I am expected to adhere to the system which demands that I show my professionalism by offering evidence of my knowledge and skills through writing about my experiences and about what I have read!! Can I gain an M.Sc., or BAC accreditation as a counsellor, or get my course recognised or accredited by a recognised body, or become a recognised supervisor, without conforming to the system that makes such demands? I fear not. It seems as though it is almost impossible to break from the norm. The willingness may be there in some cases, but the strategy becomes so cumbersome that it seems almost too big to 'hold' and manage.

So many activities in counsellor training, higher education and accreditation processes require evidence in the form of writing. So let me describe some of the difficulties I experience, with the hope of provoking some discussion around issues of providing written evidence.

As with reading, the first hurdle comes from past experiences, experiences such as having a piece of work read out in class. Most people laughed as it was being read, including the teacher. I had misspelt words, left words out, used wrong language. My writing made a good laugh for others, but left me cringing in the corner, a corner I have never been able to come out from, except when I write poetry. I appreciate that forty years ago, little was known about dyslexia. But experiences with my own children, two of whom are dyslexic – one now carrying a 'statement' – highlight the damage which can easily be caused by a teacher's ignorance of or disbelief in this condition. There are clear early indicators which help in the diagnosing of dyslexic tendencies. For adults like myself, who were not diagnosed in childhood, such a list is useful to reflect upon, and for trainers of adults, a useful aid.

When I write I often use letters incorrectly, for example I may write *ofr* instead of *for*, I may put *for* instead of *four*, I may scribe *four* instead of *five* and so on. Usually, in these circumstances, when I read my work back to check it, I do not spot the mistakes. My brain reads what it knows I am trying to say. It is only if I read the work some time later that I may spot the mistakes, and then only if I am able to read it objectively. I know, for instance, that what I have written so far today in this, makes a great deal of sense to me, but tomorrow when I feel differently and perhaps less passionately I will find it hard to gauge its usefulness. I will have to rely on external feedback and validation. Tomorrow I may have completely lost the force of my argument. That is not about lack of consistency or validity of the material, but simply a memory problem. Something would need to trigger my thoughts in order for me to recapture or remember what I was feeling or trying to say.

The frustrations of losing material are tremendous. I may think of something very important or valid to say and within seconds have lost it. Unable to retrieve it unless it is triggered or brought into awareness via a different medium, I seldom capture in writing the knowledge and ideas within me. They flash like a light which has so much energy it fuses the circuit, and is lost to the written experience.

As with this essay, I have no knowledge of whether my writing flows from one paragraph to another. As my mind flits about, so does my writing. Usually I try to check on whether what I write makes sense, and flows appropriately. That checking creates another break in the circuit, which, of course, taking the analogy of a lighting circuit, stops the light from being constant. Flickering is very distracting, and is usually associated with a fault of some kind. Like the effect of a 'strobe' light, I see images that jerk and move like individual pictures strung together, like an old-fashioned movie, not at all smooth. Without that smoothness I am unable to 'hold' what I have written. This means I have absolutely no idea how it sounds and if it flows, each paragraph being written in isolation. There is also some lack of co-ordination between my brain and my hand. Frequently I cannot physically manage to write the words in my head down on paper, although using a computer has helped this immensely. The following poem written in 1993, not long after I had bought a computer and learnt how to switch it on, offers an example of this:

> One hour ago I knew what I wanted to say,
> But the pen in my hand took those thoughts away,
> What made it so hard my words to write?
> I wish I could be rescued from this frustrating plight.
>
> I can be rescued – at last I know,
> The computer helps to let my words flow,
> I can chop and change to my heart's delight,
> Have I been rescued from my frustrating plight?
>
> (Maybank 1993–95)

The transition from writing in longhand to writing by computer was an interesting process in itself. Needless to say, my computer does not understand my dyslexic ways, and I am still often left frustrated when I reread some of my work which, after much effort, still contains gross errors.

So both reading and writing cause me great difficulties and although some authorities are sympathetic they are not very proactive in offering alternatives. Let me offer some more of my poems, that illustrate the pain experienced through reading and writing.

> *Like a blind baby*
>
> I feel like a blind baby
> who nobody knows is blind
> because it is too young,
> I am blind,
> but I can see,
> I can see feelings,
> I can see thoughts,

I can see the world,
I can see,
but I can't see words,
I can't feel written words
I can't think written words
I can't read about the world,
I can't see.
I feel like a blind baby
helpless when I need to read.

Books

When I look at a book I stare right through
When I look at a book I see nothing new,
When I look at a book my mind goes blank,
When I look at a book it's like walking the plank.
When I look at a book I begin to feel sad
When I look at a book I feel somewhat mad
When I look at a book there's a stab in my heart
When I look at a book there's no place to start.

Writing

Tears run down my cheeks
Pain around for weeks and weeks
Why do I need to suffer this way
Isn't there another way to play?

(Maybank 1993–95)

If the world of counselling is to be congruent with fostering the core conditions of acceptance, empathic understanding and genuineness, how can we facilitate a climate where individuals can offer evidence of their learning, understanding and knowledge, in whatever form they themselves can speak? Do trainers, facilitators and assessors need to be more open to receiving information through different media? Perhaps more importantly do they need to be more proactive in facilitating ways of, and giving permission for, alternative methods of offering evidence? What expansion needs to take place? Are we offering equal opportunity and appropriate access, if we continue to demand written information? How can this minority speak out?

And just in case you say to yourself, 'She can write, she has written this piece', I know I can, but it has taken me 132 hours to write, it does not include all I want it to, the process has been horrendous, and, most importantly of all, *I would have liked to have done it in a different way.* It is now just over ten days since I completed the M.Sc. dissertation. My feelings and emotions are all at sea: feelings of relief at having completed it, feelings of disbelief at the same; feelings of anger at myself for not including things I had planned to but had forgotten about, despite notes; annoyance at noticing some mistakes (but I guess that is quite normal). But most of all I notice that I have no sense of joy, no affirmation, in fact not many positive feelings at all. My children have commented on how, towards the end of writing the dissertation, I was unable to speak clearly. The words that came out of my mouth did not match what I thought I was saying, I spoke almost gibberish. I became stuck on several occasions, lost time and was very vague. My capacity for absorbing more information was severely restricted, and following instructions became completely impossible. The symptoms which manifested themselves in me were similar to those attributed to post-traumatic stress. Was it really that bad?

What I have decided through doing this paper, is that I will challenge the system when I apply for counsellor accreditation with the British Association for Counselling. I will give myself permission to offer *my evidence* in the way that is *true to myself,* and in a way that allows me to express more of what I know and understand. As a facilitator and trainer of adult learners I will commit to do more than offer the 'token', 'you can present your work in *any* appropriate form'. I will endeavour to facilitate alternative methods of recording, offering evidence and expressing meaning as an integrated part of any course.

Much of what is written about learning disabilities relates to children, but I urge the world not to forget about adults. Some of us missed out on diagnosis (I was not diagnosed until 1988 when I was 37 years old), and some have slipped through the net altogether. For instance, I have worked with adults (clients and students of counselling) who have presented all sorts of problems, concerns, frustrations, blocks and the like, relating to difficulties within this field. To my knowledge seven out of an approximate total of 140 adults, while working at what I would call a 'below the surface' level with me, discovered they had a learning disability, and have since gone on to have that confirmed and diagnosed by an educational psychologist. Facilitators in adult learning environments need to be aware of the manifestations of unrecognised and undiagnosed learning difficulties and disabilities. And assessors need to be more open to alternative ways of collecting evidence. Finally a powerful poem written by my daughter Janine:

I want to be normal

I sit in the corner
All very quiet,
Bowing my head
As the teacher walks by.
He comes over to me
And picks up my work,
Reads it out aloud,
I bow my head even more.
My face goes red,
My eyes fill with water,
My hands begin to shake,
My voice goes wobbly.
The class goes quiet
They listen to him,
He begins to criticise my work,
'This doesn't make sense.'
'What does this mean?'
I cannot say anything,
I feel embarrassed
I feel hurt
I try not to cry.
Why did the teacher pick on me?
Why not somebody brainy?
Why can't *I* be brainy?
All I want
is to be able to read,
To be able to spell
To be normal.

Conclusion

That essay reflected my frustrations and struggle to match the demands of the formal academic training world. Feeling 'an academic invalid in a world of academic excellence' is a difficult place to be. But it does not have to be a terminal condition. It helps to remember Friedman's words (1972), 'If I keep from imposing on people, they become themselves'. There is treatment ... hope ... alternative broader possibilities for assessment: for instance, audio visual recording; alternative creative presentations backed by live interview; raising the profile of collected peer assessment; portfolio of achievement gathered from both internal and external sources; verbal presentations; or perhaps the acceptance of mind maps, bulleting, image writing instead of essay writing. Of course this is not only about assessment. To be congruent, alternative resources in counsellor training and an increased openness to the issues put forward in this chapter have to be addressed. Taped books; alternatives to reading lists; computer based 'visual' books, are not the only answer. I beg the counselling training world not to confine some of its learners to a metaphorical wheelchair, purely because of tradition and lack of insight. There are many alternatives to the wheelchair for academic invalids. It is time for the training providers, assessors and those with learning disabilities to get together to find ways forward, to open up to new methods of assessment tools. A whole new era could be around the corner for learners like myself. The training world could be our oyster. I want to be included, not excluded. The prognosis? – Good!

References

Friedman, M. (1972) *Touchstones of Reality*, London, E.P. Dutton.

Maybank, A.J. (1993–95) Collection of unpublished poems.

Maybank, A.J. (1995) 'Creating a Water Garden', unpublished M.Sc. dissertation, University of Bristol.

Mearns, D. and Thorne, B. (1988) *Person-Centred Counselling in Action*, London: Sage.

Rogers, C.R. (1980) *A Way of Being*, Boston, Houghton Mifflin.

Rogers, C.R. (1983) *Freedom to Learn for the 80s*, New York, Merrill.

Sanders, P. and Liptrot, D. (1993) *The Incomplete Guide to Basic Research Methods and Data Collection for Counsellors*, Manchester, PCCS Books.

Chapter 12

A trainee's experience of trauma

*Christabel Fey**

In early spring a young woman in her mid-twenties walked into a women's counselling organisation and revealed her intention to kill her ex-counsellor. She described in detail how she had stalked this woman for almost a year and how, when and where the imminent murder would take place. When she had carried out the deed she would kill herself.

I was the counsellor she intended to murder; for the year leading up to her confession, during which I was undertaking a part-time higher degree in counselling, I had been grappling with the horrific and life-threatening effects of her psychotic transference.

In this chapter I will explore some of those happenings and their impact on me and the people around me, illuminated by research findings regarding the roles of 'bystanders' and 'rescuers' in extreme situations. Much of this research concurred with my own findings after these events, for an M.Sc. dissertation. The purpose of my research was to understand what enabled some people, both on the course and in my life, to respond to me by being supportive and intervening while others felt hostility or became passive observers. Questions also arose relating to the work of counselling and to myself as a counsellor. Finally, I will look at recovery from such traumatic events in terms of effective treatments.

Stalked by a client

John Lennon said in a song: 'Life is what happens to you when you're busy planning other things.' In the song he plans to be with his son while he grows up. John Lennon was shot dead in 1986 by a 'stalker', an obsessed fan. His son was still a child.

---

* Names, including the author's, have been changed throughout this chapter.

I was working privately as a qualified and experienced counsellor, and had begun an M.Sc. in counselling at university. I planned to study and to develop my practice, expanding my work into training and supervision. Then my life changed abruptly: every value, belief, assumption, goal and relationship was challenged and thrown into a whirlwind of fear and powerlessness.

During the first weekend of July 1993 I went camping in Dorset. On returning, I was told that a client had been found living in my home. A friend had been feeding my cat and had suddenly found himself locked out. With great difficulty he broke in and discovered a young woman desperately trying to escape through the front windows. They talked and she told him she was a client of mine. He was struck by her pathetic and waif-like appearance. He became concerned for her and offered her assistance, which she declined. In his presence, she wrote a note apologising to me and left.

After leaving, the young woman, Joni, thought better of the apology and returned to put a brick, the first of many, through my bedroom window. She then sat outside all night; she threw a second brick through another window at some stage and then a third – creating a hole in the glass through which she walked into my bedroom, for a final 'smell' of my room, removing her note as she left. I later discovered she had also removed my door lock, had a key made and replaced the lock – all without being found out. The image of Joni walking through that hole in the glass haunted me. It gave weight to her later assertion that, no matter what I did, I could never keep her out – she would always get to me if and when she wanted. I felt both terrified and vulnerable after this first invasion. But I also felt responsible: she was still a client and I was concerned how best to handle this incident.

Clearly, I could no longer work at home with her as she had breached all boundaries. Nor could I work at home with anyone else, as I could not predict her next actions. Within a week I moved my practice to a psychotherapy institute which had a locked front door. Moving a practice creates work and stress for clients and therapist, just as holidays and illness do. I had cancelled a week's work, found new premises and shifted my practice within a week! This was not exactly ideal for anyone concerned, yet I had no idea what I was in for. The phenomenon of stalking was unknown to me. The only references I had heard were in connection with famous people, and even of those I had little knowledge.

In his paper 'Psychology of Stalking', Badcock (1996) says:

As a general group stalking victims stand out from other victims of personal crime in that they tend to be successful in their work, in their level of personal maturity and in their general sense of energy and vitality. In short they are a group of people who would be seen as being at low risk of becoming victims of crime generally, but who have qualities of liveliness and accomplishment that may make them attractive to stalkers.

It is important to recognise that stalking, in the sense of actually following the victim, is only one of a range of behaviours employed in this activity. Individual behaviours can seem almost unimportant but the effect of cumulative actions over a period of time is to produce states of utmost intimidation, control and fear. Victims report the experience of feeling increasingly controlled by their stalker and of becoming progressively isolated and alienated from their normal life. Their very sense of their own identity and autonomy as a person is directly threatened.

At first I tried to carry on working with Joni by establishing a new counselling contract or, at least, attempting to do so. After a few weeks it was clear this would not be possible and with the support of supervision, I ended the therapeutic contract. However, any agreement to have or end a relationship requires the consent of both people or sufficient respect or adaptation to the wishes of one person by the other. Joni would not or could not make such an agreement. It became clear that she had no boundaries and no respect for mine. A drama unfolded; the arena was as much in the psychic or transpersonal world as the physical. The images which came to my mind were often mythological. I felt caught up in a battle between light and dark, between good and evil. I was haunted by a presence which wanted to destroy me or be destroyed by me; to be loved and cared for by me but so completely that she would suck me dry, fill every pore of my being, merge with me. For ten months she followed me, haunted me. She broke into my house several times, broke my windows, attempted to set fire to my home at 2 a.m., followed me by car and on foot, telephoned me frequently, usually not speaking and leaving long, silent messages on the answer machine. She broke into my car, and smashed its window. She frequently appeared at my place of work. At times it was as though she had materialised through the pavement, suddenly appearing in front of me. Sometimes I would turn around and find her behind me or catch a glimpse of her disappearing round a corner. She took away my rubbish and pieced together letters. She obtained personal addresses and telephone numbers, and intercepted my mail. She telephoned all the people on my itemised telephone bill, obtained their addresses, and then sat outside their homes, or broke into them, or broke their windows.

If I managed to escape her, she would escalate her activity to draw me from cover or would simply track me down. When I left the country for two weeks, she went berserk and graffitied the front of my house with twelve-inch high letters. She did this again the next night and then, having failed to flush me out, travelled 150 miles to my parents' home. After spending twenty-four hours watching their house in a small village, she was picked up by the police.

At this point she was charged for going equipped to commit burglary. Staggeringly, this was the first and only time she was arrested for a criminal offence although, by this time, I had been granted many injunctions in the Civil Court.

It is hard to describe how she managed to terrorise me, committing many criminal offences without ever getting caught. There were no witnesses and she repeatedly eluded psychiatric treatment.

Survival and surrender

I remember one morning, some months into these events, lying in bed, exhausted, unable to move. I felt her presence invading, seeping through me, taking over. And I said 'OK': I surrendered. The image that came to me was from the film *The Servant*, about the relationship between a servant, played by Dirk Bogarde, and his employer, James Fox, in which one is manipulated, submerged and destroyed by the other: an image of darkness and sickness. As I lay in bed, I saw her moving in with me to be looked after. I saw myself decline, give up work, drift and shrivel – reduced to existing in dark corners and dirt with no friends and no life – while she came and went, thriving in a dark and sinister way, like a leach growing fat on my blood and spirit. I remember the exhaustion of that moment, no strength or energy left. I had dug deeper and deeper into myself and been amazed by the depths of resources in my being. I was full of wonder at human beings and the seeming endlessness of our resources and I was equally amazed at that moment, lying in bed, when I knew I had come to the end. There was no longer anything to draw on. I knew I had to get some energy from somewhere, just to move. I breathed in and, from outside myself, drew in energy to keep going.

I am aware, from watching programmes on stalking, how difficult it is to convey the terrifying nature of the experience. To be stalked is to discover powerlessness, to lose the ability to predict in even the simplest way what the next moment will hold.

As Badcock (1996) writes:

> The process of stalking forces a relationship on the victim whether they want it or not – it is impossible to get the stalker out of one's life for the duration of the activity. The relationship may be traumatic to the victim but it is often close – again something which is forced, of necessity and against the victim's wishes.

Every moment I was overwhelmed with extreme emotions of terror, anger and aggression. I was physically adrenalised, hyper-vigilant: watching, listening and working through extreme emotion and stress. I was tempted by madness, suicide and murder. The experience was so enormous that it is hard to find words to describe it or even, sitting here, to quite believe it happened to me.

Counselling and studying under siege

During this time I was fighting for my life: my physical, mental, emotional, financial and professional life. I had to plan constantly how to keep myself physically safe. At times I had a bodyguard to sit near the room in which I saw clients, as Joni easily found ways to pass the locked front door and reception. I could only give my attention to a client if I knew for certain she could not burst in and I could only work with a client if I could assure myself that they were physically and psychologically safe while with me.

I was facing the fact that I would have to close my practice, yet I needed to maintain my work to support myself financially and to prevent her completely taking over my life. I would call the police to remove her from my office or garden, but they could not remove her from the road outside my house or prevent her from following me despite their desire to protect me and their fear for my safety. Watching and following are not as yet criminal offences.

In the following January, Joni followed me to what had felt the last safe place, the university. I was in the middle of a two-year M.Sc. course and was determined, at least at the beginning, to complete it. This became very difficult as my tiredness and stress increased. During this time the support of friends, supervisor, police, and solicitor were crucial to my survival. I lost some friends who could not take the pressure and the fear, while others became very important to me.

Nobody wishes to give up freedom. But the issue is much more complex when the decision is: how many possessions am I willing to risk to remain free, and how radical a change in the conditions of my life will I make to preserve autonomy.

(Bettelheim 1991)

Finally, in May, after ten months the nightmare ended, brought to a close through my efforts and on my behalf by the intervention of the courts, the police, the prison service and a therapeutic community.

This was a momentous time, even magical, a time that was both traumatic and healing. The stress seemed to burn neurosis out of me, I had no energy for anything except the present and staying alive and holding on to what was important to me. But what was important had changed over the months as I had let go more and more of my life.

Involvement of others

Throughout all these months of trauma, the attitudes of the people around me had been mixed. Some thought I was making a fuss about nothing. This is a common reaction experienced by victims of stalking. Often the actions of the stalker are perceived as fairly ordinary, such as hanging around on the street. People seem to think you can just ignore the stalker and the person will go away. When the stalker persists and escalates the activity, the victim is considered to be encouraging and, perhaps, even secretly liking the attention. The publicity that stalking has received recently will, it is to be hoped, go some way to change this attitude. Others around me understood the terrifying nature of stalking. These were people who either had very close contact with me and witnessed Joni's activities or were part of a small group with whom I discussed decisions – supervisors, close friends and later the police and my solicitor – or they had some previous knowledge of stalking behaviour. Joni's impact on my life and relationships followed a fairly similar pattern at first. Any relationship would be affected by how I was feeling, how stressed, tired or terrified. Her activities also affected my ability to keep appointments. How I was, with friends or in the M.Sc. group, affected them and aroused feelings of anger, loss, relief or care and concern. As one member put it:

'This is taking a lot of time, I wish you were in the group more. Also (I'm) envious you were getting special treatment.'

A second stage that sometimes developed in her activities was where she would focus on particular friends or family and sit outside their homes, at times breaking in or putting bricks through their windows. In terms of the university training group, the second stage was her turning up in person at the university. Joni would appear at some stage in the day and be seen lurking outside a door or round a corner. University security guards would chase her all over the large building, police would be called in to remove her. I spent hours sitting with a fellow student in an office. 'Business as usual' could not take place.

After these events, in order to complete my M.Sc., I had to write a dissertation demonstrating appropriate research methodology, on an area of specific interest in the field of counselling, supervision and training. After extensive discussion of the ethical issues, the only meaningful subject for me was the process I had been through and the reactions of other people involved, particularly those in my training group. I interviewed people who were a mixture of friends, professionals and a group of counsellors/therapists on the M.Sc. course.

The M.Sc. course members were particularly interesting, because they were almost as caught up in events as I was. Unlike me, they had the possibility of ending their involvement by either leaving the course themselves or requesting me to do so. Both these would have been very extreme and costly options. They provided instead a live experiment in 'rescuer' and 'bystander' behaviour, as reflected by some of the direct quotations which follow.

Bystanders

This group is difficult for me to talk about or even to see as a group. The individuals ranged from those who had been friends to people I knew only a little. They seemed to have confused, ambivalent feelings: concern for me; anxiety about how to help; feeling childlike, not 'grown up' enough to take action; not wanting to interfere, even having a value of non-interference which supported this; guilt at not helping; a sense of powerlessness of not knowing what to do. They had feelings of being excluded, combined with resentment and anger at their lives being disrupted. They seemed to hold me responsible for all that equally with Joni – possibly more so. There was also jealousy at the attention I received, and disbelief. It was as though the waves of events broke against a rigidity in them: they felt their lives disrupted, they feared the loss of their goals. Those on the M.Sc. course resented course time being taken up with these dramatic happenings. Unresolved past experiences were triggered. They were battling against something, feeling threatened. Significantly, they were far more disturbed by events than those who were supportive.

Lantané and Darley (1970) made similar findings among the bystanders in their research experiments who were:

> worried about the guilt and shame they would feel if they did not help the person in distress. On the other hand they were concerned not to make fools of themselves by overacting. If anything they seemed more emotionally aroused than did the subjects who reported the emergence.

One of the themes which stands out is how in some way almost all of these people disbelieved me, either directly, as with the person who thought I was attention-seeking, or, even more disturbing, with the suggestion that I was stalking Joni. I was told by one person:

> 'I went from curiosity to concern, to a negative period of feeling that you were perhaps, possibly, attention seeking, then Joni turned up and I felt really quite bad about that, because you obviously weren't, it was really quite real. That was also questioned by another course member, who said: "I think it could be that the psychotic transference is Christabel's, not the client's." '

The disbelief was expressed indirectly, as they refused to accept my powerlessness to stop the stalking. They came up with logical answers: if I had terminated the counselling relationship immediately she had been found in my house; or if I had terminated it differently, or not at all, the stalking would not have occurred. People even invented things, for example believing the stalking had occurred as a result of my terminating the therapeutic relationship. Others seemed to hold me responsible and saw a lack of aggression on my part as the problem. One said:

> 'I felt angry with you for not being able to deal with it much more assertively. ... I felt that if you could only somehow have handled it positively, and firmly and even aggressively, it would have been good for you.'

This disbelief of the victim seems common in stalking, as in other crimes against the person; of the prosecutions for rape only a very small proportion result in conviction. Powerlessness is so terrifying a concept that people do not willingly embrace it. If the victim can be found to be at fault, others can feel safe, for they would have acted differently. To be disbelieved is very isolating and destructive of friendship. Those around the victim who either disbelieve or blame the victim reinforce the attack and increase the sense of isolation and alienation. Badcock (1996) describes the victim's sense of 'identity and autonomy as a person being directly threatened'. Not to be believed, or to have one's experience reinvented and given back as an explanation as to why something is happening, can only add to this. Re-inventing the story to fit the bystander's view of the world was a thread throughout the year from some casual witnesses, group members and police. Such disbelief was vividly illustrated by the following example. On one occasion Joni broke into a friend's house at 4 a.m. Disturbed by a noise, he saw her climbing through a window and called the police. He explained who he thought the intruder was and the danger of the situation. Joni returned at 7 a.m. and my friend called the police again. He later discovered that the police had done nothing to pursue her, as they had disbelieved him and written off the incident as a 'domestic' with Joni featuring as the injured party.

Exclusion and jealousy were also strong themes. Possibly bystanders in any situation are jealous of the victims: their own need for attention may be triggered and, though they do not want to be the victim, they do want the attention and support they see the victim getting. The bystander is the audience and the only way into the drama is on the side of the persecutor or the victim. In contrast, a rescuer is able to see a clear way in, has a sense of her own potency, is able to take action, is possibly neither in need of attention or scared of it – polarities which often go together. Perhaps a part of the bystander's personality supports the persecutor, while hatred, fear, jealousy, are all motivational factors for persecuting a person or group. Certainly, by simply remaining bystanders, any of us inevitably collude with the persecutor.

For another member of this group, none of this was relevant: she was simply thrown back in time.

> 'What she (Joni) did was force me to look at aspects of myself I didn't like. ... There was almost a constant fear of my Mother's anger and what she might do. ... If you'd been a man, I'm sure I can say I would have felt differently. I think I would have been able to offer you more open support.'

One of the most striking examples of bystander behaviour came after eight months of being terrorised. The police of two major cities were involved and numerous court injunctions had been granted. As I described at the beginning of the chapter, Joni went to see a counsellor in a women's counselling organisation. She revealed to this counsellor what she was doing to me and her intention to kill me and then herself. She gave details of how, when and where this would take place. The counsellor informed Joni's GP who got word to me. The police contacted the organisation for a statement, hoping to be able to prosecute Joni for threats to kill, which can carry a substantial prison sentence. The counsellor and the organisation refused to give the statement as they were frightened by what they had heard and did not want her to turn her obsessive behaviour on them. What was striking was both their willingness to admit that their refusal to testify arose from fear and that they did not seem to have any trouble living with this. A policewoman involved responded to this later by saying:

'They were not prepared to help another woman, or somebody in the same profession. I thought that was appalling, I thought that was awful.'

Rescuers

These people were a mixture of professionals, police, a solicitor, supervisors, tutors, friends and fellow students on the M.Sc. course, some of whom I had known well before these events, while others were strangers. They were remarkably alike in some ways. They spoke with a calmness and clarity, involving not a lack of feeling but a lack of anxiety. There was an acceptance of me, and mostly, though not exclusively, they believed me. They did not feel personally threatened. They had less to say when interviewed than the group I experienced as unsupportive and disbelieving of me. They all had a strong core value system; many had interventionist parental role models, experience of being an outsider and a sense of adventure. Some admitted to a liking of drama which meant they felt excitement rather than fear. All had some past, sufficiently resolved experience which acted as the basis of a value which supported their involvement and gave them insight or empathy for me and in some cases for Joni. Some felt a great anger towards her; many felt both anger and compassion. When I compared my research with other studies of bystander and rescuer behaviour, I was struck by the similarity in findings: the unequivocal belief of those who intervene, that to help is what you do; it is not thought about but based on a deeply held value. One said:

'I think if I see somebody suffering and there is something I can do, I ought to do it'.

Another said:

'If you see someone who needs help then you help them regardless, and would expect them to do the same for you or other people to do the same for you. There wasn't a choice; not that I was forced, but basically, if human beings don't do that for each other, they may as well pack it in.'

The same conviction was expressed by another:

'If there is nothing you can do to stop something, you can be there with someone and looking for ways out.'

In the literature on rescuer and bystander behaviour (much of which relates to the Holocaust) I found some examples. Dr Janusz Korczsak, head of the Jewish orphanage in Warsaw, who went with the children into the gas chambers of Treblinka said:

One does not leave a sick child in the night and one does not leave children at a time like this.

(Bettelheim 1991)

and the Danish fishermen who ferried Jews to safety said:

someone came who needed help, we did not think about the risk.

(Fogelman 1995)

Other studies have found that rescuers tend to ask themselves the question: 'If I do nothing, will I be able to live with myself?'. I felt moved by the timeless quality in the voices of these people, and moved that fifty years ago, in far more dangerous and harrowing times, those who went to the aid of their fellow human beings sounded so similar to those who came to my aid.

Those who were supportive of me saw Joni as responsible for her actions and therefore as the person who had the power to stop the drama. They were able to tolerate the powerlessness. Perhaps they found relief in the actions they took. At least one person had a spiritual frame of reference which enabled him to accept he could do nothing to alter the situation. Another shared theme was the attitude that all situations, however awful, are opportunities for learning and self-development.

Being there, listening to me, believing me while I worked through how I felt or what I needed to do was the greatest support. The person most constantly involved put it like this:

> 'I kind of feel, that given what was happening we did the best that was possible in the circumstances. It would have been very easy to have blown the whole thing up. We could have or I could have acted as crazily as she was and I think that was what she was inviting really to reinforce her world view by responding in the way she expected.'

Lantané and Darley (1970) described five stages through which a person moves from bystander to active participant: (1) noticing something is amiss, (2) interpreting the situation as one in which people need help, (3) assuming responsibility to offer help, (4) choosing a form of help and (5) implementing that help. Woven into this are a number of other factors, which may be described in terms of personality and also moral and value systems which influence what a person notices and whether or not he chooses to do something about what he notices.

Noticing seems to be the single most powerful thing we can do. It is the ability really to see and to care about what we see. Maybe it is seeing, perhaps momentarily, without fear for ourselves. In the words of an American soldier in Vietnam:

> This one time I saw the guy. I mean I saw him. He was that guy, that person. I didn't shoot. I didn't even think not to shoot. I just didn't shoot. ... Then I realized that ... how can I say this? ... that I saw everybody. I mean the VC, and this guy next to me, and myself. And at that point there was no way I was going to be able to go out and fight anymore. I was going to be dangerous to my outfit, in fact; I wasn't about to be shooting.
>
> (Dass and Gorman 1994)

Seeing in this way is presumably seeing with empathy or understanding or identification. It is seeing which comes to rest on a value such as: this is another human being; I don't want to kill him; or, this person needs help so I will help. Fear, survival, ambition, hate, anger, jealousy and obedience to authority, all get in the way of this kind of seeing. If all the soldiers in Vietnam had experienced what the soldier above described, the war would have stopped. If we were aware of the connection between ourselves and our world, of that creative connection that exists for example between a counsellor and a client, between a gardener and a garden, a painter or photographer and a picture, we would no longer be able to tolerate a world in which there is so much alienation and isolation and harm. We would have to find a different way to live.

> The ability to strip away the gauze of Nazi euphemisms and recognise that innocents are being murdered is at the heart of what distinguishes rescuers from bystanders.
>
> (Fogelman 1995)

Doubts and questions

My experience of being stalked and the attitudes and responses of the people around me raised many questions. If we, as counsellors, see ourselves as people who help, what does this mean? How far do we go? Indeed, how far should we go? How is it possible to carry on 'business as usual' when someone is trying to kill you? Is it always possible to learn and grow from all experience, however threatening? When we see a new client and agree to work together, just what are we committing ourselves to? How dangerous is this work of counselling/therapy?

We have codes of ethics to protect our clients from us; insurance policies to compensate clients if need be. But, as I discovered, the insurance will not pay to protect me, to take out an injunction or to compensate me for the traumatic stress of being stalked.

What did I learn? I learned that powerlessness is a part of life, that as long as I can choose my own attitude, I can retain my sense of self. In the moment of accepting I was powerless, I paradoxically discovered my power. I learned unexpected things about boundaries. Both my supervisors and tutors were flexible enough with their boundaries for me to feel like a human being in trouble, rather than a dangerous creature to be kept within certain perimeters.

The accepted boundaries moved and changed. My supervisor spoke to my ex-client's GP. My tutors spoke to the police, gave me shelter in their homes and one came to court as a witness. At times even my supervisor's husband became involved, talking with me on the telephone when she wasn't available. I noticed that what was healing and really mattered to me were people who behaved as caring human beings. They had boundaries that were about them as people, not rooted in their professional roles. My boundaries changed in a way I might not have expected. They did not become rigid, but actually much lighter: less about the counsellor role and more about who I am and who my client is. I heard other people make decisions that they would never work at home again and that they will adhere to strict boundaries. Much of this was about their need to believe that it is possible to prevent something like this happening. To protect ourselves is important; to weave magic circles around our work with hard and fast rules merely provides an illusion of safety which is as dangerous as it is an illusion. Sometimes bad things happen.

I can also afford to allow clients closer to me now, as I have found my aggressive self and I know that I can fight and maintain my boundaries however close the person gets. My own boundaries are therefore much more solid and more intrinsic to me.

I learned from Joni to listen very carefully to clients; to believe and take seriously any fears they may have of being evil or too much for me or dangerous in some way. On the whole, these fears will stem from beliefs about themselves arising from the way an important adult treated them in childhood or fear of the emotions they sense in themselves. However, some people are dangerous; some people are right to fear what they might do. I am wary of clients who want me to do all the work, who want a magic wand, while knowing that the wish for a magic wand is very human and that we all want one sometimes! I do not know that there is anything I could have done differently that would have prevented this. I have gone round in circles often enough and am inclined to agree with Judith Lewis Herman (1992):

> To imagine that one could have done better may be more tolerable than to face the reality of utter helplessness.

I believe that any situation, however awful, can be an opportunity for growth and learning. I also believe that this attitude itself provides a vital support, a life raft for surviving as long as humanly possible in threatening situations.

It appears that the world is at present more willing to listen to victims of trauma, for example the banning of most hand guns in response to the massacre of children at Dunblane in 1996. However, it is alarming to hear people described as 'evil' as though that is an explanation for their actions. The actions themselves may be evil; people may become so dangerous that they need to be locked up for life, but I do not believe that anybody is born dangerous. They are made that way by other human beings.

So, if we as counsellors and therapists are not to be bystanders in the world, we need to find a way of putting into the world what we know: that our stories and our parents' stories are acted out in the world or on the self, if not told and witnessed in any other way; that respect, support and love are essential requirements if a child is to grow up to be respectful, supportive and loving; that clean air, shelter and nutritional food are needed.

With all of the above and the conviction that all children and adults are unique and valuable, we would have more people who cared and were ready to intervene and therefore fewer bystanders and fewer perpetrators.

The limbo of recovery

As a postscript, I want to outline the calm after this storm, to describe briefly what helped me recover, and suggest what any victim of stalking may need.

After it is all over, the tension eases, the support drops off, the adrenalin is gone. Celebration is incomplete as there is no certainty that the haunting is over. There is a void. Life which had been completely filled with dramas is suddenly slow and empty; the reality of lost friends and lost life is felt, balanced by the bliss of being alone. There is no energy to make new friends or do new things. Lying staring at the ceiling was at times all I was capable of; at times I felt as though I would die because my body would simply stop breathing, yet because of the lack of energy this was not frightening. There was a delicious relief in this blankness, at other times a desperation: would I never be well? I felt old, 100 years old. Death seemed acceptable, I had survived, I had completed the M.Sc., it would be an OK time to die.

So I was physically and emotionally exhausted, I felt as though there was nothing left, not even in the marrow of my bones. Sleep brought no benefit; I remembered that sensation of waking up refreshed after a good night's sleep, but I no longer experienced it. Often I had little sleep because as I lay down, my body became alert, listening for sounds of someone entering. When I did sleep my dreams were full of nightmares. When I was awake I was for a long time still vigilant as I walked the streets.

So what helped? Post-traumatic stress counselling eased some of the emotional and psychological scars. I was still left with the physical stress and the interrelated emotional injuries. After some searching, I discovered acupuncture. I remember the first session when I described my symptoms and was understood, the relief of finding someone who knew what I was talking about, who could ask me if I had experienced other symptoms and who was clear they could help. During that first treatment, I felt as though something went into my bones; though treatment was a slow recovery process over three years, I never again felt as low as I had before that first treatment. At a later stage I seemed to hit a plateau; at this point I went to see a homoeopath. He too had a framework in which he could understand my symptoms and treat them successfully. As I felt stronger I was able to take exercise and am now fitter than I have been, perhaps ever.

Finally, a word about the need to stay with and keep working through events until they resolve or fade: I was surprised by how often people, many of them therapists, urged me to forget and get on with my life, leave the experience behind me. It was unnerving to be confronted in this way when what I wanted was support to work through it. At times I doubted myself and thought maybe they were right and I was in some way clinging to it. So gradually I stopped talking to most people, gave up the attempt to be understood, and settled for believing myself. I was fortunate that, at any one time, there was at least one person who did understand, who could support me. This support was vital.

To anyone working with a client who has been stalked, I would say: remember you are working with someone who has suffered gross invasion and been forced into an intimate relationship with a person who wishes to cause her terror. This is akin to torture. What is also common is the experience of being disbelieved and abandoned by friends. So your client will need to be believed, need to feel in control, need to be respected and listened to, and held safely enough to feel the extreme emotions, the depression and the grief. Then she will need a place to be tired, safe and accepted and a relationship in which she can learn to trust again, to discuss how the experience has changed her, what she wants now from life, who she is now. These clients need acknowledgement that they will never be as they were before the stalking, and that this is not necessarily a bad thing.

Recovery is a lengthy process.

References

Badcock, R.J. (1996) 'Psychology of Stalking', in *Report of the Suzy Lamplugh Trust Conference on Stalking Laws*, London.

Bettelheim, B. (1991) *The Informed Heart*, Harmondsworth, Penguin.

Dass, R. and Gorman, P. (1994) *How Can I Help?*, London, Rider.

Fogelman, E. (1995) *Conscience and Courage: Rescuers of Jews during the Holocaust*, London, Cassell.
Herman, J.L. (1992) *Trauma and Recovery*, London, Pandora.
Lantané, B. and Darley, J.M. (1970) *The Unresponsive Bystander: Why Doesn't He Help?*, New York, Appleton-Century-Crofts.

Chapter 13

Healing the 'wounded healer'

Larry Parker

> When we become personally responsible for the healing of every
> thought, action, intention, and deed in our lives, the rest of the world
> will heal along with us. ... no healer, psychologist, doctor, medicine
> person, or teacher can do it for another.
>
> (Sams 1994)

Introduction

One of the things which I know to be true of myself is that I am a slow
starter. This is not a self-fulfilling prophecy, it is simply the way things
are. Childhood trauma set me back; I was mesmerised by painful experiences and transfixed into a kind of psychic immobility. Jung believed
that only the wounded physician heals – meaning that people who are
wounded are fated to have to deal continually with their own inner life
and unconscious, which may enable them to contribute to others' healing. My journey in life has involved learning where I was wounded and
what the wounding meant. I wasted a lot of time in the futile hope that
some external source would assist. Eventually I reached the inescapable
conclusion that I would have to take personal responsibility for my own
healing. I needed an energy to help me help myself, and I finally found
this in the form of experiential adult education. I owe a large debt of
gratitude to the Diploma and Master's degree in Counselling at the University of Bristol. Those experiences provided an impetus to speed up
changes, which involved a synthesis of mental, emotional, physical and
spiritual healing.

Life, if it does nothing else, offers the opportunity to form one's char-
acter – although for a very long time I seemed to be hell-bent in the
opposite direction. Today I am neither proud nor ashamed of my story, it

simply happened that way, almost as if by chance. I have made good choices and decisions, and bad ones. I have taken some opportunities, and missed others. I am simply the aggregate of all the haphazard experiences which came my way, given whatever situation or milieu I was in at the time. I am no longer attached to my wounds and I do not live in the past. Yet, on a soul and cellular level there is an indelible imprint of pain, which can be heard like an echo. I am driven to respond to the suffering of others as soon as I reverberate to the echo of their wounds, which is why I regard myself as being an example of a 'wounded healer': the counsellor I have become is the product of my learning from life experiences, with the training I found as a significant catalyst.

Woundable and wounding parents

It was early in my lifetime that I came to understand the meaning of Wordsworth's conundrum about the child being the father to the man. It became apparent, as soon as I could think for myself, that my parents needed parenting. Their inadequacies meant that they were unable to meet any of my archetypal needs. My mother and father were hopelessly trapped in their own adolescent psychology. She had been thrown out onto the streets to fend for herself at the age of 15. He had been endowed with beauty and high intelligence and was idolised, at least in the initial stages, by most people. This went to his head and put him permanently into a narcissistic downward spiral.

As parents they were almost totally deficient. He was everlastingly self-absorbed with gambling, drinking, and womanising. She, wraith-like, trailed wearily behind, chronically ill for most of her life; always suffering in silence. 'I didn't ask to be born' was the catch-phrase which I used so often to them that it became a litany. Many writers have acknowledged that family pain can set individual children off on a pilgrimage to search for those things which were missing, with the objective of putting them in place in their own life, and perhaps into the lives of others. Although family sorrow is a painful wound, it may in fact become the seed that gives birth to spiritual healing and awakening.

The problems of family life soon made it clear that my parents were not going to be able to take care of me. This also applied to my brother and sister, and I still feel rather uncomfortable when I remember that together we often toured the local streets knocking at the houses of friends, and saying to their parents 'Would you like to adopt us?' There is a popular sophism that psychotherapy and analysis are all about blaming one's parents for one's miseries. The time came in my life when it became necessary to understand my parents' wounds because, in order to move on, I needed to forgive. Before that could happen I had to work with suffering people on the London streets. Hollis (1994) says that the more sensitive we are 'to the fragility of the human psyche, the most likely are we to forgive parents for being woundable and wounding'.

Childhood illness: suffering and stoicism

I was born in London in 1942. My mother refused to be evacuated and, as a consequence, we spent a lot of time in the air-raid shelter. In infancy I dreaded being put to bed because for a long time I was plagued with horrible nightmares, the details of which I still remember. I wonder how awful nocturnal apparitions could have entered into the thinking mind of a child, either consciously or unconsciously? I can only deduce that I was 'infected', on a soul level, with the fear which then stalked the world. Nostradamus ('the healing prophet') is reported to have said, 'fear is the door, through it comes all sickness. … it creates war'.

From birth I was frail and sickly. The family photograph album shows pictures of a grim unsmiling child. I felt that life was a troublesome burden to be endured with stoicism; my mother had passed on to me the art of silent suffering. At the age of 7 I was put into hospital with glandular tuberculosis. I remained there for two years, during which time streptomycin was discovered as a cure. I have often tried to fathom out where the roots of such an illness could be buried. There is research to support the hypothesis that tuberculosis can be related to upheaval in society, and esoteric writing always associates TB with loss.

Hospitals, in 1949, were not children-friendly. I was kept in a large ward of terminally ill men, without the company of other children. I became intimately acquainted with death. I was not particularly concerned about my own death, because I reached the conclusion that it would simply be a matter of time. The stratagem which I deployed as a coping mechanism was to escape into an inner world. Dissociation helped me to survive traumatic experiences; 'we escape the pain around us by retreating into the safe haven of fantasy, illusion, or the transpersonal realms' (Grof 1994).

I did not receive any education in hospital, but I became an avid reader. I consumed most of the novels of Charles Dickens, and found it easy to identify with Oliver Twist, in terms of deprivation and victimology. I listened endlessly (on headphones) to the radio which developed in me a passionate love for music. Somebody once told me that music is the way that the angels have of communicating with us – and I have never had the slightest trouble in believing that. It was terrible and dreary being in hospital so long, but I can see that I owe a debt to that experience of watching others suffer, and suffering myself. I was taught compassion.

Sexual abuse creating narcissistic wounds

One day an adult patient was pushing me in a wheelchair around the hospital environs. He raped me in a goods lift which he stopped between floors. I didn't cry out, because I had learned to be a brave little boy. I think that I was so traumatised by the hospital experience that the rape did not seem to be much more invasive than the procedures which represented my medical treatment. I was eight years old: I told nobody.

A year later I was suddenly taken home without warning or preparation. I left hospital having cultivated, as do all damaged children, a heightened awareness. It was like having been given an emotional radar system. The price which I had to pay was that illness and abuse had violated my core self. James Hollis (1994) warns that if one has been narcissistically wounded 'one tends to view the world through that Gestalt only'. I arrived home to find that my father's gambling and drinking had forced my mother into taking a lodger in order to make ends meet. He was allowed to take me away on holiday as a 'treat' for being so long in hospital; Margate, of all places, was the location. On the first night he raped me in the guest house, and then for the ensuing three years. As with the earlier experience in the goods lift, I was mute. I often tried to tell my mother what was happening, but no words came. The resultant secrecy created what Summitt (1983) describes as 'the accommodation syndrome' where the victim child 'threatened, helpless and entrapped ... carries the burden of the abuse and assumes responsibility for the situation'.

In his American study of sexually abused boys, Hunter (1990) found that 'fear, guilt, shame, loneliness, and anger' were the commonest emotional problems following abuse. The sum total of those five states coalesced for me into a mind-numbing depression; but nobody in my orbit took any notice of what was going on. A contributory factor to the depression was that the secrecy of the abuse had catapulted me willy-nilly into a double life of lying and subterfuge. As far as I was concerned, dissociation was the only way of containing what was happening to me without going mad. It is known that sexually abused children tend rigidly to compartmentalise deeply negative emotional experiences. I sometimes felt like breaking down, but the spectre of a further admission to hospital acted as a strong deterrent. I did not then know that those events were to be the formative experiences in preparing me for a career, later in life, as a social worker.

Introduction to pedagogy

At the age of 11 I was educationally backward. Schooling was the least of my concerns, especially after the setback of having missed so much of it. I flopped the eleven plus exam and was sent to what was thought of as being a rough comprehensive school in Battersea. This actually turned out to be helpful because the school had a raw energy which worked as an impetus to jolt me out of my somewhat effete self-absorption.

There were other counterpoints to help me to think about standing up for myself, even though at this stage I was still being abused. I think I deflected the energy of unexpressed anger at being abused into areas in which I had some control, and was more able to express genuine self-assertion. Such a focus was our local evangelical church to which my brother, sister and I were packed off every Sunday. My parents had no religious convictions whatsoever, it was simply their way of getting rid of us for the day. I was in the process of being prepared for baptism by a hectoring bully of a minister. I dreaded the sessions with him in the vestry where he tried to coerce me into believing things which in my heart I could not accept. It was a poisonous experience of the worst kind of didacticism; and I refused to be trained in religious sheep psychology. Also, I knew that in the eyes of the church I was, as an abused boy, a sinner. In the face of a resulting furore I simply refused to go to church any longer.

Then, there were the piano lessons – a further repellent pedagogic experience. I was longing to express myself in music, but the piano teacher had other ideas. She taught entirely by rote and I found myself caught up in what Hermann Hesse describes as the struggle between rule and spirit. I loathed hacking and grinding my way through endless scales and arpeggios, I just wanted to play music, preferably something with a good tune. The piano was located in the lodger's bedroom where most of the abuse took place; this was not helpful. I failed all the grade exams because I was so nervous, and, probably, as a subtle form of revenge. Eventually I had to dig my heels in very hard in order successfully to terminate those dreary lessons.

Prostitution as a legacy of abuse

Two important events occurred when I was twelve: the lodger suddenly moved out, and I got a bike. Like a homing pigeon I cycled furiously into the West End of London at every available moment. I was happy just to be on my own, hanging around railway stations and mooching up and down Charing Cross Road. I was totally without supervision at home, my parents never cared nor queried where I was. At least I felt some identity as a street kid, a runaway. The pace and excitement of London offered powerful adrenalin and literally took me out of myself. But I was left with a legacy from those years of sexual abuse and over-stimulation: I had become programmed into believing that sexual activity was inevitable for me, whether I wanted it or not.

I became a prostitute. In my muddled thinking sexual activity was synonymous with being cared for. Charging for sex helped me compose a sense of my own value. That lifestyle rapidly became hideously addictive: 'he (the survivor of abuse) is only a sexual object attempting to prove his worth and desirability through repeated sexual encounters which are neither satisfying nor uplifting' (Lew 1988). So, in about 1954, I became one of the first 'Dilly (Piccadilly Circus) rent-boys. Having a rather inflated view of myself and my potential to attract, I preferred not to be draped over the iron pedestrian railings, known colloquially as 'the meat rack'. Instead, I lurked enticingly in the foyers of nearby hotels. My 'earnings' introduced me to a fantastic and grandiose world of escape. I had beautiful clothes, stored in the house of a friend. Every night I went to the ballet, opera, restaurants. I looked older and developed poise, and people assumed that I was a rich kid. I truanted from school, but the teachers either did not notice or were not bothered. Like Oliver Twist, I fell in with a gang of thieves and delinquents, and in order to be acceptable to them I committed serious offences throughout the span of my adolescence.

BBC and addiction

In 1960 I took the decision to bring prostitution and delinquency to a conclusion. My reason for doing so was that I had got a job in the BBC, and I was fearful of jeopardising career prospects. I was also very well aware that I was probably running out of time with the chances I was taking on the streets and from detection by the police. Since the days of listening to the radio in hospital, I had cherished the dream of working at Broadcasting House. It was indeed a strange experience to get to meet the owners of the voices that had been the friends of my inner world in childhood.

I had managed to scrape through a couple of 'A' levels at school, although they were the only subjects in which I had the remotest interest – music and English. For some long while I had been given to announcing, in my most grandiose manner, that the BBC had a job awaiting me – which was not at all the case. I solved that problem by the simple expedient of turning up at Broadcasting House and refusing to go away. Eventually a nice lady came down and gave me a job as a clerk. I remained with the BBC for thirteen years, rapidly being promoted to studio manager, and then music producer.

It was a struggle to hold my own in the world of broadcasting. I felt desperately ashamed of my background and increasingly conscious of my educational deficiencies. I set about obliterating my cockney accent. 'Oxford' English was *de rigueur* in those days, before the arrival of the Beatles, who popularised regional accents. I bluffed my way through an appointment board to become a music producer, and I lied about non-existent qualifications. Later, on more than one occasion, my fabrications were revealed. This was so mortifying that I decided it was essential to remedy the situation. As far as any use of my mind or intellect was concerned, I was simply going around like a somnambulist. Ferguson (1981) tells us that 'if we are not learning and teaching we are not awake and alive ... learning is not like health, it is health'. So I did course after course at the City Literary Institute and in the extra-mural department at London University. I auditioned for the Guildhall School of Music and Drama and was accepted as a part-time student of singing and piano. I was able to do this alongside my BBC job, and I remained with my teachers for five years.

It was exhilarating to be in the music industry in London during the 1960s. I gravitated towards a hedonistic lifestyle like an iron filing to a magnet. I was no longer charging for sex, but I continued to be promiscuous. I had good friends, but found it impossible to settle into an ongoing emotional relationship, despite several attempts to do so. I was drinking alcohol every day, often in very large quantities. Actually, I had had a taste for alcohol all my life ('like father, like son'). Drink had been freely available at home and as a youth there had been numerous instances when I had got myself paralytically drunk. Many programme negotiations took place in the BBC club or in local pubs. Alcoholism was seen as an occupational hazard.

Inwardly I knew that the drinking did not relate to the hurly-burly of my job; it served a more sinister purpose. It was an attempt to blot out the memories of my abuse and illness, the facts of which I had never disclosed to anyone. So, the crazy paradox was that on one hand I had acquired some personal and professional power, which, on the other hand, I was intent on destroying by reverting to the victim status of becoming a slave of alcohol.

Probation training

I have always relied on intuition to help me make important decisions. I am usually willing to trust the inner voice. I resigned from the BBC on what seemed to be impulse; at least I had not given the decision very much thought. I had seen a newspaper advertisement inviting mature entrants to train to be probation officers. As a producer I was in fact more like a social worker. I had developed a reputation with singers and musicians as being understanding, able to coax forth a performance even under the most trying conditions. As a singer I knew full well the technical, emotional and spiritual problems which faced performers, and I was much more fascinated by the psychology of performance and programme making than by the content or material.

In those days probation training was a twelve-month course, run directly by the Home Office, leading to a professional qualification. Despite the damage I was doing to myself by drinking, the other side of the coin was that I invariably demonstrated to others the milk of human kindness, and I genuinely thought I could become a successful helping professional. A motive which was not quite so clearly in my consciousness was that 'many, and probably most psychotherapists are drawn to their work because they themselves grew up in unhappy families and early conceived a desire to repair the hurt in others' (Lomas 1981).

The Home Office course, in 1973, had its own didactic bias. Casework, as it was then called, was taught from dusty books, the contents of which were treated as if they were words direct from God. The overall tone was one of patronising moralisation and do-goodery. It was a far cry from Lao Tsu's dialectic that the perfected man does not interfere in the life of beings, he does not impose himself on them, but he helps all beings in their freedom. Groupwork was reckoned to be a fashionable way in which to proceed. I had previously experienced this form of torture at the age of 16, having consulted my doctor because I was worried about my sexuality. He panicked and sent me to the nearest psychiatric hospital. The psychiatrist to whom I was assigned quickly recognised a hopeless case when he saw one (in terms of 'cure') so he arranged for me to attend group therapy.

This turned out to be a horribly distressing experience; in retrospect I am amazed that I kept going for so long. Once a week, in a large bleak room, a motley group of people were assembled. I was the youngest, and we all carried the label (and stigma) of being sexually 'dysfunctional'. The meeting was presided over by two sullen, stony-faced, silent psychiatrists. Microphones were suspended from the ceiling, almost obscuring our view of each other. In a wall of the room a one-way mirror had been fitted, on the other side of which (I was perfectly sure) was grouped a collection of medical students, likely to be helpless with hysterical laughter. It was a grim atmosphere, not conducive to self-revelation or catharsis.

Groupwork, at the Home Office, was remarkably similar. Our facilitator was our course tutor as well as being a Home Office inspector. I remember that she always arrived wearing dark glasses and a fur coat. Her technique was to sit in total silence for the entire duration of the group: in terms of her own self-control it was undoubtedly a *tour de force*. This threw us all into a terrible panic, especially as she refused to answer any questions which were put. We felt that the slightest degree of self-disclosure, however innocuous, would have been negatively interpreted, likely to result in our being thrown off the course. My method for surviving those ghastly sessions, steeling myself not to blurt out anything personal, was to recite (silently) the Lord's Prayer and to count endlessly the leaves of a tree on the street outside.

Working on the London streets

When I qualified from the Home Office course I was appointed to work in the West End of London at a probation office attached to Bow Street Magistrates Court. It was ironic that I was employed by the criminal justice system in the very location where my own delinquency and offending had taken place. I could see the point of not over-identifying with my clients, but I could also see ever more clearly that I had been unconsciously drawn in this direction because I was impelled to find answers to my own experiences of childhood traumatisation.

I worked on the streets with people who were homeless and depressed, addicted to alcohol and drugs, psychiatrically ill and socially disenfranchised; with prostitutes and runaways. Park (1992) has written that 'therapists should have had early experiences that sensitise them to the complexity of people's emotional lives'; I think I satisfied that criterion. He adds, 'they must be people who had suffered enough to understand other people's pain' – I could also offer that as a qualification. But it would have been fraudulent of me to have pretended to satisfy his third requirement that therapists should be people 'who are no longer controlled by their disturbance'. Never having dealt with my trauma, I was still, obviously, controlled by it. In addition, I did not have the slightest idea how to cope with all the pain, distress, and misery that I was meeting on a daily basis in the lives of my clients.

Illness and alcoholism

Working with the pain of others hurt me. Depression seeped across from my clients almost as if by osmosis. I formed the ludicrous opinion that it was permissible, even heroic, to carry the pain of others. Over a period of years I became wearied with exhaustion, and I drank more and more. By then I had formed a relationship (which is now in its twenty-fifth year), and my partner watched my antics with a kind of horrible fascination and disbelief, impotent to intervene or to arrest my downward spiral. Alcohol and malnutrition had wrecked my immune system. I went abroad to try to recover from glandular fever, but I collapsed with pneumonia and pleurisy. I was hospitalised in Germany, and eventually flown back to University College Hospital in London, where pulmonary tuberculosis was diagnosed. None of the hospital staff ever questioned my drinking habits. I lay in bed for week after week in indescribable pain, struggling to gasp tiny breaths, and feeling overcome with shame: I knew that I had brought this upon myself.

The hospital finally got the disease under control by way of chemo-therapy, and I was frantic to return to work as soon as possible because I feared that the probation service might not want me back. At the philosophical level, a disease, though considered to be a disgraceful episode, may, according to Yaryura-Tobias and Neziroglu (1983), 'be beneficial, since it gives an awareness of psychological and corporal zones that normally work silently. ... this knowledge of one's self enriches personal experience'. Sadly I had the insight, minus the benefit and enrichment. Nor did I fit neatly into May's (1989) schema 'that human beings will not change their personality patterns until forced to do so by suffering'. Although endangering the success of treatment, I carried on drinking. How true is the premiss that people who do not learn from their histories are condemned to repeat them.

Every drunkard has his or her fund of maudlin anecdotal stories, some of which, at least on a superficial level, can appear to be highly amusing. Beneath the storyline will invariably be histories of self-torture and spiritual pain. Sometimes hacking laughter can be the only defence for the alcoholic pursued by the demon. I have my own sad compilation of drinking stories which still make me flinch with embarrassment and disgust when remembered; but (and I accept that this may be self-justification) I always went to extraordinary lengths to try to conceal my drinking from others. Apart from when I was in hospital, I never took time off work; in fact I worked harder in an attempt to salve a guilty conscience. Later, when I had finally stopped drinking, I explained the reason to my friends and family. They greeted my admission with incredulity: 'We knew you liked a drink, but you never had a problem, and we've never ever seen you drunk.' Only those in my closest circle knew that – as far as alcohol was concerned – I was almost past redemption.

In my heart I knew that time was running out, so I dragged myself off to a local meeting of Alcoholics Anonymous. I attended meetings throughout the length and breadth of London for the next two years. I hated them all. Try as I did, I continually felt like an outsider. At the very first meeting I had been befriended by a young cockney plumber, with a warm and generous personality. I went to AA as much to please him as anything else. He was loving and supportive and is still a friend. When I felt suicidal, he was the only one I could bring myself to phone in the middle of the night. AA is a wonderful organisation that has undoubtedly saved countless lives; but my personal and academic knowledge of the theories of addiction supports Ellis and Velten (1992) in their conclusion that 'addiction is a mental state, a thought process, a purpose. It is a meaning we give to feelings and experiences. It is not a disease.'

Search for a 'cure'

There is a saying in addiction recovery groups, 'through humiliation comes humility'. Christina Grof (1994) is a psychotherapist who has conquered alcoholism; she wrote, 'we must feel as though we are reduced to nothing before we give up our defences'. I understood very well the feelings of humility and nothingness she described, but I could not find anyone or anything that would help me take down the barriers which had been fixed in place by illness and abuse. I scrabbled around in a frantic search for some external entity that would heal me. I flapped and floundered my way through a tangled maze of therapeutic activities which included encounter groups, spiritual healing, AA, deep tissue massage, radionics, homeopathy, addictions counselling, psychic surgery, and … this is embarrassing to admit: exorcism. My pathetic search for the perfect therapy to provide the perfect cure was nothing more than a long and expensive wild goose chase. In his research into smoking and overeating, Schachter (1982) makes the interesting point that people who had never been in therapy had a higher remission rate than those who had. This led him to conclude that it was possible that the very act of turning oneself over to treatment 'was antagonistic to the feeling of self-efficacy necessary to succeed at cure'.

The final, the most abysmally inefficacious of all the therapies with which I struggled, was psychoanalysis. I could not endure this longer than six months, during which time I went to my analyst's house on the other side of London thrice-weekly for sessions which commenced at seven o'clock in the morning. What did I want from this expensive and time-consuming process? I wanted to be 'heard', that is, to have my story validated ... by an 'enlightened witness'. I wanted to be 'held' (therapeutically), at least for a while, until I was strong enough to move onwards and outwards from my woundedness. I wanted to be loved – in the agape sense of the word, a strengthening love, which by definition does not burden or obligate the loved one. I wanted a simple common or garden boost to my shattered self-esteem, such that it would be like a kick-start onto a course of self-healing.

I was sure that I made those needs explicit to the analyst at the exploratory interview, and I assumed that he must have had the experience of working through some of his own traumas and neuroses. Alice Miller (1990) believes this to be an essential prerequisite for the practitioner in accompanying patients on the path to truth about themselves and in not hindering them on their way. She stresses that the remembering and reliving of traumatic experiences can only be transmuted into healing power if the aid given by therapists will not confuse their patients, make them anxious, or educate, instruct, misuse, or seduce them. With my analyst I felt more alone and abandoned than ever. My neuroses were not becoming any more intelligible to me than to him. He expressed a total lack of human warmth; worse almost, I felt he was bored with me. My friends said, 'well, find another analyst'. The mere thought of doing so pulverised me with despair.

This lack of warmth in the therapeutic relationship is a theme which emerged frequently when I did my own research into the phenomenon of the 'wounded healer'. A yoga teacher who had experienced childhood illness and sexual abuse, resulting in depression and suicide attempts, said (of her psychiatrist and psychologist), 'I found them so cold, so cut-off. They weren't able to help me at all.' In the alternative therapies field she found an acupuncturist and a healer – 'they totally empathised and were warm and loving, and they helped me tremendously. The healer was able to spark something off within myself; she was able to light the flame which produced the healing within myself.' As my respondent felt she had no alternative but to move away from psychodynamic practitioners, so did I. Malcolm (1982) in her funny and lucid book defines what constitutes analytic behaviour. She observes, 'if the patient sees the analyst as a cold, callous person of limited intelligence and unbounded tactlessness, he may decide to quit the analysis'.

I regard myself as being a tenacious person who does not lightly accept the notion of quitting. Before aborting psychoanalysis, I thought carefully to try to discover if I had failed in my responsibility to the treatment alliance. I felt poisoned by the negative therapeutic reaction which had appeared in the relationship like an uninvited guest. Therapy was exacerbating the symptoms of alcoholism and depression. I questioned myself honestly to see if my shadow had activated the defence of self-sabotage, that is, the opposition of my will to his. I came to the conclusion that I genuinely wanted healing and wholeness, and that I was not 'cutting off my nose to spite my face'.

The kindest explanation is that my analyst and I were hopelessly out of kilter with each other. He seemed not to understand my story or my thought processes. After extensive research into therapy, Masson (1988) has concluded that 'therapists attempt to impose their own structures on patients ... each shows a lack of interest in physical or sexual abuse'. I was elated when I terminated treatment because I felt that there was now no option but to do therapy for myself. Nowadays I would not interfere in anyone's decision to embark on lengthy analysis, but I think I would suggest that they be aware that the superior–inferior, therapist–patient relationship may actually stop us from coming to value and accept our own self.

Sobriety and the emerging child within

Thirteen years ago, not long after I had finished with psychoanalysis, I stopped drinking. No climactic moment helped me to take that decision. In existential terms I had become sick to death with myself and with the way in which I was living my life: 'if one is sick of sickness, then one is not sick'. From that source of nothingness, I slowly sensed the appearance of my inner abandoned self, no longer as a victim, but as an ally and healer. 'That child', according to Marion Woodman (1991), 'is our very soul who cries out from under the rubble of our lives, often from the core of our worst complex, begging us to say "you are not alone. I love you." '

As I began to make a relationship with my inner child (my soul) I understood what Jesus meant when he taught about becoming again as little children. Reading about the shamanic traditions helped me to realise the necessity of seeking within for a magical guru or teacher. In shamanic terms, becoming whole means finding your ally and asking it to help you find other lost or missing parts of your soul. I knew that with this new Gestalt I was committed to a lifetime of reorientation. Capacchione (1991) captures how I felt: 'in order to heal the wounds of childhood you become your own counsellor, and counsel the child of the past'. I decided to train to be a counsellor.

Reparation: counselling training

My partner and I moved from London to a remote location in Dorset. I was accepted on to a part-time postgraduate Diploma in Counselling course; this was at the University of Bristol, and run by Hazel Johns (1996) who observes that 'personal development is not an event but a process, life-long and career-long: it must and will happen incidentally before and after any training course, through all aspects of life and work.' On the diploma course I was detached and watchful. I was trying to work out how much I could trust others, and indeed, how much I could and would trust myself. I learned four important things – to accept myself for what I was; to study, practise, and integrate humanistic psychology (a person-centred approach) with existential counselling; to read widely; and to accept responsibility for ongoing development. Addiction groups have a saying about 'walking your talk'. Because the diploma course was part-time I had the immediate opportunity to put the Bristol experience into action in my working life as probation officer, with a large client group, in Bournemouth.

It was evident that my colleagues on the diploma course were equipping themselves (often at their own expense and in their own time) with a qualification which would encourage enhanced counsellor professionalism. We were from a variety of disciplines – social work, teaching, medicine, the church. My impression is that most of us struggled with the concept of self-love. On the diploma course there was the therapeutic freedom to say 'This is who I am! This is my background! This is how I think, feel, believe, and behave!' Since self-empowerment necessarily involves understanding the individual reasons for distress, David Smail (1996) stresses that it is important to remember that we are our own psychologist.

As I write this chapter I wonder if I am presenting myself as a self-absorbed egocentric. It is true that childhood and adolescent experiences had produced a narcissistic Gestalt, but I think that the Greek mythological story of Narcissus is often misunderstood. Narcissus became fixated with his own image, such that, literally unable to move, he died of starvation. Narcissus died of self-hatred, not self-love. The roots of narcissistic disorder lie in the child's fear that nobody will love him as he is.

My 'child' (or soul) had to wait until I had battered my ego into submission with alcohol and depression before it could reveal itself. Adult education provided the metaphorical bridge that would 'take over what we would call the true life (the inner child) into adult life' (von Franz 1981). While awaiting the appearance of the healing forces of the inner child, I had always peered out of the Gestalt spectacles, wanting for others what I desired for myself. Childhood days in hospital had engendered a vivid emotional identification with the underdog, the victim. As I received the impetus to try to put right what was wrong in my own life, I realised that the reparative task could be seen from the viewpoint that 'if one can become the therapist one never had, then one has already become a therapist for others' (Dryden and Spurling 1989).

On the Diploma in Counselling course the opportunity was provided to experiment with a variety of counselling theories and approaches. Having experienced a good deal of disintegration in childhood, I was now keen to synthesise an integration (or re-integration), combining all the parts of the human experience into a functioning (not dysfunctioning) whole. Psychodynamic theory proposes the integrating function of consciousness. I became aware of the possibility of trying to make conscious what was unconscious – not by psychoanalysis, but by the self-analytic process of attempting as rigorous a combination of self-awareness and self-knowledge as was possible. Karen Horney (1942) approves of this process, reminding us of the self-evident point that analysing ourselves 'is different from analysing others. The difference most pertinent here is the fact that the world that each of us represents is not strange to ourselves; it is, in fact, the only one we really know.'

More than anything else, self-knowledge and self-awareness meant that I needed to relive, retell and reframe the sexual abuse which I had experienced. I did this by careful thought and appropriate self-disclosure in written work, group seminars, and individual tutorials. I was, in fact, collecting what Miller (1990) refers to as 'a sufficient number of enlightened witnesses ... to create a safety net for the growing consciousness of those who had been mistreated as children so they do not fall into the dark of forgetfulness'. Alice Miller (through her writing) became a friend and ally: I wept when I read her books. She distanced herself from all methods for addressing abuse based on forgiveness and reconciliation. Instead she proposed the much healthier energy of rebellion. She was vehemently against 'a quasi religious act of forgiveness ... which can never resolve patterns of self-destruction'. In a very tangible way I was able to transmute the anger and vitality of her words into self-healing. I stopped feeling guilty and responsible for causing the abuse because of the arousal, excitement, and pleasure which I had experienced during sexual contact. I included in the abuser list all the hundreds of men who had used me for sex when I was a boy prostitute.

As the Diploma in Counselling course neared its conclusion I started to go regularly to experiential workshops at the Findhorn Foundation in

Scotland. For me Findhorn has become a spiritual home, and it is a source from which I can always draw a deep, nourishing energy. Findhorn is an archetypal listening community, and various friends there convinced me that the 'awakened heart' is an essential element of human development as well as being the most powerful resource for self-transformation. I met and worked with Caroline Myss, who is an astonishing medical intuitive and international lecturer in the field of human consciousness. One afternoon, working with a large group of participants, Caroline helped me to understand the human heart, groaning with compassion. I felt channelled with a Christ energy of healing that awakened my heart in a totally unexpected moment of initiation and numinous insight. Later, Caroline told me that without the participation of the human spirit, nothing could remain in healthy form – and that this was absolutely real in the world of healing; she said, 'Those who heal have spirit. Spirit is essential to the healing process, and where any individual is unable to engage the power of the spirit on the healing journey, that person is preparing to die.'

Life can be full of joyous paradoxes. I was now 49, and looking back I could see that there had indeed been many periods when, on one level or another, I had been preparing to die. That was especially true of the two decades when I had been intent on drinking myself to death. Also, I am sure that I had a death-wish as a child, when illness had robbed me of basic human energy; but now, it was as if I had been given the opportunity to start life all over again. Caroline Myss encouraged me to think about applying for the Master's degree course in Counselling Supervision and Training at Bristol University.

Master's degree course in Counselling Supervision and Training

The M.Sc. is a unique course with negotiated learning at its heart. It would not be too far-fetched to say that its origins could be traced back to the inscription 'Gnothi Seauton' at the Delphic Oracle: 'Know Thyself'. The Greek philosopher Socrates was said by the Oracle to be the wisest man in the world. He did not teach, as such, but devised a system of drawing forth knowledge from his students by pursuing a series of questions, and he examined the answers. This became known as Socratic Dialogue, or Dialectic. Plato (Socrates' disciple) believed that dialectic was the sole method by which truth was arrived at. Carl Rogers argued that Socratic person-centred teaching should not be the exclusive domain of adult learners. He believed that this approach could be used to meet the challenge of the education of students of all ages.

The most important learning experience when I discovered the Socratic approach was the discovery that the process allowed individuals to seek within to find answers. For me this was the other end of the continuum to the way in which I had learned the piano, or had the Christian faith drummed into me. Feelings of success are promoted 'when you are encouraged to take as much responsibility for your own behaviour as you can handle ... you must believe that you are in control of your learning in order to feel psychological success' (Johnson and Johnson 1994). I was introduced to the work of Paulo Freire who passionately condemned pedagogy – the process by which the teacher narrates and the pupil becomes a patient listening object. Freire (1972) regarded dialogue as being an existential necessity, not only in teaching, but in any encounter in which the united reflection and action of the dialoguers are addressed to the world which is to be transformed and humanised. Using these methods, the interaction achieved on the M.Sc. course between students and tutors created an exciting and vital transpersonal education. We were all reminded, too, that training never ends; Clarkson and Gilbert (1991) see it as 'a lifelong, continuing, cyclic process'.

It was moving and encouraging to work intimately with a group of peers, who became a community of friends. Many people are now drawn into some form of community life and group living can do away with much of the spiritual and personal loneliness from which people suffer. Groups can achieve collectively what the individual cannot achieve alone, 'the whole is greater than the sum of its parts'. Synergy is the chemistry that transforms group activity into something much more than the aggregate of individual contributions. Sometimes for us the contribution was tears, at other times anger or hostility or frustration or perplexity. More often than not it was the nourishment of laughter; laughter until the tears ran down our faces. We developed the ability to laugh 'lovingly at ourselves, at our humanness, at the entire cosmic game ... the capacity to recognise life's drama as not only extremely serious but also exquisitely funny. ... this compassionate recognition of the comedy within tragedy can be very healing' (Grof 1994).

Conclusion

I do not know the meaning of my life past the point of understanding that I am here to serve. Suffering is an integral part of the human condition, but so also is the need to share suffering with others. My strange route through negative experiences must, I think, be viewed as a blessing: it took me in the direction of healing, and strengthened me in the realisation that I would have to do the healing for myself, alongside any loving help which I might find. The turning point, or healing spark, was the descent into total acquiescence. When I reached nothingness, I knew I could go on.

I am still a probation officer, now working in a prison for young offenders, where we are attempting to create a drug therapeutic community. We are all caught up in the struggle between rule and spirit, between poisonous pedagogy and the chances of joyous liberation through transpersonal education. Education seems pointless to me unless it meets the needs of the human spirit. Our teenagers are sometimes young in psychological years, at the same time as being prematurely aged; some have suffered a lifetime in a day.

As a counsellor, the only thing that I have to offer them, in the final analysis, is my own state of being. If nothing else, I hope that I model humility – my own experiences frightened me into a position of complete acquiescence. Brief appropriate self-disclosure can be helpful, especially in unlocking the door of childhood sexual abuse. With their own psychic radar scanners, most of my young clients seem quite capable of having some intuitive sense of my history; but I say to them, 'I am not my wound or my defence against my wound. I am my journey' (Hollis 1994). I accept the view of many shamanic cultures that a person is not fully healed unless they become a healer themselves. Of course, no woman or man ever heals; what heals is individual consciousness lifted to the height of Christ consciousness. Healing, for me, is nothing more complicated than what the Dalai Lama believes to be at the core of all healing – loving kindness; he says, 'my true religion is kindness'. For our own safety, that loving kindness needs to be in full focus all the time, equally directed outward to others and inward to ourselves.

References

Capacchione, L. (1991) *Recovery of Your Inner Child*, London: Simon and Schuster.

Clarkson, P. and Gilbert, M. (1991) 'The Training of Counsellor Trainers and Supervisors', in W. Dryden and B. Thorne (eds) *Training and Supervision for Counselling in Action*, London: Sage.

Dryden, W. and Spurling, L. (1989) *On Becoming a Psychotherapist*, London: Routledge.

Ellis, A. and Velten, E. (1992) *When A.A. Doesn't Work for You: Rational Steps to Quitting Alcohol*, Fort Lee, NJ: Barricade.

Ferguson, M. (1981) *The Aquarian Conspiracy: Personal and Social Transformation in the 1980s*, London: Paladin.

Freire, P. (1972) *Pedagogy of the Oppressed*, trans. M. Bergman Ramos, London: Penguin.

Grof, C. (1994) *The Thirst for Wholeness: Attachment, Addiction, and the Spiritual Path*, San Francisco: HarperCollins.

Hollis, J. (1994) *Under Saturn's Shadow: The Wounding and Healing of Men*, Toronto: Inner City.

Horney, K. (1942) *Self-Analysis*, London: W.W. Norton.

Hunter, M. (1990) *Abused Boys: The Neglected Victims of Sexual Abuse*, Toronto: D.C. Heath.

Johns, H. (1996) *Personal Development in Counsellor Training*, London: Cassell.

Johnson, D.W. and Johnson, F.P. (1994, 5th edn) *Joining Together: Group Theory and Group Skills*, London: Allyn and Bacon.

Lew, M. (1988) *Victims No Longer: Men Recovering from Incest and Other Sexual Child Abuse*, London: Cedar.

Lomas, P. (1981) *The Case for a Personal Psychotherapy*, Oxford: Oxford University Press.

Malcolm, J. (1982) *Psychoanalysis: The Impossible Profession*, London: Karnac.

Masson, J. (1988) *Against Therapy*, London: Fontana.

May, R. (1989) *The Art of Counselling*, New York: Gardner.

Miller, A. (1990) *Banished Knowledge: Facing Childhood Injuries*, trans. L. Vennewitz, London: Virago.

Park, J. (1992) *Shrinks: The Analysts Analyzed*, London: Bloomsbury.

Sams, J. (1994) *Earth Medicine: Ancestors' Ways of Harmony for Many Moons*, New York: HarperCollins.

Schachter, S. (1982) 'Recidivism and self-cure of smoking and obesity', *American Psychologist*, 37, 436–44.

Smail, D. (1996) *How to Survive Without Psychotherapy*, London: Constable.

Summitt, R.C. (1983) 'The child sexual abuse accommodation syndrome', *Child Abuse and Neglect*, 7, 177–93.

von Franz, M.-L. (1981, 2nd edn) *Puer Aeternus*, Boston: Sigo.

Woodman, M. (1991) 'The Soul Child', in J. Abrams (ed.) *Reclaiming the Inner Child*, London: Thorsons.

Yaryura-Tobias, J.A. and Neziroglu, F.A. (1983) *Obsessive-Compulsive Disorders: Pathogenesis, Diagnosis, Treatment*, New York: Marcel Dekker.

Postscript

Chapter 14

Rainbows and shadows

Hazel Johns

We have reached the end of a balancing act very familiar to counselling trainers: we must end, even though we have by no means covered everything; we have run out of time and space; and must send these pages, like our counselling trainees, out into the world – ready or not.

'Balance' has many meanings: stability, equilibrium, weight/authority, harmony, evaluation, difference – and aspects of all of those are present in the preceding chapters, in the many themes which the contributors have explored. We have touched on the tensions between stresses and rewards, personal and professional, content and process of training, planned and incidental learning, power and empowerment and individual and group or organisational needs. Of particular significance are the balancing acts outlined between action and reflection, co-operation and competition, creativity and standardisation, risk and safety, growth and pain, teaching and learning and inclusion and exclusion.

Some key issues have emerged: the apparently relentless juggernaut of professionalisation has costs as well as benefits; oppression comes in many forms; the needs of trainers are as crucial as those of trainees; the quality of relationships is as central in counselling training as it is in counselling. The developmental stage of trainees and trainers matters a great deal, as do past and present life-experiences, while the integration of continuing professional development and supervision is essential to provide the most effective balance of support and challenge. Supervision, indeed, about which we have been able to say little here, is a vital forum for the exploration of all the puzzles and paradoxes of both counselling and counselling training.

Many of the contributors have raised, either explicitly or implicitly, issues about selection, accountability, the gatekeeping of power and all the ethical dilemmas which any single training course, trainee or client can generate. These glancing lights on aspects of counselling training invite us as trainers to be vigilant, self-critical and alert to all the possibilities of oppression inherent in the complex human activities we undertake. We run the risk of becoming too precious in our attitudes and pretensions, yet we manage a deeply serious and responsible task. It is not too much to expect us to undertake our own learning journey alongside trainees and clients, in order to optimise our own 'emotional intelligence' (Goleman 1996). Our task is to live and work in accordance with our values, so that we manage to respect and not exploit our colleagues, trainees and clients.

Counselling training is complex and full of ambiguities and paradoxes. Like counselling, it offers at best a relationship both 'passionate and ethical' (Aveline 1996), equally necessary if change and growth are to occur. If balancing acts are at the heart of counselling training, then trainers and trainees need a good head for heights, a suitably wary (though not crippling) awareness of depths, a fine sense of balance and excellent co-ordination of eye, mind and heart. Counselling training can be, to adapt Aveline's words about therapy, 'a rather ordinary encounter ... but one of exceptional promise'.

References

Aveline, M. (1996) 'The Training and Supervision of Individual Therapists', in W. Dryden (ed.) *Handbook of Individual Therapy*, London, Sage.
Goleman, D. (1996) *Emotional Intelligence*, London, Bloomsbury.

Index